My Darling Patty

Ellen Heenan Reddy

Suite 300 - 990 Fort St
Victoria, BC, v8v 3K2
Canada

Copyright © 2019 by Ellen Heenan Reddy
First Edition — 2019

All rights reserved.

No part of this publication may be reproduced in any form, or by any means, electronic or mechanical, including photocopying, recording, or any information browsing, storage, or retrieval system, without permission in writing from FriesenPress.

ISBN
978-1-5255-2895-8 (Hardcover)
978-1-5255-2896-5 (Paperback)
978-1-5255-2897-2 (eBook)

1. BIOGRAPHY & AUTOBIOGRAPHY

Distributed to the trade by The Ingram Book Company

Prologue
January 2018

It all started with a plastic bag from Target.

That bag, adorned with the omnipresent red circle with the red dot emblazoned in the center, was among the myriad of things I hastily packed almost eight years ago today, as I assumed the unenviable, unwanted task of moving my eighty-seven-year old mother out of her house and in with me and my husband, who was at best unenthusiastic and at worst, completely opposed to this relocation plan. After Mom suffered from a stroke, it became obvious that she could no longer function independently. One of her children had to hunker down, and apply the badge of "caretaker". Unfortunately, none of us wanted to adorn that emblem and take on the task. After all (and perhaps, selfishly) what child wants to assume the burden of adopting a parent in need of care and obviously declining both mentally and physically? What skills did I have to assume that role? What would I do with this person I called "Mom" but didn't really know?

Many years ago, I had tried to talk Mom into moving to Wisconsin to be closer to family and to be proactive about her future, but she refused. She was absorbed in her own life of beach time, wine, travel, and a living the life of a gadabout, and didn't have time for what she perceived as a slowdown in her lifestyle. So she remained in her house until one day she blacked out and fell flat on her face, loosening her front teeth and leaving a trail of blood as she crawled nearly 200 feet back to her home. The inevitable had arrived. Now she needed me to become the parent as she slowly slid in to the descent of her journey on earth.

After Mom's stroke, my siblings and I realized that she could no longer live the nomadic life she had chosen. We had to make drastic decisions about selling her belongings and moving her to a place where she would be safe and eventually in the care of professionals who would tend to her daily needs. One of the problems was that, growing up, I felt that I hardly knew her – she busied herself with bridge clubs, entertaining friends, shopping, and other activities that appeared to come before parenthood. But that was life in the 1960's. Kids poured a bowl of cereal when the sun rose, and came home when the street lights turned on. We rode our bikes wherever we wanted (or needed) to go – the park, the dentist, to friends' houses. My guess would be that a majority of the time, my parents had no idea where all of us were, but again, it was a different era.

But back to The Bag. I did what needed to be done. My sister and I hosted an estate sale to quickly and brazenly purge Mom's homestead of virtually all her belongings, and then we crammed as many things into my car that would fit (Mom included). I hastily grabbed that "Expect more. Pay less" bag and recklessly tossed it into my car. I had seen that there were a bunch of envelopes inside and assumed they held potential importance to her, but then Mom was known to be a letter hoarder. I thought I would keep those meaningful notes she so carefully guarded and expose them at a date undetermined, so she could reminisce about twenty-something year old Christmas cards and that she might find solace and companionship in their messages.

That bag, stuffed with envelopes of unknown origins and authors, found a new home in my closet. There it festered, dormant, ignored, for years.

Finally, that lonely bag was emancipated from that dark corner of ignored storage when my husband and I prepared to downsize our home. While Dave and I sorted through our belongings amassed from thirty-plus years together, we were also purging Mom's remaining possessions, items that had been ignorantly stuffed in that closet. It was all headed for the recycle bin. The Target bag and its unknown contents was marked as a victim for the refuse collection team.

But something in my subconscious compelled me to look inside that wrinkled, neglected bag for giving it the heave-ho. I had to peek and see what lurked within.

Inside were letters—scores of letters—which my dad wrote to my mom while he was deployed as a soldier during World War II. I realized that I had held captive these precious missives in the bowels of my musty closet for years, without realizing the story they told of my parents as they met, courted, and survived the tumultuous years of sacrifice, anguish, despair, confusion, and commitment that defined our country during that world changing event.

My mom, the third daughter of a Methodist pastor, had lived a disrupted, yet ironically charmed life. Because her father was reassigned every two years to a new parish, she was regularly uprooted in her childhood to start afresh in a new school, a new neighborhood, having to find new friends that she knew were only temporary companions. During her senior year of high school, she was abandoned by her parents and left alone under the care of regimented elderly guardians who took her in out of a sense of religious duty, and not of a desire, nor energy, to nurture another child. She was alone at a time of uprising and uncertainty as the United States embarked on a mission to save the world.

By happenstance, she met a college boy who would ultimately change her life, and she would have to make decisions about her path in life amidst societal pressures to "contribute" and "sacrifice" as the war escalated. It was daunting, overwhelming, and confusing. Mom coped with her lot in life as best that she could, given her lonely, yet undefined circumstances.

I can't pretend to understand what people went through during that era of love grasped, love realized, then for many, love erased by untimely death. Many veterans do not like to share their experiences during the war, not only because of the anguished relationships they desperately hung onto (or lost), but because it was a time of such loneliness and despair that they choose to hide the experiences in the depths of their psyches. My dad was one of those soldiers. He rarely talked about anything that happened during his years as a trainee, then as an active participant in Europe. His letters are the only connection I have my parents during that tumultuous time – and I'm sure that I still can't comprehend the pain, the loneliness, the hopelessness that was felt by those who served our country. The only knowledge I have of my father's experiences of those and other feelings is what I have learned and experienced through his letters.

"The Greatest Generation" is a misnomer—an understatement—incomprehensible for the generations that have followed. We will never, ever, grasp the hardships those brave, patriotic warriors endured. The soldiers of WWII were adult orphans, alone and with limited means of communicating even the simplest of messages of how they were coping, or to convey messages of love, longing, and dreams of the future.

What you hold before you in this book is rooted in those real letters from my father to my mother during their courtship and then when he was away at war. From them I began to learn the story of my parents - a story of a young man and a girl who found love at a time when they enjoyed a carefree, simple unencumbered life. Then all hell broke loose as the Japanese army attacked Pearl Harbor. Nothing in their lives, just like nothing in the lives of their fellow Americans, would ever be the same.

This is the story of my parents, beginning when my mom was sixteen, and my dad was a freshman at Milton College, age eighteen. I don't want to give away the ending, but since I am writing the story at the age of fifty-nine, it must be obvious that things worked out for them. Sort of. It is also a story of struggle, love, and loss and ultimately, eventually, how a charmed life can be robbed by the cruel invasion of Alzheimer's disease.

Life wasn't easy, as I learned from reading the "air mail" letters they exchanged sixty-seven years prior. Before discovering the letters, I had no idea what they went through to fall in love, raise a family, and survive the crushing aches and dreamy aspirations of everyday life. The archaic United States Postal Service was their only means of connecting with loved ones abroad. Sending cryptic "I love you, Soldier" notes was the only way to help the cause and to keep the spirits of our heroic armed forces sane for another day. They needed love and the promise that there was a happy ending awaiting them upon their return from the retched war.

It seems that my dad wrote a letter to my mom almost every day that he was deployed overseas. I'm honored to be able to share those missives with you, and to pass on the importance of the two most meaningful messages I think we need to keep in our hearts: love and forgiveness.

Mom's method of coping with the anguish and loneliness was to save all correspondence she received throughout the years. Every missive was carefully tied up in twine – organized by author. She wasn't a demonstrative person – she didn't really know how to outwardly show love and affection, but the fact that she held on to boxes full of correspondence shows how deeply she cared about her friends and family.

This book is a tribute to my mom, beginning as she was a teenager in 1941. The book travels to yet undetermined end of her life, as she clings on to life at the age of ninety-three. She faltered, she struggled, but she lived a life gifted. Hers was a life where she was infinitely loved, but ironically, she really didn't know how to give love back. This inability sounds like an anomaly – a quagmire, an enigma – given how deeply she was loved, but within her past there was also a chaotic, unpredictable life. My guess is that she was a pampered child and was crushed to find that Nirvana only exists in fiction as she watched her parents leave her behind when they slipped out in the middle of the night due to her father's indiscretions. She learned to accept love, but not how to give love back. I'm not sure that any of us – myself and my siblings, learned the true meaning and appreciation of love. And now, as she struggles with the ugly disease of Alzheimer's, she occasionally, unpredictably, flashes back to those times of love, loss, tragedy, and celebration. The only thing she knew how to hold onto were the written words that she infrequently received from friends and family or letters exchanged between family members that she lovingly kept in her belongings.

My dad was an affable, loveable guy with torrential mood swings and an inability to control his obsession with alcohol. He grew up in a loveless family – his mother probably suffered from some kind of mental illness that resulted in neglecting her children and consequenly forced to raise themselves. My dad learned to control his destiny from an early age knowing that his parents wouldn't provide much guidance.

Unfortunately, my father picked favorites, and I drew the long straw. He was mean to my siblings and singled me out as the chosen one. I was, in his mind, cute, clever, and inquisitive – qualities that he found endearing. My siblings worked hard to please him. Perhaps that is why I ended up as being my mother's caretaker – it was something willed by my dad.

Patricia Marie Gaskill Wise was born on July 20, 1924. She was, as she reminded me to her last days, a "PK", aka Preacher's Kid. When I asked if that was a good thing or a bad thing, she can't remember. She tells me that she was belligerent just because she was expected to be the opposite. She ran away from home – twice – but always returned to the comforts of the parsonage. At the age of seven, she boarded a train from Kenosha to Milwaukee (a forty-five minute commute) to go visit her dad at his place of work. A rebel, but ironically, a follower without much direction.

Her eventual husband, my father, David Kyle Heenan, was born on February 16, 1922. The son of Irish immigrants who came to the United States in 1919, David decided early on that he did not want the label of "immigrant" and worked every day to prove himself otherwise. He had a paper route at the age of ten and picked up as many odd jobs as he could to scrape enough money to enroll in college.

Mom and Dad met at a high school church group gathering. Dad had just returned from a trip to Cuba and he was the guest speaker at their weekly high school church meeting.

The letters from my dad you find in this book are authentic. By contrast, the letters from my mom are fictional, as I have no proof of what she might have written back to Dad or to her sisters. They are products of my own creation, though all of their writing stems from what Mom has told me over the last few years as she descends into the depths of her long-term memory, slipping back to her days as a child and involuntarily erasing the last decades of her life.

The letters from Dad in 1946 were obviously written during a period of boredom and frustration for him, so many of them are repetitive. I have removed some of the information that was written over and over again to spare you having to read the same stories, but also wanted to convey the deep loneliness and anguish he must have felt during that time.

Dad was a stickler for spelling and grammar, so I was a bit flummoxed to find that every reference he made to writing a letter, he used the word "missile" instead of "missive". I assume that he was making a feeble attempt at some kind of humor here (maybe a subtle suggestion that her infrequent letters dropped on him like a bomb?), but it escapes me. So – I have taken some journalistic liberty and changed each use of missile to missive. Forgive me, Dad, but missile just doesn't make sense.

Letters to my dear cousin, Barby, are also fabricated, but I hope that in telling the story, it helps to demonstrate what we were experiencing with our family and friends during that time. Barby is a real person, and she was a true sounding board. I just don't have any of the letters written to her to prove her existence, (failing to inherit my mother's penchant for archiving all correspondence) but we were in constant communication about the dilemmas of dealing with parents suffering from dementia.

The alleged relationship between my grandfather, Harry, and his secretary, Nancy, is based on a story that my mother told me just a few months ago. She was unusually glib that day (by this time, her ability to speak was slipping away) and regaled a memory of her mother standing up during a church service and announcing the affair to the entire congregation. Her recollection was so vivid and convincing that I decided to include it in the story. It might explain Harry and Zella's abrupt departure from the Janesville parish, however, I have checked with other family members, and no one recalls any evidence that these events occurred.

Finally, I continue the antiquated tradition of writing old fashioned letters with pen on paper—with my dad, hovering in spirit over my shoulder. I end each missive to my children with the closing, "Love, love, love, Mom". I encourage you to practice the same.

Bottom line: nothing else really matters other than love, love, love.

Real people involved in this story (in order of appearance):

- Patty Wise (later Heenan, my mom)
- Rachel, Patty's eldest sister
- Harry Wise, Patty's father
- David Kyle Heenan, my dad and author of most of the letters – zealous cad pursuing Patty
- Zella Wise, Patty's mother
- Ellen, me, daughter of David and Patty
- Barbara (Barby) Simpson Blume, cousin to David and Patty's children, daughter of Rachel and Merlin
- Jean and Tim, my siblings, children of David and Patty
- Jean Wise Douglas, Patty's sister
- Nancy, church secretary for Harry and the Methodist Church in Janesville, Wisconsin
- Roy, my mother's second husband

Book One
1941

12 January 1941

Dear Rachel,

Oh, Sissy, I miss you so much! It just doesn't seem fair that we are so far apart, and that you are establishing your new home in St. Louis. It's not that I am not happy for you, for I love you and your Merlin so much! I guess I'm just wallowing in my selfish sorrows of being an "only child".

Our second semester has begun—what is worse than being a junior in high school? I have to deal with the typical high school issues—boys (although I'm still sweet on Prescott Lustig), rumors, and my never-ending problems with carrying a few extra pounds.

I haven't heard much from Jeannie. I think she is loving her life at college and can't be bothered with correspondence. It makes Mama and Daddy quite crazy that they aren't able to get in touch with her and find out what activities she is pursuing. My guess is—boys!

I have a little news. I was attending the meeting of the Epworth League at church on Sunday, and they had a featured speaker by the name of David Heenan! He had just recently returned from a trip to Cuba, and he told us the stories of his travels. What an adventure! He is intriguing (and cute!) And the best part, Rae, is that he offered to give me a ride home!

Oh, please, please, don't tell Mama and Daddy. It was just a ride and I'm sure I will never see him again. He is a college boy, and he has a gal at Milton—one "Jo Gray". Why would any Miltonite favor a high school girl like me?

Anyway, I am planning on attending the January ball with Prescott! Mama is making me a blue chiffon dress, and I get to buy a new pair of shoes to match! I'm so excited that I could just die!

Everything else here seems to be okeydokey. We miss you and can't wait for you to make a visit!

Your loving sister, Patty.

20 January 1941

Dear Patricia,

I appreciate your letting me drive you home after that dull diatribe I put on for your Epworth League … I'm surprised that you weren't bored to tears! By the time it was over, I was sure that you had had your fill of me.

We are having a formal dance here at Milton on February 1st. I would be honored if you would attend as my guest (date). I would pick you up around 5 p.m. We would have dinner, then the dance starts at 7 p.m. You might have to put up with the antics of my roommate, Kenny, who is giving me the business for being so bold as to ask you out via air mail. Kenny and his girl, Mona, will be our "double date". I'm certainly hoping that you say "yes". Please reply ASAP!

Fondly, David

21 January 1941

Dearest Sister Rachel,

We miss you so much! When can you come to Janesville?

I mentioned in a previous letter that David Heenan gave me a ride home from Epworth a couple of Sundays past. The most incredible thing has happened—I just got a note from him, asking me to attend a dance at Milton!!! I would like to say "yes", but as you know, I'm going already going steady with Prescott, and I don't know how to tell him that I'm interested in someone else. What are the proper words to use when you would like to give your hand from one to another? Help!

How are you coping with Merlin being away? Life in the South Pacific is such a combination of unknowns—I can't imagine having to agonize over your beloved facing deployment and unfamiliar surroundings, much less imagining their living conditions and having to survive every day knowing it is a brush with death –a challenge to their safety and wellbeing.

I hate to bother you with my childish problems when you are so burdened yourself. But if you could call on the telephone, and give me some advice, I would greatly appreciate it. I can stand by to receive your call if you let me know a date and time.

Sending love, Patty.

24 January 1941

Dear David,

You were incredibly wrong in your assessment of my interest in your presentation last week at Epworth. I found your travel log quite fascinating. Who in their right mind would choose Cuba as a destination? It was an honor to get a ride home from you.

I would like to accept your invitation to attend the Milton Ball on February 1st. I'm assuming that it is a formal event? I have a blue chiffon dress that I hope will be suitable for the occasion.

Thank you again for the invitation, and I look forward to seeing you again.

Patty.

27 January 1941

Rachel dearest,

It is with heartfelt desire that I inquire about your welfare. A father shouldn't worry about such things with children who have grown into adulthood, but I can't help myself. Your happiness will always be of grave concern to me and your mother.

We try to imagine you in a large city like St. Louis, and it is hard for us to digest that you are happy and safe there. Have you found a church? How do you occupy your days?

I am told that David Heenan has requested the hand of our Patty at an upcoming Milton College function. We know the Heenans from church, and although I feel that he is an honorable, career-driven young man, it is disturbing to think that he is preying on high school girls. My secretary, Nancy, is familiar with the family and vouches for their upstanding reputation. I will not make an issue out of this, as Patty seems to be quite pleased with the prospect of attending a college mixer. We will be waiting for her timely return after the dance and importing on Mr. Heenan that she is a simple sixteen-year old girl with no intentions of continuing with a long-distance relationship.

Totidem verbis, (in so many words) we are happy, healthy, and in pursuit of great things in life. We miss you terribly and look forward to a visit in the near future. May God guide you as decisions are made and hardships are endured.

With warm regards, and love, your padre.

February 3, 1941

Dear Patricia,

Thank you for accompanying me to the Milton Winter Ball. Many of my buddies commented on what a swell date I had! They were surprised that a guy with a mug like mine could attract such a beauty!

We are knee-deep in studies here. Along with Glee Club and intramural sports, my dance card is full!

I would like to see you again, and hope you feel the same about me. I can get a ride to Janesville next weekend, on the 15th. Could we catch a movie together? Please let me know if you are interested.

Fondly, David.

Saturday, February 8, 1941

Dear David,

I had a wonderful time at the dance last Saturday. Thank you for inviting me and for showing me around Milton College before the dance. What a beautiful campus!

I received your letter requesting a "date" to the movies on February 15th. Before I accept, I have to know the status of your relationship with a one "Jo Gray", who, according to my friends, has been seen on your arm at a number of Milton events. I do not want to be a person who "steals" a boyfriend—especially a sorority gal who is obviously smitten with you!

As you may have heard, I have been seeing Prescott Lustig. We have attended a number of school events together. I am fond of Pres, and do not want to hurt his feelings if you are going to be "two-timing" me.

Please respond as soon as possible.

Patty.

February 11, 1941

Dear Patricia,

I'm not sure what crowd you are running with, but their information source is foul. I am no longer seeing J. Gray and furthermore, I would never ask you on a date if I was involved with another woman. It is a bit insulting for you to suggest that I would be such a cad.

I will take your response as an affirmative reply and will pick you up at 6 p.m. on the 15th.

Yours, David.

ps – What about this Prescott Lustig character? Might I throw back the same accusation to you, that you are "two-timing"? I will assume that by the 15th he will no longer be a part of your social life.

David

February 16th, 1941 – my 19th birthday

Dear Patricia,

Thank you for attending the movie "Pinocchio" with me! That was very entertaining! It's amazing how they can do the animations like that. I'm sorry that I had to race back to Milton that night, but I have a number of tests to study for and our Glee Club was holding a rehearsal on Sunday afternoon.

I hope that we can go out together again soon. We have a spring break in mid-March, so I will be in Janesville during that time. How about dinner and a show?

The boys are hosting a little birthday party for me—I really don't want to attend, but they are always looking for a reason to hold a bash! It is amazing that any of them continue on in college—their number one priority is drinking beer!

Yours, David.

February 20, 1941

Dear David,

Thank you for your most recent letter, and yes! I would love to go to dinner and a movie with you.

My connection with Mr. Lustig has been severed. I am completely available and ready to see you exclusively.

I know that you are very busy with your Milton obligations, so I don't expect an immediate response. However, if you could call me between now and your spring break, I would greatly appreciate it.

FYI, I have notified my parents of breaking ties with Prescott. They are not completely happy with my decision to be dating a college boy, but they know your family and they are cautiously supportive of our relationship.

Warmly, Patty.

March 1st, 1941

Dear Patricia,

I haven't heard back from you since my last missive. I hope there isn't a problem! Perhaps I was too bold to suggest that you sever your ties with Mr. Lustig—needless to say, I am hoping that we can become "exclusive" and commit to just seeing each other from now on. Let me know what you think about that!

I will be home on March 21st for Spring Break. When can we get together? Does your high school have a break at the same time?

Please let me know ASAP. I am on edge until I receive a reply.

Yours, David.

March 17, 1941

Dear David,

It has been a pretty busy time since our last correspondence! I have gotten involved with the Drama Club, and we are posting our upcoming events with the Yearbook Group. While I don't expect to be the next Ida Lupino, I am having lots of fun with these wacky characters, and I'm hoping that next year, I can build up the courage to try out for a part in the fall play. Right now, I'm just helping with set building and advertising.

I must warn you that you will have to meet my sisters, Jeannie and Rachel, when you arrive on the 21st. Jeannie is a sophomore at MacMurray College in Jacksonville, Illinois. She will be home on spring break and is curious to know about this fellow of mine! Be prepared for a thorough interrogation.

My older sister, Rachel, is married and living in St. Louis with her husband, Merlin. He is in the Army and has been sent to the South Pacific, but when he returns, he plans to open his own hardware store! She will also be visiting and looks forward to meeting "my guy". Rae will take the train to Chicago, then Jeannie will pick her up at Union Station. Jeannie is such a daredevil—she drives back and forth from Jacksonville to Janesville! I can't imagine DRIVING, much less going downtown to Chicago!

I look forward to seeing you on the 21st. I hope this letter arrives before then to warn you of your unenviable fate of meeting my whole family.

Warm Regards, Patty.

April 1st, 1941

Dear Patty,

I had a swell time with you during Spring Break—thanks for everything! Your family is really great ... I can't wait to see you again, if you will allow such a meeting to occur. Possibly now you have gotten an idea of what it is like to hang around with DKH and you have changed your mind about this being a good idea. If so, I would reply like Irving Berlin, "Say it isn't so!"

I like your sisters and their families/beaus. I think that we all have a common element that will last for years to come – forever!

I'm busy with classes and thinking about running for Student Body President in the fall, so I have to make a lot of contacts now. In addition to all that madness, I am "rushing" to join a fraternity, Alpha Kappa Pi. They only allow five new members every year, so I doubt I will make the cut.

I'll write as soon as I can again ... please include me in your list of missives! I know that sisters come first, but I always love to hear from you and to learn what you and your little friends are up to.

Thinking of you! David.

April 15, 1941

Dear David,

As you can see, I'm afraid I'm not much of a correspondent, but I haven't had time to write for the past couple of weeks. The Drama Club is really taking a lot of my energy, and church life is very busy as well!

I am wondering what your plans are for the summer, as I will be going to Lake Winnebago and spending a few weeks in July at the Downing's home—they let Daddy use it for a respite. I may try to find a job working in a local restaurant, but more than likely, I'll just be hanging around on the beach, enjoying my last summer as a high schooler.

Let me know what you are doing—maybe you could figure out a way to come up to the lake! I'm sure that Mother and Daddy wouldn't mind!

Yours, Patty.

May 1st, 1941

Dear Patty,

I'm sorry that I haven't written in a few weeks. The end of the semester brings many obligations—classes, fraternity activities, and as the acting Class President (YES! I won the election!) I have a ton of things to get done. Most importantly, I have to see that the younger students keep to their books and aren't out carousing rather than studying! I don't really know how I am going to do that, but I plan to set a good example and hope that they will follow suit.

Final exams are in two weeks, then I will return to Janesville, where I hope we can see each other every day until your departure! I miss you so much and hope that you are well.

With love, David.

May 13, 1941

Dear David,

Congratulations on winning the election! I know you will make a good leader for the student body at Milton. I realize that you have been busy getting ready for exams, and I wish you all the luck in the world! I, too, have exams coming up during the first week of June, and then summer break! Hooray!

I will be traveling to Lebanon, Illinois, at the end of school to visit with Aunt Tillie, then to Normal, IL, to visit with my Aunt Jane and Cousin Helen. I guess I've never asked—do you have aunts, uncles, and cousins in the area? I know you have one brother and three sisters, but that's all I know of your family.

Gee, I don't really follow the news too closely, but it sure seems like things are heating up between France and Germany. I just hope that the United States doesn't get pulled into the fray. A lot of the boys at school are talking about "signing up", and it just scares me. They wouldn't be recruiting college boys, would they?

My sister, Jeannie, wonders if you have any friends for her to date! Just kidding, you know. She goes on dates with a number of boys, and Eugene waits patiently for her to return. He is a swell guy, but she just doesn't take a shine to him. But for Jeannie to suggest that she would be interested in your friends tells me that she approves of you.

I know that my parents like you, too. And Rachel was so happy to have finally met you! She may have received a few letters in which you were mentioned!

Well, I have to go! I have homework to get done, and Mother is expecting me to help with some chores around the house. I hope I can see you the minute you return to Janesville!

Sincerely, Patty.

May 17, 1941

Dear Harry,

Today is our anniversary. I have been your secretary for two years. I believe that I have displayed dedication, attachment, and unity with you to the point where I know the feelings of love and devotion are real. You need to make a decision about our future – although it may be difficult to leave your family behind, you know it is the right thing to do.

We are destined to be together. We spend endless hours in each other's company, reviewing the weekly program for the Sunday service. Your eyes meet mine, and there is a definite connection. We were meant to be one. I am committed to make a relationship deepen between us despite the consequences, and then the rest of our lives we can enjoy growing old together.

My love for you grows stronger every day.

Your love always, Nancy.

May 20, 1941 (Tuesday)

Dearest Patty,

I arrive home next Monday night—can I see you then? It just seems like SO long since we have been together, and I really miss that.

Most of the chaos here has ended, but as you can imagine, there were plenty of hijinks going on as most have finished their final exams and are bidding the college one last adieu, accompanied by their friends Miller, Schlitz, Blatz, and Strohs (oh, honey…you may not know … those are names of beers!)

I have a number of things to finish up after final exams in preparation for my return in the fall. As President of the student body, I'm in charge of holding a "Newcomer's Meeting" for all freshmen before school begins in the fall. I also have to find some volunteers to show the frosh around campus and help them get their class schedules, etc.

Warmly, David K.

May 23, 1941

Dear David,

Yes! We can meet on Monday night when you return. Let's go bowling! That would be a hoot.

Mother and I leave on June 10th for a month-long visit with extended family. It will be a good time for us to get away, as my father seems to be having a difference of opinion with the elders at the Methodist church. I'm not sure what it is that they are in disagreement about, but he has been very cranky lately, and I have heard him and Mother exchanging harsh words late at night. Daddy's secretary, Nancy, seems to be acting oddly when I stop into his office and at Sunday service. I don't think she likes me.

I am so excited to be ending my junior year at JHS!!! Just think—soon I will be a senior, then graduating from high school, and on my way to—Milton College? It would be a dream come true!

Yours, Patty.

. . . .

June 2, 1941

Harry my love,

I hate to communicate via notes left on your desk, but I haven't seen you in a while and I am resorting to the only way I know how to reach you without dialing you up directly. Could you please come by my house? I have some troubling issues that I need to discuss with you. The sooner, the better. I don't know if I can carry on without your advice. We have been together for two years now, and I think it is time we had a candid discussion about what our future holds. I can't be a church secretary forever. I need a husband, a family, and possibly a different career. You will probably be reassigned in the next few months – have you ever stayed at a parish for longer than two years? Your assignment affects my future plans as well. We need to talk.

Yours always, Nancy.

. . . .

June 7, 1941

Dearest Nancy, my friend and confidante,

I am deeply grateful for the years you have served as secretary to our congregation. How fortunate I am to have met your acquaintance and to have developed a relationship so deeply intense! You listen when I am troubled, and you are intimately aware of the private and personal matters that our members bring to me for reflection and prayer. I am infinitely thankful for you serving as a sounding board and shoulder for me to lay my heavy burdens upon. The life of a minister is a paradox – a daily mixture of sadness and joys. Sometimes it gets to be too intense, and I appreciate your kind and supportive words.

I do acknowledge a bond that we have melded over our days, weeks, months, now years together, but to walk away from the life I have established seems an impossible feat and a cowardly action. Please allow me some time for further prayer regarding this matter.

In His Service, Harry

If one gives an answer before he hears, it is his folly and shame (Proverbs 18:13).

June 11, 1941

Dear Harry,

Now that your family has left town, our opportunity is imminent. The only chance for us to be together is when Zella is out of town. This is the weekend that we will become one. Our destiny will finally mesh, and she will be a faded memory of days gone by. After all, two of the three girls are off on their own—there's only the one left, and she is old enough to fend for herself. You and I can finally seal our passion and destiny for being together. Let bygones be bygones! We are about to embark on a new adventure – side by side, hands entwined, lips softly touching. I can't wait to embark on a new life with you!

Nancy.

June 17, 1941 4pm

Janesville, Wisc.

My Darling Patricia,

I received your cards this morning and your letter this afternoon. I just finished a long letter to you and you will find it waiting in Illinois at your aunt's house. You seem so distant in your letters although it's a wonderful feeling just to hear from you. Perhaps I did something wrong in my letter as I write too much as I feel (it is a bit sentimental in most parts).

How are you, hon? I promise you that Janesville is pretty dull without you. I guess there is no reason to keep you waiting until you get to Lebanon for the big news. I have a job at the Parker Pen Co. and I am going to work on Monday! Therefore, I will be in town all summer, and I would appreciate the honor of seeing you the night you come home.

This is slightly off-the record, as I was sitting in the Church office this afternoon with the secretary, Nancy (she's SWELL) …we called the operator to see how much it would cost to call you in Normal. Nancy is very interested in what you and your family are doing this summer! She's a peach!

Getting back to the phone call, I crawfished because I feared your mother might not approve of it, but right now, the sound of your voice would be a welcome tune in my auricles!

Right now, I am basking in the sun in our backyard (I'm home all of the time). When I received your letter, I became very excited and that is the cause of this short letter. I will resume my correspondence tomorrow and will probably mail it to Aunt Jane's again (I don't know Aunt Tillie's last name). I am expecting a letter a day and I hope it isn't asking too much. Goodbye for now, hon.

Love, Dave Kyle Jr.

June 23, 1941

David dear …

Thank you for the fun things we shared while you were in Janesville before I left for vacation. I had such a great time! It will be hard to come back and then leave again for Lake Winnebago, but I'm afraid I don't have a choice in the matter.

Things with Daddy don't seem to be improving. They are very tight lipped about the disagreement they are having with the church elders, and I'm afraid that he may leave before reaching an agreement. He is a very stubborn person (it must be the German in his genes), and he holds his ground to a point where he would rather lose his position than give up on a stance. I am trying to find out what the issue is that is polarizing them, but everything is quite hush-hush. Right now, things have quieted down since we are soon leaving for Fond du Lac for a couple of months. I'm looking forward to a relaxing stint in the lake and sun.

I hope that you find a good job for the summer, and I look forward to seeing you again when I return from Normal, Illinois! That sounds so funny, it's not like I am coming back from Abnormal … ha ha.

Yours, Patty.

- -

June 27, 1941

Harry dear,

You haven't replied to my request to get together, but I know you want me as much I want you. The fear of leaving your controlling wife and escaping from your mundane life as a pastor and father. Why can't you see the light? Well, I'm just going to stir the pot a bit—won't it be interesting to the church Trustees to find out that there has been an ongoing tryst between the church secretary and the pastor? Who are they going to believe? Commit to our future, or the thing we have established is going to end.

Nancy.

- -

July 2, 1941

Appleton, Wisc.

Dear David,

I'm sorry that I disappointed you by not writing "a letter every day" as per your request back in June, but why write when I got to tell you all about my trip in person when I returned? Isn't it better that way?

It was wonderful to see you during the few days that I got to spend in Janesville before leaving for Lake W. My favorite time was roller skating in Delavan! Well, I should clarify that to say that my favorite time was spending with you (I'm blushing now).

I hope that you will be able to get some time away from the Parker Pen Company so that you can make a trip up here! Mother and Daddy said that it was okay, but you will have to stay next door at the Mulligan's. We can have bonfires down by the lake, roast marshmallows, and maybe sneak in a kiss or two! (now I'm REALLY blushing!)

Yours, Patty

July 7, 1941

My Darling Patty,

Thank you for the delicious letter—you keep me wanting for more! Please don't worry about writing things that make you blush—I enjoy it!

I'm afraid that it is impossible for me to get any time off work to visit you at the lake. We are working six days a week, twelve hours a day, and even if I could travel up on a Sunday, I don't have access to a car. This news hurts my heart, as there is no place that I would rather be than by your side. A bonfire and a kiss sound blissful!

I can't wait for your return in a few weeks. We'll plan a special celebration, and hopefully, we'll have most of August together. How wonderful that will be to have you within arm's reach for almost an entire month!

With love, David.

Ps…I'm sure there are a lot of eligible bachelors around the lake, you're behaving yourself, I'm sure???

July 18, 1941

David dear,

Correspondence just doesn't seem to suit me well. I always feel that the drivel I spout is juvenile and inconsequential—silly talk that you would roll your eyes at! I want you to be proud of me and I want to impress you as more than just a simple high school girl who is enamored with a college guy.

So I'm not going to bore you with the goings-on of a nearly seventeen-year old girl (yes, that's a hint! My birthday is in two days!) who is on vacation and spending her days soaking up sun rays and sipping on root beer.

I'm sorry that you couldn't arrange to come up here this month, but I understand the demands of your job and your limited funds. Just think—in two weeks, I'll be back home! I can't wait to hug you (blushing again)!

Until we meet again, a kiss through the postal service (I'm sure the postman won't mind).

Patty

August 21, 1941

Dear Rachel,

It was with horror and astonishment that I discovered the following excerpt from last week's minutes from a council meeting:

Minutes from the Janesville Methodist Church Special Council Meeting. Date: 8/17/41

Agenda Item 4: Discussion of future relationship with Rev. Harry Wise. Trustee Ralph Walters made a presentation to the board regarding some clandestine meetings between Rev. Wise and his secretary, Nancy Andrews. Miss Andrews has suggested that Rev. Wise has made some unwelcome and inappropriate suggestions with regard to an enhanced relationship between the two parties. After much discussion, the Council decided to offer Rev. Wise a severance package in exchange for his timely departure from the church. Miss Andrews was present at the council meeting but offered no comment. Rev. Wise maintained his innocence and denied any such interaction took place. He urged the council to follow their instincts and offered a prayer that God would direct them to the true path.

Having no further testimony or discussion on this matter, the Council voted to seek the resignation of Pastor Wise. This motion passed on an 8-1 vote.

Trustee Perkins made a motion that the Church Council table the consideration of writing a recommendation regarding Rev. Wise's future assignment within the Church. The motion was seconded by Trustee Williamson and passed unanimously.

It does seem that your father has been particularly on edge during the past few weeks. Some of our discussions about matters relating to the church have gone well into the night, but I never dreamed that they had escalated to this level. What provoked Nancy to make such ridiculous claims? Just what does she hope to accomplish, and why is she trying to ruin his career? The whole scenario is so outrageous that I just don't know where to turn or what to do. Naturally, your father denies any existence of an inappropriate relationship.

Whatever would we do if the church passes him over for his next assignment? We have lived in a furnished parsonage provided by the church since I married your father. We have no home and scant belongings. You can bet that this will be a topic for conversation when your father arrives home.

Listen to my ranting – all over some fabricated accusations -- and I didn't even ask about you. What do you hear from Merlin? How is the baby, and how are you getting along without a hand to help?

I must go as the hour is getting late and I need to prepare for what will be said (or not said) tonight. I will be in touch soon.

Love, Mother

August 18, 1941

Dear Harry,

Obviously, our relationship is over. You have chosen to stay with your family and I must move on. We could have made it all work if you would have stayed with our original plan to be together. I'm sorry that you chose otherwise. We are no longer one – I will miss you, but you made the ultimate decision. And, the council has made their decision to dismiss you as pastor – I feel vindicated, and victorious. Goodbye forever.

Nancy.

August 25, 1941

Dear Rachel,

I have very sad and disturbing news for you, and I apologize in advance for placing this burden on your shoulders. However, as the oldest of our children, I feel you must know the truth. I am sparing your younger sisters from the sordid details.

Your father has now confessed his indiscretions with Nancy. Apparently, they have been engaging in secret trysts for the past two years. I had absolutely no idea – the life of a pastor often requires the keeping of odd hours and calls from desperate souls needing immediate spiritual assistance. When your father would leave the house after dark, or before sunrise, I always assumed he was tending to a member of his flock. We have always had an understanding that his meetings with members of the congregation were of a confidential nature, so I never asked about his whereabouts. How silly and ignorant of me! I thought he was tending to his sheep, while all along he was shepherding a clandestine romance.

Of course, he was falling over himself with apologies, and promises that this was an isolated event, one that will never happen again. His groveling almost makes the situation worse. In my eyes, he has transformed from a kind, loving, devoted husband and father to a lecherous, deceitful cad.

I'm afraid I caused a bit of a scene in church yesterday. When your father offered an opportunity for attendees to make announcements, I stood up and declared, "I'd like you all to know that my husband and his secretary have been having an affair." A dead silence swept through the room, and Father was visibly shaken. What could be said after such an announcement? That the church potluck begins at noon?

I don't mean to make light of the situation, but I am dealing with it as best I can. If you agree, I plan to move to St. Louis and stay with you, but I will not impose for long. My friend, Essie, lives at the St. Louis Branscombe and she is keeping an eye out for an opening for a room there for me. What your father does is of no consequence to me at this point. He may plead to you to allow him to come along – that is up to you.

I'm sorry for the vulgar tone of this letter. My faith tells me that when a window closes, a door always opens. That is the message I am holding in my heart right now.

Much love, your mother

Ps – after my announcement, the Council President told the parish that the church would be closing for a week to "investigate".

August 28, 1941

Via telegraph

ATTN: REV. HARRY WISE
FROM: JANESVILLE METHODIST CHURCH ELDERS
THIS IS OFFICIAL NOTICE TERMINATING YOUR CONTRACT AS PASTOR DUE TO CHARGES OF INAPPROPRIATE CONDUCT. YOU WILL BE COMPENSATED UNTIL THE END OF THE YEAR.

1 September 1941

Dear Rachel,

I fear that emotions have swelled to a point where I am going to have to depart from my beloved Methodist church. Unfortunately, it has come to a point where Mother and I will be leaving immediately. Our original plan was to relocate to the Fond du Lac parish, but alas, that itinerary has been redirected to the south. I know that your mother is deeply aggrieved by the situation at hand, but I have faith that all necessary reparations will be made and life will return to our otherwise quiet and normal existence. Your mother has a forgiving heart and I'm sure that this bump in our journey will be behind us soon.

I have no choice but to ask you if we could respite with you for a couple of months until I find suitable employment outside of the church. As you may know, your mother is quite distraught about this change of events and she is buried in the agony of departure, so I am speaking on her behalf.

Our arrival will be on September 6th. Sadly, we are leaving Patty behind so that she can complete her high school education. Our dear friends, the Kruegers, have agreed to take Patty in until she completes her time at JHS. Janesville is now home for Patty, and I don't want to interrupt her studies because of my unfortunate situation.

I'm certain that you are curious about how a turn of events such as these could have happened given my history of my commitment to this faith. An explanation will follow post haste, as soon as I am able to humbly face my indiscretions without the presence of angst, regret, and I fear to admit, a waterfall of tears.

Begging your forgiveness, and understanding, Your devoted Father.

September 3, 1941

Darling Daddy,

I already have received correspondence from Mother regarding your move. While I don't like to pass judgment, I always believe that there are varying versions of every story told, and I hold on to the hope that the truth will prevail.

Of course, you and Mother can come and stay with us as long as you like! It will be nice to have the company as my days while Merlin is on the other side of the planet fighting for our freedoms. Right now, the days are long and tedious waiting for word of his safety. I could use some company.

I'm so disappointed that Patty won't be joining us, but I understand that she might not want to miss the revelry and finality of her last year in school. Since being on my own, I have learned that relationships can be strengthened when necessity dictates. I know it has been the case with me and Merlin.

So come quickly, my door will be open!

Love, Rachel.

September 10, 1941

My darling Patty,

Well, I just can't tell you how much fun I had during our August together in Janesville. It was hard to go back to Milton, but with my new responsibilities as President of the student body, my days are full with attending classes, athletic matches, and nightly social events. I would rather hunker down in my dorm room, but duty calls!

I'm sorry that you have been left in the manipulative clamps of the Kruegers. I know that they are God-fearing Christians, but they are sure to make your final year in high school restricted and lonely.

Despite your living conditions, I hope you are enjoying your senior year at JHS. What's going on there? Have you seen your former beau, Prescott Lustig? I would be very upset if I hear that you have been spotted painting the town with him while I agonize my way through another semester a mere fifteen miles north of you.

Yours, David

September 20, 1941

Dear David,

As you know, my parents departed from Janesville a couple of weeks ago, and are now living with my sister, Rachel, in St. Louis. Daddy is looking for a new job. The Kruegers own a house on top of the hill right above the high school. Momma and Daddy didn't want me to miss my last year in high school so they decided to leave me behind and quite frankly, I am pretty happy about that! It would have been terrible to have to start anew at a high school as a senior, but at the same time, I am lonely for my family.

Actually, I think there are other reasons that they left me behind, but I'm not in the mood to ponder those ideas. I believe that something happened at the church that I am not being informed about, and they are protecting me with their silence. I hear a lot of whispers and see inquiring eyes around me, and I feel like my church friends are avoiding me. At least I have our occasional times together to keep me grounded.

I hasten to suggest that our relationship is more than a boy/girl thing – in the event that you don't share the same sentiment! We have been seeing each other for 9 months now, doesn't that deserve some kind of milestone to show that we are a couple? I know that my friends tease me about being a "spoken for" woman, and I consider myself off the market. I hope that you share the same sentiment.

Love (hope that's not too bold!) Patty.

September 26, 1941

Dearest Little Patty,

How I miss my little sister! I'm sorry that I haven't written sooner, but I have been busy keeping up a household and tending to little Susie's every demand. You wouldn't believe what it takes to be a mother, but thankfully, Mother and Daddy are helping out and occasionally, I get a full night of sleep.

I hope that you are not struggling too much about them leaving you in Janesville, and that you have the support of your friends at this difficult time. It is an uncomfortable situation to deal with, but we have to believe that good will prevail when the dust settles and everyone recovers from the shock and sadness of Daddy's departure. Someday, little sister, when the time is ripe, the entire scenario will be brought to light, and we will work hard to understand, to forgive, and to keep love foremost in our hearts. You have to believe in that, Patty. Are there any whispers amongst the church folk? Are your cohorts at the Epworth League still treating you with kindness and respect?

We miss Merlin. He is so dedicated to his army, and to our family at the same time! We think of him daily, and our heart aches terribly.

When will you come to visit? What are your plans for after graduation? Merl,

Susie, and I are hoping to be able to attend your graduation ceremony.

How is life with the Kruegers? I'm sure that they are keeping a strong thumb on your comings and goings.

Sending much love your way, your adoring sister, Rae.

September 27, 1941

Dear David,

I have decided that I am going to get more involved in the Drama Club at school. It might help to take my mind away from the gnawing feeling that something isn't right with my folks. Anyway, the club is in need of a Treasurer, so I have agreed to assume the role. It isn't very taxing (ha ha, is that a pun?). We have very little money, and our expenses are few as most of the set items are donated. This year, we are doing a production of "Cock Robin", and I will be playing the part of Carlotta Maxwell. I can't believe that I have a role in a play! Normally, I wouldn't do anything as outrageous as this, but I seemed to have gotten caught up in the moment, and the next thing I knew, I was cast in the Carlotta role! It is a barrel of fun, and it will keep me busy during my senior (!) year. Can you believe it? I'm a senior! It's fun but I worry about what I am going to do after high school ends.

Will we be able to meet sometime in the next month or so? I know you are busy with your presidential duties, but I would hope that you could carve out some time for us to go on a date. The Kruegers are very strict about my comings and goings, so it would have to be pre-arranged and okayed by my parents. Perhaps we should think about the Homecoming dance? That's on October 26th.

Thinking of you, Patty.

September 30, 1941

Dear Rae,

I miss you terribly! The letter that you sent saying that you and Merlin (and baby Susie) were planning on attending my graduation sent me into orbit! What a wonderful thing that would be!

In answer to your inquiry about church scuttlebutt, I'm afraid that I have been kept out of the whisper and innuendo circle. I am still attending church and the Epworth League. Although there has not been even a mention to me about Daddy's departure, I have a feeling that there is talk going on when my back is turned. I am going to garner up my strength and ask Sally Wuthers, whose dad is a member of the elders, to see if she knows anything. It sounds as if Mother and Daddy have confided in you, so why am I not privy to the details? Sometimes you all treat me as if I were a child.

What, if anything, are you hearing about the war escalation? I am worried for your Merlin, and I hear that the government is starting to draft eligibly aged young men for service. I may sound selfish, but I am concerned about David's fate.

Love forever, Patty.

October 2, 1941

Boy's dorm
Mildew, Wisc.

Dear Patricia,

I apologize for being incommunicado during the past couple of weeks. Life is quite crazy here, and I have very little time dedicated to the things I enjoy most, i.e., YOU!

Monday night has rolled around and as I sit here nursing an over-stuffed abdomen I feel that studying is piling up all around me. Right now, this place is going mad, as is usually the case immediately after supper and the whole place is rocking with music, jokes, and general chaos and turmoil.

I locked my door but that is just a farce because "the boys" are so insistent in getting in that they will break the door down. My gallery is coaching me on what to say. By the way, Charlie Banks, a fellow roomer, saw you Saturday night and he thinks you are positively B –E –A-U-T-I-F-U-L.

Tomorrow I have but one class (and Glee Club) which I might take up if my working schedule will permit. I have almost lined myself up for a straight "A" in one course. My instructor in Speech heard the football broadcast the other night and commended my speaking voice.

Say, how about next Saturday? Are we still going through with that little "cottage deal" we had planned? If we are, I would like to know so I could further my plans. As yet, I can only think of one or possibly two couples I could ask. There is going to be a roller-skating party at Delavan in the evening so if we could go out in the afternoon and eat supper then we could all go out to the party – if you want to!

I attended five classes today and now I am pretty tired. The boys are going out on a rampage tonight so I think I'll go to bed around 8:30. Part of my fatigue is due to the fact that I had to chase a bunch of unruly freshmen who haven't been able to abide by the rules. We put Mercurochrome on Bob Tolen's face after a bit of a battle.

I am fairly sure that I can break away to attend your Homecoming festivities, although I must admit that I feel quite removed from the high school atmosphere. But if it is important to you, I will sacrifice and attend, albeit a bit unwillingly.

Right now I am going to mail this letter and if I don't get a line or two from you tomorrow, I'll be down to see what's wrong! I'm really emphatic about this issue.

So long for now, darling, and please write.

Love, Dave Jr.

October 10, 1941

Dear David,

I don't think that the cottage idea is going to work out. We don't have proper chaperones and I just don't see how we could get away with being alone. I am disappointed, but I know that we will be able to work something else out.

I am very busy with the upcoming play, and I hope you can break away from Milton to come and see it! There are only two performance dates, on the 28th and 29th of November. I think you might enjoy it.

I am very thankful of your friend, a Mr. Charles Banks, that he finds me to be attractive! I hope that I can meet him the next time that I am able to travel to Milton. Did you mention that because you are interested in pursuing other women?

Warm Regards, Patty.

October 13, 1941

Men's Dorm
Milton, Wisc.

My darling Patricia,

I received your letter this morning and was so shocked at its contents! I nearly fell off my chair when I read it. What the heck is wrong? Did I sound like I wanted to date someone else? After all, who started it all? I think you said something about wanting to "meet" this Chas. Banks because he said you were beautiful. Let's get this straight ... I have positively no desire to take out anyone else. I was almost ready to spank you when I heard that you ever thought of anything like that. We'll get off that subject now ...

Tomorrow, Milton plays Mission House at Plymouth and the boys want me to go. However, I don't think I will because I would have to "cut" my English Literature class and I don't think my Prof would be very agreeable. My Spanish Prof called off the Friday session because he's on the Athletic Board and is forced to attend the game which starts at 2 p.m.. It nearly broke his heart and he is trying to arrange an evening class for us so we won't get behind (nice guy).

The other night, when I was in Janesville, we got back at 10:35. I waited in the lobby for about thirty minutes and finally got disgusted and was ready to leave without them but being the "good fellow" I just went in and dragged them out by the nape of the neck. I took my history exam the next morning and I think I did all right on it.

Love, Dave Jr.

p.s. I think our Saturday night escapade is off, as for the little cottage deal! We will have to plan something different unless you can think of some kids to invite out. Banks is going to Manitowoc and Lucy is going too "steady" for the little plan. I'm afraid I don't care to invite any of these Miltonites. We can discuss it further tomorrow; please don't hesitate to ask any of your little friends if you still want to go through with this arrangement.

October 16, 1941

Dear David,

I'm so sorry that I missed you during your brief trip to Janesville on the 12th. My obligations with the school play, along with Homecoming preparations, have kept me quite busy. We are building a float for the Homecoming parade that looks like an argyle sock, and the theme is "Argyles will win!" We think it is a winner—how clever of a play on words!

I want you to know that I have no designs on your friend, Mr. Charles Banks. While it was flattering to hear such high praise, I will not submit to the pandering of a simple cad with the likes of him. Please do not speak of him in future missives.

Must go! Write soon! Fondly, Patty.

October 19, 1941

Dear Patricia,

Here is the letter like I promised. I got back here about 8:30 p.m. and the place was in one "ungodly mess". I began studying immediately and about 10:00 I became so disgusted that I turned off my light and climbed in bed.

I was up at 7:15, took my shower, and made my first hour History class. My program (I was supposed to see that those crazy ninnies were to put one on for radio speech) was a miserable failure. My "radio prof" consoled me in that none of the members were unwilling to cooperate (I set myself up for an "A" a long time ago).

After lunch this afternoon, I lay on my bunk studying in a free hour before my Survey class and I fell asleep dreaming of you; so I missed my Survey class.

Hon, I suppose we're going to the "mixer", aren't we? There isn't much going on this weekend so we will have to amuse ourselves in a dance or somethin'! Well I am going to close now and I had better get a LETTER from you … or ELSE!

So long for now, darling, Love, Dave.

October 22, 1941

Dear David,

You still have not confirmed whether or not you will be attending the Homecoming festivities this weekend. My girlfriends have been asking if I will be there … but I can't imagine going without you! Please let me know ASAP!

Patty.

via telegraph October 24, 1941

WILL BE THERE WITH BELLS ON. LOVE DAVID.

October 28. 1941

Dear David,

Thank you very much for attending the childish antics that comprise the Homecoming experience … it was very important to me that you were on my elbow. Janie and Stella remarked about how impressive it was to have a Milton man as a date! You are raising some eyebrows around J'ville!

Your college life sounds quite intriguing! Both of my sisters have experienced the "yoo-rah-rah" of college excitement, and I know it has been fascinating for them. I can't wait to get beyond the clutches of the Kruegers …God bless them both for agreeing to take care of me, but their rules are WAY too restrictive! Some days, I feel as if I am a prison mate. I am saddled with chores (which, to be honest, I am not accustomed to). It won't be a day too soon until I can be reunited with my family.

I am sorry that I broke the joyous spirit of the celebration by confiding in you about the ongoing dilemma and mystery surrounding my parents. I just know they are keeping some sordid details from my delicate ears, but I am determined to discover the root of all this alleged evil. I just hate to see the toll that it is taking – especially on Daddy, who seems particularly morose and downtrodden.

Thank you again, my knight in shining armor! Patty.

November 2, 1941

Dearest Patty,

I'm so sorry about the news regarding your padre. He is a stand-up gentleman and I'm sure there must be some kind of misunderstanding that led to his abrupt departure from the Methodist church. It is certain that he will find likeable work in the St. Louis area.

I had a great time at the Homecoming Dance last Saturday! Although it made me feel quite elderly … I was one of the older attendees, other than the chaperones. Your boyfriend is an antique!

I am quite busy handling my classes and planning for my responsibilities as President of Student Body. Given the national atmosphere of things going on in Europe, one has to be a little worried about when we will get involved in a war, and when I will be called to duty. I am not inclined to sign up, but if called, I will respond.

Let's try to get together before Thanksgiving! I think I can get a ride home either this weekend or next—maybe we could take in a movie together?

Sending a smooch through the mail, David.

November 5, 1941

Darling Daughter o'mine …

The days hang heavy as a London fog here in St. Louis as I ponder the 300-plus miles that separate us. My heart sinks down past my navel when I think that your own flesh and blood abandoned you with virtual strangers (may God's grace fall upon the Kruegers, but they must be like Nehemiah to live with). May your heart find peace in knowing that your mother and I made this painful decision to separate with your best interests in mind.

Your sister Rachel has been a gracious hostess, but soon we will be wearing our welcome thin. With God's grace upon us, we will find housing of our own and allow Rae and Merlin to resume the life of a newly married couple upon his return, absent the burden of aged parents.

Sending my heart to you … wherever it may rest between sternum and abdomen. It is difficult to locate at this time.

With heartfelt love, your humble father.

November 10, 1941.

Dear David,

My fall play is nearly approaching … I hope everything goes well! We are having a grand time! The plot is hilarious and intriguing—I hope you can find the time to attend one of our performances.

Thank you again for attending our Homecoming dance. I know it is hard for you as a graduate to come back and pretend to be excited about our event, but it meant a lot to me!

Today I received a letter from Daddy that almost reduced me to tears! No further explanation of the source of his sadness, but my heart seemed to rip as I read the brief note bereft with despair.

I hate the stories I am reading about the increased tensions in Europe, with this Adolf Hitler dominating the scene. It seems that he is hell-bent (sorry for the offensive wording!) on taking over every European country. Now I understand that he has a hatred for the Jewish population and is seeking to destroy their culture and populace. That doesn't seem very rational to me. Father always taught me that every person, regardless of race, religion, or beliefs, is the same in God's eyes. Even the negroes!

We are having cast parties after each show. It would be swell to have you there to show you off to my friends. I hope I'm not sounding too forward, but so many of my cast mates are wondering about this "mystery man from Milton" that I keep referring to. They must not have noticed us at the Homecoming Dance—did we stay in the shadows for too long? The thought of that makes me blush!

Mother and Daddy are going to try to come up for the first show, but it is unlikely that they will make it. Daddy is still struggling with finding a new job, and I'm sure their finances are strained. I don't think I will be able to go down to Thanksgiving to be with them because of limited time, money, and play practice.

I enjoy your letters, please keep writing!

Yours, dearheart, Patty.

November 27, 1941 – Thanksgiving

Dearest little Patty,

It is with a soul weighted down with a sack of rocks that I sit here at my typewriter and compose a letter to you, when you should be here with your family. Not only do I feel that we have abandoned you, but here we are at the holiday that celebrates family connections, and we are hours and hours apart. I hope that the Kruegers had a nice dinner and gathering for you to enjoy.

I'm sorry to report that my job search has been in vain. There are very few calls for a retired pastor/aged teacher/son of a gun like me. I have an interview on Monday with a small college in Illinois teaching divinity classes. I would hate to be apart from your mother, but necessity usually requires change.

Nothing will keep us apart from celebrating the next holiday together - please plan on packing your bags and heading south come Christmas break! We just are busting with anticipation until we can see you again, my darling.

Sending God's grace, and a bucketful of hugs, your father.

November 30, 1941 – Sunday after Thanksgiving

Darling Patty...

It was wonderful to spend most of the weekend with you. Most importantly, kudos! Your performance as Carlotta was quite entertaining, and a little seductive, if you don't mind me saying so! I hope that you consider pursuing a higher education in the dramatic arts, as your sister Rachel is doing. You are considering college, aren't you? We really haven't talked about it, but I think you would be an excellent student! Really, what else is there to do? Unless, of course, you got married right away as many girls your age do, and then settled in to run a household. Maybe that is an option!

Maybe we're too young to start thinking about it, but someday, I would love for you to be my wife! I've dreamed about it, having kids and living our lives together. We'd make a great married couple, don't ya think? I hope I'm not scaring you!

The natives are restless here ... lots of ruckus with everyone returning with a full belly and four days of freedom ... it's hard for some of them to buckle down again and remember what we're really here for. Honestly, Patty, I don't see some of these young bucks making it through the year. Their inability to control their impulses is only trumped by their ability to consume massive quantities of alcohol. Sometimes I feel like the headmaster rather than the class prez.

You mentioned the unrest across the ocean ... honey, that's been going on for a long time ... those Germans can't get along with anyone! I think their troubles will stay on their soil ... we learned our lesson getting involved in the World War. So you just concentrate on your studies, and enjoy your senior year (but steer clear of any activities involving the opposite sex)!

Must go ... things are getting out of control here, and I need to instill a little "parental discipline". Write soon!

Love to you! David.

December 5, 1941

Dear David,

School has been a riot since the play's debut! I must admit that I am enjoying the notoriety of having played a part in the production. Maybe you're right, I should consider pursuing college and the theater! I just haven't given it much thought up to this point. If Mother and Daddy were here, I'm sure they would be asking lots of questions about what I am going to do after graduation. The Kruegers are simple people—neither of them went to school beyond the 8th grade, so they don't care much about my future.

Guess what? The Drama Club president got mad about our choice for the spring play, "The Nutt Family", so she QUIT in a fit of rage! We voted 5-1 in favor of this production, and she stomped off like a spoiled child.

I am planning on going to St. Louis for the Christmas holiday. School lets out on the 19th, and I have off until January 5th. I will take the train down—it is a ten-hour ride, but I am excited to see my family again! I'm sorry that I won't be able to spend time with you, but I'm sure that you understand. I have been apart from Mother, Daddy, Rachel, and Jean for so long that I am just bursting with anticipation about being with them.

I can't understand your indifference about the developments in the war in Europe. The Japanese are also being quite aggressive. It worries me because if we are called into duty, all of the young men (you included) will have to report for duty and become part of the U. S. Army. I know that they take college men last, but it is a real concern for me.

I am going shopping today after school for Christmas gifts. Do you have anything in mind that you would like? I am getting Mother a new apron, Daddy a tie clip, Rachel a set of kitchen linens, and Jean, a pair of nylons. I have been saving my allowance since August to make these purchases … I hope they are all happy with my choices!

Maybe we can talk on the telephone soon! I know it is bold for me to make that suggestion, but with our limited time together, I just thought that it would be a good idea.

Warmest Regards (and love! Blush!) Patty.

8 DECEMBER 1941

LEARNED OF THE ATTACK ON PEARL HARBOR. AM SIGNING UP FOR THE US ARMY RESERVES OR AIR CORPS. MORE INFORMATION LATER.

DAVID.

Book Two
1942

January 5, 1942

Dear David,

It is positively mortifying what has happened over the last month! Who would have ever thought that the Japanese would attack us? The reports from Pearl Harbor have been devastating—so many lives lost, and so much destruction! I just hate it, but I understand your decision to enter the military to fight for us. It is scary, but I admire your commitment and patriotism. Lots of boys from school are signing up as well. I will stand by you during your service to our country, and beyond!

Your Patty.

January 8, 1942

Darling Patty,

Well, today is Thursday and I received your letter this morning. Thank you for your pledge to stand by me as we enter these troubled times with the European enemies. I have never felt such hatred toward a country in all of my life! Whatever made them feel compelled to attack … other than sheer arrogance and a need for control … I will never comprehend. Whatever the motivation, I will stand by my country and do whatever it takes to avenge the horrendous attack on an unsuspecting island hours from our shoreline.

We played our b-ball game last night and, as you will read in the paper, we were beaten 48-26! Whitewater is not in our conference so we still are unbeaten in conference competition.

I haven't heard back from the military board, but I know that sometime soon I will be called upon for service. That's okay, because I think that the raid on Pearl Harbor makes us all want to wage a war on the Japs to defend our boundaries. I want to finish my education, but more importantly, I want to serve my country.

I think I will be home Friday but I still don't know for sure. If I do get home I will call you immediately. It will be anytime from 4:00 to 8:00 depending upon the length of basketball practice and the difficulty of getting a ride home. So I'll see you, hon!

Dave Jr.

January 9, 1942

Dear youngest daughter,

My spirit has collapsed since the invasion on our Pearl Harbor. How can humans be so aggressive and bullyish? I fail to understand this need to control, to dominate, and to conquer. What has happened to the basic need to love?

I wish I could report some positive news about the job front. Apparently, there are many openings with the increase in draft notices being sent to our young men of this country, but nothing that employers would like to fill with an aging, mechanically challenged male. I must admit that I haven't been seeking the type of employment that uneducated, unskilled men would gravitate toward, but still, you would think that there might be some call for a handsome, humble, intellectual like me.

We miss you terribly and hope you understand that our motive for separation was purely for your well-being and not for ours. We plan on attending your graduation in June, then hope that you will be willing to pack your belongings and return to St. Louis with us. By that time, we hope to have established our own abode, and ceased to rely upon the kindness of your sister and her husband for our accommodations.

When I privately grieve of our distance, I try to console myself with the following:

The Lord is my shepherd;

I shall not be in want.

He makes me lie down in green pastures

and leads me beside still waters.

He revives my soul

and guides me along right pathways for his Name's sake.

Though I walk through the valley of the shadow of death,

I shall fear no evil;

for you are with me;

your rod and your staff, they comfort me.

We must all have faith that this outrageous demonstration of power and control will cease in the near future.

With much love, your loving Padre.

January 10, 1942

Dearest Patty,

Although I signed up to be a part of the Reserve Forces, I haven't heard anything back yet about my assignment. So for now, I will continue on my duties as class president and trying to rein in this rowdy group of ne'er do wells that they call our student body.

Our Glee Club is performing on Sunday for the Milton Alumni Association … we're doing a bunch of numbers from "Crazy from the Heat", a short-lived Broadway show. I just love to sing I know that you are interested in the theatre, but I've never asked if you prefer singing, dancing, or just performing in front of an audience. My favorite thing is to sing a cappella with a bunch of guys who can carry a tune and hear good harmony. I can't read music, but for some reason, I'm able to hear a melody and pound it out on the piano without the benefit of the written note.

I want to see you … soon! When can we meet again?

Sending love (I hope that's not too forward!) David.

[Author's Note: this is true. Dad had perfect pitch, couldn't read a note of music, yet was one of the best piano players I've ever heard. We used to gather around an old pump organ and he would blast out any request thrown his way.]

January 12, 1942

Baby sister,

I'll admit that I am no fan of this crazy war—I just can't believe it is happening! But it is putting bread and butter on our table while Daddy is out looking for some kind of employment. If you decide to come to St. Louis, I know that I can find a job for you here at Emerson Electric. They are always hiring girls to support the cause. You could help Momma and Daddy through this difficult time if you agreed to move here and work. Emerson builds gunnery machinery, but there are a number of different jobs you could take … honey, just come down here and join your family while we wait out the war.

Now I must tell you something that Momma and Daddy don't want you to know – because they are afraid that you will worry too much, and you are too young to understand. Because they have left you alone, wondering and worrying, I feel that I need to tell you what is going on. Rachel may disagree with me, but she is not my boss, so I will say what needs to be said.

Daddy was accused of an uninvited approach by Nancy, the church secretary. It was her word against his, and I'm afraid that the elders believed her story over Daddy's. At first he maintained his innocence. Nancy is a bitter old spinster who would stop at nothing to gain favor with the church elders. There were two meetings at the Janesville church where Daddy tried to explain the circumstances, but the elders took the side of Ugly Nancy. However, Daddy finally admitted to Momma that there had been some sort of clandestine relationship between him and Nancy. I don't know the exact details but I'm sure it involved some kind of misunderstanding on Nancy's part, and confusion on Daddy's part. His kindness and compassion could have easily be mistaken for a deeper bond existing.

As you know, Daddy is insanely in love with Momma! There have been times when I have sneaked in late at night after a date – way past curfew – and peeked in their bedroom door to find them entwined in in each other's arms! In the same bed! Even if there was some hint of indiscretion, I think we all need to embrace the story that we know is the final truth – Momma and Daddy are meant to be together eternally.

I don't know why Nancy would accuse Daddy of wrongdoing, unless she has a crush on him and he spurned her advances. I feel horribly for him. He has been made a scourge by church members who believe Nancy's story. Of course, Momma is stoically standing loyal by his side, but they have both been humiliated by the charges brought forth. Daddy will no longer be able to be a pastor of any Methodist Church, but I don't believe that after what he has endured that he would want to be a part of that group. This humiliation leaves him a pariah in the eyes of the parish and the church as a whole, regardless of where the truth lies. His move to St. Louis was one of desperation—to shield his family from the scorn of judging parishioners and to escape the sting of the vote of distrust from the church elders.

I'm sorry to have to inform you of the true details of Momma and Daddy's departure from Janesville, but hopefully it has blown over by this time, and there aren't rumors floating around that are soiling your reputation during your last months at JHS. I can't imagine the taunts, the skepticism, the hateful eyes. Regardless of any gossip or innuendo that falls on your ears, keep your eyes focused and your head held high.

Oh, Patty, I love you so much, and can't wait for a family reunion in St. Louis. Be strong of heart, keep your chin up, and remember that you are loved!

Your loving sister, Jeannie.

ps…how are things going with that college boy, David? It was nice to meet him. Is there a future with you two? Now that the war is going on, it might be smart to get engaged and marry him before he is called to duty. It's what all the girls are doing.

January 15, 1942

Dear David,

The situation with the war in Europe has me crazy with fear. All of the boys in my class are talking about enlisting, and how important it is for everyone to do their part to protect the world from Germany's dominance. I don't have plans for what I am going to do after high school, but all this talk is making me think that I should do something to help with the war effort.

I have heard from Mother and Daddy that he has found a teaching job in Lavelle, Illinois. Mother is going to stay in St. Louis until Daddy is settled and knows this is a sure thing.

I hope that you are enjoying your college life and aren't too worried about what will happen. What good does worrying do, anyway?

Sending love (also hoping it is not too forward), Patty.

JANUARY 20, 1942

HAVE BEEN CALLED TO REPORT FOR DUTY. TRAINING IS IN LAREDO, TEXAS, THEN I REPORT TO YUMA, AZ, FOR ADVANCED EDUCATION. I GUESS MY COLLEGE EDUCATION IS ON HOLD FOR NOW. LEAVE HERE ON FEBRUARY 1.

DAVID.

January 22, 1942

Dear David,

I received your telegram today. What do you mean that you are leaving? Don't you college boys get a special dispensation? I would like to see you before you depart. When can you come to Janesville? We must have a proper goodbye before you shipping out to parts unknown. I would not be able to cope with your departure without saying adieu (that must be the dramatic side of me coming out).

Your girl, Patty.

January 25, 1942

My darling Patty,

I could come to Janesville on January 29 for a farewell gathering. I hope that date works for you. I leave on January 31st to muster with my unit on the 1st.

It appears that the Army doesn't distinguish the college boys from the working boys anymore. The good of the nation is at stake, and I need to reply.

I hope that you are able to meet with me during those few days I have before I am sent off for basic training.

Your David.

January 27, 1942

David dear,

I will be waiting for you on the 29th, and I hope we can spend some time together before you leave for Laredo. My heart and prayers go out to you. Please telephone me when you get to town—the Kruegers will surely understand the urgency of our call.

With love and concern, Patty.

February 1, 1942

My dear Patty,

Today I reported for duty with 140 other recruits. We were stripped, shaved, examined, questioned, and run through a bunch of physical agility tests that Ulysses himself would have had a hard time passing. I'm afraid this will be my last correspondence until I am through with basic training. If I haven't said it before, I LOVE YOU!! Please stand with me until this ordeal is over.

David Jr.

ps. It would help me get through this training if you would respond with the same sentiment.

Here is a picture of your pop trying to understand the new concept of "Daylight-Saving Time" that the government is instituting next week. I really like your Dad, hon, but he just overthinks some ideas. He might be in bed for a week getting used to the change!

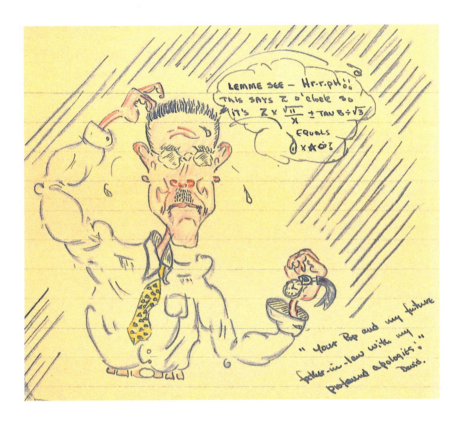

Harry Wise trying to figure out how Daylight-Saving Time will work

February 15, 1942

Dear David,

It is with a heavy heart that I hear of your deployment into the Army. I haven't written in the past two weeks because it is just too much for my heart to bear. Where will you be once you are done with training, and what will happen to you? I know that you have no answers to these questions, but it is difficult for someone in my position to respond appropriately.

I think that the best thing I can do at this point is to say "I love you, too!" and I can't wait to see you again.

Your Patty.

March 1, 1942

My darling Patty,

Our ability to communicate with the outside world is somewhat restricted at this time. I hope you understand that this is the first time I have been permitted to write a letter, and of course, the first person I wanted to write to was YOU.

The one thing that is getting me through this induction to the Army is your last missive ... reading that you LOVE me put me through the roof!! I can now face any obstacle or hardship, knowing that you will be waiting for me when this is all done and over.

Basic training is quite grueling ... we are up at 0500 hours for calisthenics and a run, then have breakfast at 0630. The food is palatable but doesn't rise to the level of "good". We run drills until the next chow time, then have two hours to eat and relax. One more dose of marching and foxholing follows, then we have chow and lights out at 2100 hours. I'm not sure what is worse—life in the dorm or life in the barracks! I have to admit that I miss those hooligans at Milton.

My training is scheduled to be over on April 15. We have a "graduation" ceremony but I wouldn't expect you to make the trip to Laredo to see them slap a stripe on my arm. The only thing I am living for at this point is to see you again. How can we meet after the 15th?

Love always, David

Book Three
1942 (continued)

March 15, 1942

Dearest David,

Thank you for your letter. I hope that your time in Laredo passes quickly. You are right—I won't be able to travel there for your graduation, but I will be available when you return to Wisconsin. With my senior year drawing to a close, I have some more flexibility with my schedule. Who cares if I miss some classes, or fail a subject or two? It's not like I am going off to college and need good marks. I just want to get through our spring production of The Nutt Family. I'll be playing the role of Mrs. Nutt … she is quirky and a little daft … it's going to be fun! That is my priority right now.

This summer, I hope to work at a restaurant in Fond du Lac, near our place on Lake Winnebago, or in the pea cannery in Janesville. After that, I just don't know what will happen! I'm feeling like I need to do something to help with the war effort. I am also missing Momma and Father terribly ... I may move to St. Louis to be with them.

Love you always; you are my soldier, my friend, and my love. Patty.

April 1, 1942

My dearest Patty,

We are nearing the end of our training here in Laredo. I have had enough of marching in heavy boots and eating bland cafeteria food! I understand why this training is necessary, but I am hoping that President Roosevelt can work out a deal with the European countries to end this war ASAP.

I doubt that I will be able to see your production of the "Nutts"—it sounds like a lot of fun. You'll have to tell me all about it when it is over.

Your letters are the only thing that keep me in step here. Please write as often as you can and remember that I LOVE you and MISS you terribly!

Yours truly (forever!), David.

April 10, 1942

Dear David,

We are finally over our spring production of The Nutt Family. What an endeavor!

So many of our classmates are talking about enlisting when they graduate. I don't want them to go, but I understand that the war effort is in need of a large number of enlistees. It saddens me to watch all of these hearty, healthy boys sign up to fight overseas. I know we have a duty to secure the world against the threat of fascism, but at the same time, I wonder how we can stop a person like Mr. Hitler. He has been able to draw in so many supporters ... how can we fight that kind of influence? It is just such a sad situation, but you know that the good ole' U. S. of A. will be victorious. I just hope this whole thing is settled before it goes much further.

I am excited about graduation! Momma and Daddy are coming back for the ceremony! Jeannie, Rachel, Merlin and Susie are also planning on attending—won't that be something if we could all be together again? It makes my heart hurt to think about them, so I try to keep busy with other endeavors. It sure is hard to do any schoolwork anymore—my mind always drifts off to that special day in June when I will no longer have to attend school! I was never much of one for studies anyway, so as long as they let me graduate, I'm fine.

Do you know for sure when you will be returning from your basic training? I hope we can see each other this summer a bit—do you think you will be returning to your job at Parker Pen? I think that Momma will want me to go to Illinois again to visit with the cousins, and I suppose I'm going to have to start thinking about getting a job. What else would I do with myself?

I'm off to get an ice cream with Ruth and June … let me know your plans for returning!

Fondly and lovingly, Patty.

TELEGRAM – 16 APRIL 1942

PATTY, I AM BEING RELEASED FROM BASIC TRAINING ON 21 APRIL, WILL TAKE A TRAIN TO CHICAGO AND DAD WILL PICK ME UP. HOPING YOU WILL CLEAR YOUR CALENDAR FOR A DATE ON APRIL 23. MISSING YOU TERRIBLY. DAVID.

1st of May, 1942

Dear David,

How wonderful it was to have you in my arms again! Basic training seemed as if it lasted FOREVER. I know that you can't go back to Milton at this point in the semester, but hopefully in the fall you will return as class president and be able to finish your degree. Don't you think that this war will be over soon?

My graduation is in six weeks, and everyone is going to attend. Mother, Dad, Rachel, and Jeannie will be in the audience. Once again, I don't know what I will do once graduation is over. My inclination is to move with my parents to St. Louis after the summer is over. It appears that this war effort is continuing—rationing of gas and sugar has begun, so I think I should probably join in and help with the cause.

Let me know what you think about this. What good news it was to learn that you will be nearby – at least until your next assignment, but from what you said, it will be a few months in Janesville and a return to college life in the fall! It's hard for me to think too far ahead, because I am just hoping to spend most of the summer with you. Being back home is probably a far cry from having your own dorm room or eating Army rations!

Your Patty.

September 3, 1942

My darling Patty,

How wonderful it was to spend time in the same town this summer! Returning to the old sots at Milton is bittersweet … I was glad to see some of these old SOB's, but their juvenile hijinks can get tiring quickly. I'm relieved to be back in the arms of Academia after three long months as best friend to a factory line at Parker Pen. I was one of the few men under the age of forty to return, so much of the season I was peppered with questions like, "When are you going over, boy?" and "Good thing you're a preppie boy, hey?" and "Wouldn't want to have to fight for your country like the farm boys".

The good news is that I have accumulated enough credits to be officially counted as a "junior". I have decided to stay on as Class President but will be living in the Psi Kappa Pi fraternity house. Whether or not that will be an improvement over the Boy's dorm is yet to be seen … they are a great bunch of guys, but they can drink circles around the freshmen and sophomores! And, our obligation with socializing with the sororities is heightened as a house resident … we are expected to host a number of parties and be in attendance to others.

I have a busy schedule this fall ... courses in History, Philosophy, Ethics, and Geography ... plus the basketball coach has been draggin' on my drawers to join the team again ... and there is Glee Club as well!

My roommate Strohbusch is jumping on my bunk, wanting me to join the boys downtown, so I had better close this. Hope to see you soon, my love!

David

September 10, 1942

Dear David,

I wanted you to be the first to know—I am leaving the Krueger residence and moving to St. Louis to be closer to my family. Being fifteen miles away from you while I am in Janesville and you are in Milton is difficult, but the thought of being 300 miles away from Momma and Father just rips at my heart. Even though St. Louis is not my home, I am homesick.

The Kruegers have been more than hospitable in caring for me during the last fifteen months, but it is time for me to find a path of my own. I cannot keep on being stagnant in Janesville, staying here because I consider it to be my hometown and holding down my mundane job at the pea cannery. There really is nothing left here for me, except waiting for the occasional weekends that you are able to visit. My family needs my support in St. Louis, and the uncertainty of when we can be together again is unnerving.

I am packing my bags as I write this letter and plan on being on the 3:20pm train to St. Louis on the 13th. Jeannie thinks she can get me a job at Emerson Electric there, which I intend on accepting.

I don't want to leave Wisconsin, or to leave you. My hope is that I will be employed with Emerson and somehow make a difference in the effort against Mr. Hitler's aggression.

I will miss you terribly.

Yours forever, although miles apart, Patty.

September 15, 1942

My darling Patty,

I can understand your confusion about a future course of action ... given your father's uncertainty with his teaching job and your loneliness in Janesville. All I can say is that I am sorry for all of the chaos and upheaval that this war- my schooling – and the situation with your folks has caused.

The Army tells me that I will be able to finish this semester at Milton, but my future after that point is unpredictable. Right now, I am trying to juggle my course load with Glee Club, President of Student Body, and being a member of Alpha Kappa Pi.

I just wish there was something I could say to relieve you of your worries .... babe, I hope it helps to know that I am in your corner, and I will do whatever it takes to make your life more bearable!

Yours always, David.

October 1, 1942

Dear David,

Well, I am settled in with Jeannie and Gerry in a little apartment and have started work at Emerson. Our war efforts have begun. I am feeling like I am doing my part to help, but yet it still doesn't seem like enough.

Jeannie and Gerry are gone most of the time, since Gerry talked Jeannie into leaving Emerson and getting jobs as stewardesses on the train. I am quite lonely in my apartment and now that Jeannie is gone, and I haven't made any friends at work. When do you think you could come to visit? Always in my thoughts and prayers, with love, Patty.

October 15, 1942

My darling Patty,

With my crazy schedule, I don't see how we could be together until Thanksgiving break. I miss you so much! Life is full here in Milton ... my "prez" duties require me to be acting as a father figure most of the time. These kids are crazy! If they're not drinking, they're finding ways to get into trouble with hijinks. The vandalism complaints are going through the roof. Somehow, that ends up on my shoulders ... how am I going to control this band of ruffians?

I'm sorry to hear of the goings on between your folks and this "Nancy" ... when I met her, she seemed like a great gal! I can't believe that she was involved with your dad and then went on to accusing your pop of unwanted advances when she didn't get her way. Your pop obviously loves your mom and is regretting his errant ways.

Must run and snuff out another "fire" of young bucks causing trouble .... pray for me!

DKH Jr.

November 1, 1942

My dear David,

It sounds as if you have your hands full with the youngsters becoming used to college life at Milton. Why does the President have to reside over the antics of all of these characters? You must also be getting ready for the basketball season ... will you be filling the position of center again?

I feel that I am aiding the war effort by working at Emerson, but it is far from what I hoped to make a difference. We are rationing our basic supplies, but somehow, that doesn't feel like we are doing enough. I continue to hope that you are not called to duty anytime soon.

Can we get together for Thanksgiving? Mother and Rachel are putting together a feast that you would enjoy, and you are welcome to stay at their apartment.

Daddy and Mother are still not talking about the circumstances surrounding their departure from Janesville, despite the fact that Jeannie has already disclosed her version of the story. They must think that I am too young to understand the details. The few times I have seen them, it seems that there is an impenetrable rift – an anger that floats like thick fog. But I am holding out hope that this is a passing fog that soon will be blown out to sea, and that their ships will stop passing and pull into port together. Hearts will soften, and they will rediscover the power of forgiveness. It's just part of who they are! I know it to be true!

Thinking of you, Patty.

December 2, 1942

My dear Patty,

Thank you for including me in your Thanksgiving feast last weekend. Mother was a bit upset that I was in Saint Louie for the holiday rather than staying home in Janesville, but it was worth it! Your family is an absolute HOOT. Playing "charades" was comical with your dad trying to display the story of Noah—hilarious! Who would have thought to point upwards to make us guess the story!

I am back at Milton with this group of hooligans that keep me busy putting out fires. If I had known what the position of President involved, I never would have run! I am the world's busiest babysitter! Today I had to traverse to the local tavern and pull some gents by the scruff of the neck out before the owner had them tossed out on their keisters!

I'm glad that we had a chance to talk about your folks … gee, I really feel badly for your folks, but it appears that they are handling it with grace and dignity. Their listing ships will be righted soon, you'll see.

Hoping to hear from you soon, sending love, David,

December 15, 1942

Dearest David,

My life working at Emerson is quite dull, and although I am happy to be with Jeannie and Momma and Daddy, there isn't much more to report. What are you doing for Christmas? We will be spending the holidays with Rachel. Is there any chance that you could come down to St. Louis again?

Daddy is still in a state, thinking that you will be sent overseas and that you and I shouldn't commit to anything long term. I just don't know what is right, other than I get butterflies in my stomach every time I think of you. Daddy just wants me to go back to school and continue on my studies and forget about boys in general, but I just can't help it! I would rather become a wife and mother than to pursue a silly career. But who knows what will happen in the world at this point? Every day, I wonder if you will have to leave school to protect our country. Of course, Daddy also thinks that I am much too young to make any promises to one boy. He probably has a point to consider – after all, I'm only eighteen!

Let me know your plans for Christmas break ASAP.

Fondly and lovingly, Patty.

TELEGRAM, DECEMBER 20, 1942

HAVE BEEN ORDERED TO REPORT FOR DUTY ON 2 JANUARY 1943. TRAVELING TO YUMA AZ FOR TRAINING AS A GUNNERY INSTRUCTOR. WILL SEND MORE INFO AS IT ARRIVES. WILL NOT BE ABLE TO CORRESPOND DURING THIS ASSIGNMENT. SENDING LOVE.

December 31, 1942

Dearest David,

Happy New Year! I wish that I were in Janesville with you. We are celebrating in a quiet way—a little champagne and many tears. Not only do we know that you are headed to Arizona in two days, but Merlin is being kept in the Pacific for another assignment. How will Rachel survive?

Emerson is a supportive place—they give us regular updates on the status of our soldiers. We are building gunnery cases—isn't that ironic? You, a gunnery instructor, and me, part of building gunnery cases! It is a sign that we are meant to be together.

And yet, there is a part of me that wonders if we can survive the strain and uncertainty that wartime creates. Not having you by my side feels like I am missing a limb, yet maybe Daddy is right about us steering away from commitment. I don't know how long I can endure that constant agony, knowing that you are in danger's path. Perhaps we should reconsider whether our relationship can overcome the loneliness and insecurity that comes hand in hand with combat, if it comes to that point in this lousy war.

With love, Patty.

Book Four
1987–1992

June 1987

Dear Cousin Barby,

I have missed being able to talk to you on a regular basis like we did as teenagers! How did it happen that we grew up and are now raising children of our own? I long for the days when we zipped around town in your mom's 1967 Cougar convertible, chasing boys and spending the evenings at the drive-in theatre.

I look back twenty-some years ago and realize how much the world has changed. Recalling those days I realize that the four of us, Dave Junior, Jean, me, and Tim, struggled with the same issues that most children of the 60s faced. Speak when you are spoken to. Come home when the street lights go on. Don't bother us unless you're bleeding. Yet in our household, the bar was raised a bit. If you didn't rise to Dad's level and earn a PhD, you were nothing in his eyes. We were all failures, and it has haunted us into our adult years. Mom chose to take the path of the passive, submissive spouse who never stood up for us and our life choices. It was a different era—when men were men, and women were subservient. I see now how the four of us just had to deal with it and figure out our own survival. We were just props for the drama played out in our parents' lives. They needed pawns in the chess game of life, posing for happy family pictures, attending uncountable university social events, pretending that we were the quintessential family others should aspire to be, and most importantly, always trying to please mom and dad. An impossible task. The sad and sorry truth was, we were alone and there was nothing we could do to measure up to the standards they set for achievement. No matter what we accomplished, we knew it would never meet the unattainable standards that had been silently, clandestinely, established for us. We were the hamsters stuck in the wheel – running, running, to no avail.

Dave Jr. continues to struggle with issues that probably stemmed from the year he spent in Vietnam. Jean is a mother of two who works menial jobs and didn't finish her college degree. I earned a Master's degree (not good enough) – tried law school and failed miserably. Tim is still selling cars at a Ford dealership, but he is hugely successful! None of that seems to matter. This was not the scenario that my dad had in mind. We were to be scholars, doctors, researchers, analysts, world changers. We ended up being disappointments, and that has haunted us throughout our adult years. Instead of making a world of difference, we have inflicted a world of hurt.

Let's go back to the carefree days of the 70s! I love my family, but rarely a day passes when I don't think about the way my dad looks at us with disdain. Why can't we just be good kids, doing good things, raising good children? When did that become not enough?

Your cousin, Elle.

October, 1988

Dear Barby,

The four of us are holding a vigil at Dad's deathbed. We know it is only a matter of hours until his demise. We are told that he is suffering from colon cancer, but all of us know that what will be written on the death certificate reflects the real truth—cirrhosis. His liver was dying because he chose to drink himself to death.

The one thing that we can't figure out is that he seemed to have had such a charmed life. Married to a beautiful, engaging woman for over forty years—he had *us*, the four offspring of his connection to his darling Patty. Why wasn't that enough? Why could we never measure up and be enough for him? Why did the four of us make him feel so pained, so inadequate, that he chose the bottle over us?

But this all sprouted in the 60s, when relationships were less open than we enjoy now in the 80s. Addictions were to be hidden, not paraded around like a participation badge. We weren't beaten (very much), we had the basic necessities. Childhood wasn't painful, it wasn't abusive, it was just deranged. Our adolescent lives were pretty typical. The rules of life were pretty simple: just shut up, you will be fed and clothed, and damn it, you will appreciate it. End of story.

I often think of how different it is raising children of the next generation. We hover their every movement – they can't ride a bike or roller skate without a helmet (I never even owned a helmet!). Every moment is to be accounted for – with schedules, play dates, soccer practices, dance lessons – no wonder we are all exhausted. When I was growing up in Thailand, our parents signed us up for dance lessons (I'm sure with the agenda that we would put on performances for their friends, showing off what a happy, well-adjusted group we were). The funny thing is that they would call a cab and have the maid accompany us to the lessons! Never once did they show up for a rehearsal.

Death stirs so many memories – I just wish that more of them were positive, happy ones. You too? Why do our brains focus on the bad? Is it a choice, or is that part of our mind more powerful than the part that houses the good?

But that was then, and this is now. Time to move along and live our own lives, and let go of the skeletons that haunt us when we have time to ponder the past. Wait – when do we have time to ponder? Must go – write soon.

Your cousin, Ellen.

January 1991

Dear Barby,

Dad has been gone for a little over three years now. Although Mom has adjusted to widowhood quite well, it wasn't long after Dad's death that potential suitors started sniffing around. At sixty-eight years old, Mom is still quite remarkable – stately, a world traveler, well read, elegant, and sharp. Not to mention that she has a beautiful condo on the shores of Grand Traverse Bay in northern Michigan.

Two of her first gentlemen callers were former friends of my Dad. Raymond had recently lost his wife to cancer. They met when Dad and Raymond were assigned to Bangkok to develop a satellite campus for Michigan State University in the 60s, and the four of them were inseparable during the 70s. Raymond and his wife were frequent visitors at our cabin in northern Michigan, which always involved a heavily imbibed cocktail hour every Friday night and lots of revelry to follow.

Raymond wasn't adjusting well to being alone, so it was just a matter of weeks after Gracie passed that he was knocking on Mom's door. Mom was having no part of that – perhaps it was too soon, or Raymond was just too familiar.

Next came John – who was still married! A retired professor who went to law school when he was fifty-five, John and Dad taught Humanities together back in the 50s. The four of them – Mom, Dad, John, and Ruth, were social acquaintances, but apparently in John's mind, there was something more.

He called Mom on the premise to discuss matters of the will, but he was definitely willing to do more than provide legal advice. Mom put the kibosh on that plan, gave him his walking papers, and never heard from him again.

Friends of Mom have set her up on a blind date to meet this new gentleman – Roy. I don't know much about him, but as soon as I learn something, I will let you know! Imagine Mom on the dating scene again – although if truth be told, she doesn't like the solitary life, and she is really quite a hussy!

Your loving cousin, Elle.

March 14, 1991

Dear Elle,

How do find time to write letters? It must be a genetic thing – your mom would write to Grandma and my mom every week. I can hardly find time to put together a shopping list – so more often than not, I just fly by the seat of my pants!

All is good here – the boys are busy with their activities. I'm putting the finishing touches on my thesis to finally finish my Master's degree! I'll be glad when school is over.

Your last letter about your mom being an unwilling female Casanova made me laugh! Do you think she is going to settle down with one of her many suitors? Knowing your mom, my guess is NO. She will be jetting off to some exotic destination, fleet of foot with chardonnay in hand. Let's hope our lives are that exciting when we get to be her age.

Love you, Barby

June, 1991

Dear Barby,

I recently told you that Mom has been set up on a blind date. She claimed that she shunned his advances and refused to go out with him, but he was persistent. He arrived at the condo promptly (no, early) at 4:30 for a 5:00 p.m. dinner. Flowers in hand, and sweet talk in mouth, he wasted no time in wooing, crooning, and eventually winning her over. I guess we have to brace ourselves that Mom is going to remarry, and that we are going to have a new "dad".

Roy is a handsome, talented, interesting person with very few words to offer, but when he speaks, you listen. At five feet-six, with wiry hair and a full beard, all of salt and pepper, his eyes penetrate your soul and reach the depths of your being. There is something magical about his presence, and as much as

I want to hate him for taking my dad's place, I can't help but feel a connection. And, most importantly, he worships Mom.

Do you want to be invited to the wedding? I have a feeling that something might be happening SOON.

Love you, Elle.

January, 1992

Dear Barby,

As I predicted, Mom and Roy have made their connection official, and nuptials are complete! They didn't even give us a chance to send out invitations. They held a casual wedding in South Bend, Indiana at the Holiday Inn. All seven children and our spouses and offspring were in attendance. Fortunately, there was a bathtub full of champagne (literally—we filled the tub in room 106 with ice, and stuffed copious amounts of the bubbly therein) which helped us all to cope with the co-mingling of two families. While the children played in the pool and the shuffleboard court, we, the adult kids, drowned ourselves in enough alcohol to ease the awkwardness of becoming a newly merged, uncomfortable, clumsy, family unit.

I know you wanted to be a part of this union, but again, they sprung it on us with a week's notice. We hardly had time to pack before putting the girls in the car and speeding off to South Bend! Crazy!

I wonder if Mom has told your mother – she has been very secretive about the whole relationship, and all of a sudden, we have a new "family"!

Cousins (but really, sisters) always, Elle.

Book Five
1943

May 1943

Dear Mom Wise (may I call you that? Apologies if I am being too bold),

Don't be alarmed when you see the mass of stamps on the envelope – I just leave a bit of extra maguna to spend. However, this epistle has a very special message and I'm sending it to you so that you can break it lightly or at least prepare Patty for the shock.

Before this reaches you, Patty will know that I'm coming home on "delay enroute" but after contemplating for a long time, I couldn't think of the proper words to tell her that it will be my last for quite some time as I have been accepted to serve overseas (unknown when that will be) after a short "refresher" course at Laredo, Texas. You have, no doubt, heard that I had volunteered for combat duty a couple times before but was rejected because of the fact that I lacked a few weeks of the required six months of instructing. Now they have issued a waiver because of previous education. Actually, it is an act of cowardice since my primary desire is to escape this &^%%$#@& desert and I'm almost ashamed to face my buddies here.

At any rate, I feel very fortunate that I could get that much time home before going! Enough of that! All I ask is your permission to bunk with you for a few days until I can find suitable accommodations.

Our life of late in Yuma has been anything but dull. Our "CO" has been having a heyday introducing new and clever schemes of keeping the boys on the ball. This has led to such disastrous things as being on time for most of our classes, attending lectures and meetings most faithfully, and putting our students on the beam whenever we suspect the gestapo around – saluting hi at the slightest provocation; oh, what the morbid existence!

Now I must pack this letter – we expect to leave tomorrow night – 'til about Saturday.

Love, Dave Jr.

Just in case you've forgotten what to expect when I hit St. Louey…

May 29, 1943

My Darling Patty,

I'm FREE! My training in Yuma is officially over, and I'm preparing to leave for home in the next couple of days. I have been officially commissioned as a "Gunnery Instructor", but I could be coming home as one of the Three Stooges and I would be as happy as a pig on wheels.

I will be heading in on a train to Saint Louie on the 5th… do you think you could meet me there? All I want right now is to spend a lifetime with my girl … but I will settle for a few weeks if that is all the Army can give me. I love you dearly!

Patty, can't you tell me once again that you love me back? I am so lonely and missing you so badly … your letters are quite cold. How about some loving? Please, I need to know.

David.

TELEGRAM – June 2, 1943

TO: PFC DAVID HEENAN
FROM: PATRICIA WISE

WILL BE THERE WITH BELLS ON! I DON'T REALLY KNOW WHAT THAT MEANS, BUT IT SOUNDS GOOD! CAN'T WAIT FOR YOUR ARRIVAL. YES, I LOVE YOU TOO. I WON'T REALLY BE WEARING BELLS. WILL YOU RECOGNIZE ME? MOTHER SAYS YOU ARE WELCOME TO STAY AT HER PLACE AS LONG AS YOU LIKE. YOUR FOREVER PATTY.

September 2, 1943

My darling Patty,

What a great summer we spent together … those nights at the drive-in theatre … hugging and kissing afterwards … I just loved every minute of being with you!

Now that the Army has postponed my training in Laredo, I am back at Milton, once again filling the role of "parent" as President of the student body … and these kids are testing my mettle, getting into all kinds of trouble that you would never understand! I don't understand it myself … throwing eggs at the President's house, tearing down the float for the senior's Homecoming parade … and dropping their drawers (sorry for the thought I put in your mind) in front of the Delta Zeta house! I just don't know how I can bring these hooligans under control.

What is happening in St. Louie? I hope that you are behaving yourself and not being a gadabout with the fellows at the Emerson plant.

Basketball practice starts in about a month … I don't know how I am going to get in shape again. Army training put me in a good place, but since my departure, I have slacked off and have avoided anything that involves physical exertion.

Can't wait to hear an update. Write soon!

d.

September 13, 1943

Dear David,

My life as an employee of Emerson Electric is quite mundane. I moved from building gunnery cases to checking time cards and hope that I am doing something to help the war effort, but quite honestly, it seems to be a hollow attempt at "making a difference". We all need to contribute, but I feel like my contribution is quite empty and meaningless. Should I join the USO?

Good luck with your basketball career, and with maintaining order as President! If I were a student, I would surely obey your directives.

Sending love, Patty.

September 21, 1943

My darling Patty,

Our football team has been dismantled due to the situation in Europe. The administration feels that every able-bodied student should be ready for deployment, so putting together a team is frivolous and extraneous. I just don't know how I will rally the troops to support our alma mater if there are no teams to cheer for.

As for joining the USO, honey – I support the war effort (as you know!) but the thought of putting you in harm's way crushes my every dream for the future. Stay with Emerson. Our future depends on it.

Your love, David.

October 1, 1943

Dear David,

I continue to grow weary of the life of a factory worker. I received your admonishment about considering the USO—now I know what I DON'T want to do in the future! The redundancy and routine of factory life are enough to make one want to pull the hairs out of one's head. College life looks so appealing right now! Maybe I should start thinking about making a change—but at the same time, I feel a duty to continue to help with the war effort.

Rationing continues to make life difficult and inconvenient – I don't know if it applies to those of you in the service. I'm hearing rumors that soon other items will be added to the list, including shoes, nylon stockings, jams and jellies – all of my favorite items!

Well, I must take a quick shower and prepare to return to my dreary existence tomorrow. I hope that this war comes to an end soon so that we can all return to our normal lives.

Sending love, Patty.

October 13, 1943

My darling Patty,

Chaos is the word that comes to mind when I try to think of one word to describe my life here at Milton. Between putting out fires set by rambunctious underclassmen (last week, they picked up the President's car and moved it on its side!), the duties of being part of a fraternity (endless parties), and my coursework ... I feel that I don't have a moment of peace to myself.

Classes are going well ... I have mid-term exams coming up next week, so that will give me a better idea of how I stand in the academic part of my life.

I just heard from Mother that brother Don is being deployed overseas in two weeks. He and Doris are going to get married before he leaves! There will not be a formal ceremony, just a trip to the Justice of the Peace. I hope that I can attend to lend some support and to enjoy their day of happiness ... maybe we should think about the same thing!

No, I know that is foolish ... you deserve a proper wedding and I hope that we can start making plans toward that end! This is not a formal proposal, for I will come down to St. Louie and ask your father's permission before I ask you to marry me, but I want you to know that it is in the works! I love you, Patty, and I hope that when the time is right, you will accept my request to become my wife. Wouldn't life be grand if we could live it together? I miss you so much!

Must go ... apparently some thugs have jumped the school mascot and tied him to a flagpole! I never get any rest from their shenanigans!

Love, David.

November 23, 1943

Dear David,

Thanksgiving is just two days away! How I wish I could be spending the holiday with you! I read the proclamation that President Roosevelt just issued, and I know that we all have to be brave and to stand firm as our troops battle for our freedom in parts unknown to us.

Mother and I are trying to concoct some Thanksgiving recipes that don't require turkey or other ingredients that we are saving to send to our soldiers on the battlefront. We will be serving a "Meatless Mince Pie" and substituting butter for this new oleo margarine that is occasionally available in the grocery store.

Love to you, Patty.

24 NOVEMBER 1943

RECEIVED NOTIFICATION THAT I AM TO REPORT TO ARMY TRAINING AT 0600 HOURS ON 29 DECEMBER 1943. TRAINING IS IN LAREDO TX. MORE DETAILS WILL FOLLOW.

1 December 1943

Dear David,

Youngest daughter Patricia has informed me that you may be seeking her hand in marriage. I would like to weigh in on your contemplation of entering into this lifelong commitment.

Patty has a mercurial temperament that you may not have experienced during your brief encounters. She is indeed the most spirited of my three offspring. She holds no bars in stating her opinions and is quite loquacious in offering her ideas in matters that affect the home front. I would not take lightly your suggestion that the two of you become entwined in a long-term relationship. She is a rogue and has not yet had the opportunity to "sow her oats" as she has been housed in the comfort of many parental situations for most of her childhood. She is flippant, and headstrong—many of the qualities that most men would find offensive and annoying.

I understand that your deployment to Europe is pending after this next bout of training in Texas. I hope that you will not enter into a rash decision about marriage as a result.

I will not oppose your suggestion of marriage to Patty, but I just want to warn you of the potential pitfalls. Why not wait until this silly war is over, and start with a clean slate?

Warm Regards,
Rev. Harry Wise

2 December 1943

Dearest David,

It is just fabulous that you can spend a few precious days here before training begins! I'll be waiting for you whenever you are free.

Daddy is still struggling with his work at Lavelle (partly due to the distance from Momma, I think, but also due to a lack of challenge and mental stimulation). As a result of his Janesville experience, I believe that he has become jaded from continuing on as a minister. Ultimately, I think he would like to teach at a seminary, but positions are scarce and the ones that are available seem to be on the east or west coast. He has fallen into a great depression, and I am terribly worried for his well being. So many difficult situations in such a short time span would wreak havoc on anyone.

Thinking about the possibility that you will be with me and my family before your departure make my heart flutter and make me lose the ability to breathe! Let me know your arrival plans (I'm counting on this, and as you know, I usually get my way), so I can wrap my arms around you when you pull into the train station! Then we will enjoy a splendid holiday together … what happens from there, no one knows, but at least we will have the joy of Christmas.

Sending love your way, Patty.

21 December 1943

My darling Patty,

I am whoopin' and hollerin' right now 'cause I just found out that we will be able to spend Christmas Day together … I have completed my final examinations at Milton and am hopping on a train on the 24th to arrive on Christmas Day. Sorry to disrupt your family celebration, but there is just no other way that I can get down there to see you again. And with my pending departure for another Army training, it may be our last chance to be together for a long while.

Much love, David.

28 December 1943

Darling David,

It was with great heartache that I put you back on that train yesterday. How could the Army pull you away from me? I am rewinding in my memory our last moments—you, handsome in your Army attire, wrapping your arms around me, and promising that you will be back soon. Me, a complete wreck—makeup amiss, hair out of place—why would you ever want to return to such a sight? It's probably better to sail off to a place where there are women who are more appreciative and attractive than I. Not that I am wishing for that, but I just don't see what you see in me that makes you want to commit to a life together, spending your life with me raising your children.

Let me know how things go in Texas. I dread to hear the news of what happens after Laredo. I may have to don earplugs and eyepatches until this war is over and you are safely back in my arms. You are missed and loved here.

Yours forever, Patty.

Book Six
1993–2009

June, 1993

Dear Barby,

Well, I guess that Mom is loving her new life with her new husband. We hardly hear from them at all, and when we do, they are always running off to some new adventure! While I am glad that she has found happiness again, I am selfishly jealous of the fact that she has no desire to spend time with her grandchildren – am I being silly?

Mom and Roy are off to meet your parents in Louisville, Kentucky – they are staying at the Newport and witnessing the "Marching of the Ducks". I think they are off to tour some horse farms after that and may stop in Nashville on the way home. Meanwhile, us minions just keep plowing away at our daily grinds. I want to be retired! Or I want parents that want to help with their grandchildren. Do I sound like a spoiled brat?

Much love, Elle.

July 1993

Dear Elle,

At the risk of sounding harsh and judgmental, don't you think it is time to let your mom live her own life, and not focus on yours? How many years does she have to be a vibrant, exciting world traveler? Celebrate her happiness – don't let it drag you down.

Carpe diem! Love, Barby.

December, 1994

Dear Barby,

Christmas is soon approaching, which means that we, the respective offspring of Pat and Roy, have to engage in that annual awkward dance of choosing which partner we will spend the holidays with. This is no Astaire/Rogers match up. This has been going on since Mom married Roy. Enter in the confusion of a blended family with adult children—Roy and Mom are both on their second marriages. Where do we go? What do we do? Should we plan a mixed family gathering and pretend that we are siblings – buying presents for each other, and cooing over the grandchildren? What is the protocol for new families? Who do we have to buy presents for? Are we going to draw names, and act like we are one big happy family? In years past, it has been our tradition to arrive at Mom's house on Christmas day, after driving six hours in the middle of the night to find that Santa had snuck in and left a plethora of gifts for the girls to rip open and revel in the magic of Christmas. Now we have new "family" members and I can't seem to get a hold on how we deal with them. Ironically, most modern families have to cope with this on a daily basis – how many people do you know that haven't dealt with divorce, second marriages, blending, etc.? I'm just being a patsy about this situation.

But the bigger issue is lodged in the bowels of our souls. We have to wonder, as Mom and Roy enter into their octo-years which one of us, or what combination of us, is best suited to care for them? This decision is looming on all of the next generation like a bad hangover. It hurts, and we want to deny it ever happened, but we still have to deal with it. No amount of tomato juice- accompanied by a chaser—can sever the pain involved when you have to choose something as simple as deciding where about your Christmas destination. The bigger issue is that sometime soon, one of us is going to have to take responsibility for Mom.

You would think that, after two years of Mom and Roy being together, that we, the separate progeny of their prior relationships, would have figured this out by now. How do once separate, now intertwined families cover all of the bases? Someone always feels left out, ignored, overlooked, dissed, indignant. Mom is now busy with Roy's grandchildren, and she seems to forget about the indigenous family of her own. It is more about appearances than love. Trips to Disney World, vacations in northern Michigan with his family are all happening with the "new" members while the original family is ignored.

I think that the hard part for all of us – the four children begat by Pat and Dave, is that we never felt loved. We were just pawns or tokens of a scene in a b-rated movie. We were neglected, yet when the scene required attention (when someone was looking) we were doted upon. Loved, yet unloved because social obligations prevailed over family. Now we are thrown into this new relationship – where Mom has a new love, and a new family, and we're supposed to embrace them as our own. It's weird. Awkward.

Ironically, Mom and Roy never seemed to be bothered by this situation. They prefer to stay at their home – alone. We, the next generation, toil over the minutiae of the holidays—where we will meet, what we will eat, what gifts will be exchanged. Mom and Roy would be completely content—no, nonplussed, even secretly elated, if December 25th was the same as any other day. They would be happy to have just one more day together, and that was all that matters to them. They are peas to a pod, matches to a fire, water to a lake. Inseparable, unified, selfishly connected with no need for outside interruptions, kids and grandkids included. They are in a fishbowl, like goldfish, surrounded by the comforts of faux castles and hiding places, just keeping their distance to be in each other's company.

Divorce and widowhood has a bipolar, yet stealth kind of reaction on the parties involved. Either you succumb to the angst and resentment that you are faced with, or you become a superpower—impenetrable, iceman—ready to face, and embrace, the new family members now absorbed into the life cocoon that you previously envisioned as normal.

Yet the inevitable is looming. One of us is going to be saddled with the care of those two in the foreseeable future. They can't keep operating independently, even though that is their wish. It's getting to be time when they have to surrender their autonomy and move closer to one of us. They want to be left alone – to forge a path of isolation far from any of the seven of us. They have their wine, their books, and their home – "please leave us alone" was the message that they convey whenever one of us tries to intervene and plan for the VERITAS—that the end is approaching.

None of the children really want to think about it, so we keep our respective craniums buried in the sand, denying the fact that one of us is going to have to step up and take charge. One of us is going to have to insist that they face the obvious. They are old, and they need help.

This diatribe might sound heartless, callous, and completely devoid of compassion, but truth be told, it was how we, as spokesperson for the children of the maternal side of the equation, were brought into the world. We were nomads, devoid of much parental direction. Those people we associated with—given the monikers "Mom" and "Dad"—were so busy with their social lives that the four of us kids (there must have been a "Dear Abby" etiquette column that suggested that four children made the "ideal" family) really never felt much of a connection to parental units. "Quality time" was not a priority in the 1960s. It was all about appearances. Dressing us up in matching clothing, having us perform at their cocktail parties with magic shows and mini-plays, not knowing that we were being humiliated at our expense. We didn't know any better – we were just pawns in their game of one-upmanship.

And now here we are—all of us "kids" have become quinto-genarians, with lives of our own, and minimal contact with our parental units—each of us secretly worried about whether we will be the one who is going to have to assume responsibility for the old folks.

I am sorry to burden you with all of this drivel about our elders – how are your parents doing? Thinking of you often, and hoping all is well,

Elle.

January 1995

Dear Elle,

I love you, but your worries are exasperating! All of us – cousins, friends, characters on TV shows – all have to deal with changes in lives and circumstances. We make choices, and then we are placed in the environment that surrounds us. What you do in your situation – you hold your head high, treat all the others as you would want to be treated (the Golden Rule) and muster on. Don't plan! Don't worry! Just press on. Live your life. If you want to buy gifts, or if you want to plan parties, then just do it. If you don't, that's okay. You are blowing up this situation into much more than it should be. Let go.

Cousins always, but friends first – Barby.

September 2004

Dear Rachel,

We are off to Spain and Italy on a tour! Destinations include Barcelona, Naples, Rome, Salerno, Tarragona, and Castellon de la Plana. Will write soon about our adventures! Will you join us on a tour of the Middle East next year? I feel as if I am hardly home anymore! If you want to stay stateside, we could plan a trip to Washington DC. Let me know your thoughts.

Love to all, Pat and Roy.

September 2004

Darling Patty,

Thank you for the invitation, but I am afraid that our traveling days are coming to a close. Merlin and I have enjoyed trips around the world during the last thirty years, but we are slowing down and we are happy with staying terra firma – at our own place. You two have a great time, and we can't wait to hear about it upon your return!

Your loving sister, Rachel.

January, 2009

Dear Barby,

I just received a phone call from Mom. She described this scenario: Roy laid motionless in a snowbank, just footsteps from the garage. Mom was paralyzed with fear, unable to coerce him to move on his own, powerless to pull him out of the icy bed his lips morphed blue. Panic overcame her sense of reason. It was one of those moments that you read about in the paper when adrenaline kicks in and miraculous events occur. At 110 pounds, she knew that physics defied her attempts to heave a man with fifty pounds of advantage off the ground and into the seat of her Mercury Sable—but what option did she have? She tried to hoist his limp body toward the passenger side of her car with the hope of dragging him to what she knew might be a final voyage.

A passing neighbor offered a hand. Between this anonymous persona and Mom, they were able to pour Roy into the car and off to the nearest emergency room.

Mom was frantic and called all of us to know that Roy was possibly inhaling his last breath. We, the offspring, faced the ugly truth that we have denied for years: our parents are OLD, and we have to do something about it. But all of us live the better part of a quarter of a thousand miles away. We are ensconced in basketball games, PTO meetings, volunteering for the Forensics fundraiser—which one of us was going to respond? And more importantly, which of us is going to eventually take care of Mom? And do we have to take Roy along?

What is our responsibility as second family members? Should I rush to Roy's bedside, and help Mom when she has baled on me during the last few years? How do we help ailing parents when they have refused in the past?

Love, Elle.

February 2009

Dear Elle,

I am sorry to hear about Roy's situation. It must be a terrible burden on your mom.

I've never had to take the reins and make decisions for my parents—they were proactive, they understood their lot in life, and they took steps to care for themselves. It seems like your mom and Roy have been in denial for a long time – hoping to fend off the need to rely upon others as they grew long in the tooth. Have you tried to talk them into moving to an assisted living facility? It's all the rage now for the elderly and infirmed! I'm sure that they want to be a part of the cool kids group, ha ha!

Love, your cousin, Barby.

ps – maybe you need to seek out some help with these decisions. An objective voice might make a difference. Perhaps there is a minister or someone from the senior citizen's advocacy program that could help. I'm sorry that I can't offer more advice.

February, 2009

Dear Barby,

You are right in suggesting that I need professional help – probably above and beyond the Mom and Roy situation!

As you may recall, I had attempted to convince Mom and Roy to face their ultimate fate when they were much younger. As each of them approached their 80th birthdays, I coaxed them over to Wisconsin for a visit – with the secret plan of visiting "care centers" that would be in close proximity to me and my siblings.

Roy has recently been diagnosed with Parkinson's disease. At this point, his mobility suffers although his hope for an unencumbered, carefree life remains. No one was going to convince him to move from their home in Okemos. He is a fixture, a monument, a recognized character in their small town. Plus, Mom owns that condominium on Grand Traverse Bay in Elk Rapids where they spend five months out of the year. Roy is a regular at the daily tennis club—they have friends, they entertain, they are part of the social scene. Wild horses or marauding pirates couldn't drive him from their homestead. He is ensconced – squatted– planted – until the good Lord calls him to his final destination. He proclaims his life mission is to stay in his home until death draws its ugly sword and drives him to the Promised Land.

Then came the stroke. In addition to the presence of unforgiving Mr. Parkinson as a life mate, it has become time for Roy to move to an assisted living facility. The throne at his home is going to have to be relinquished. There will probably be no return to Comanche Drive, no return to the tennis court in Elk Rapids, no more cocktail parties. Their lives as they have experienced have vanished as quickly as a meteor sails through the sky.

Mom is faced with a dilemma. Given Roy's latest setbacks, should she move to a multi-level senior home, waiting for Roy to rebound, or is she going to stay in the Okemos house? At eighty-five years of age, blind in one eye, her options are limited. Up until Roy's setback, they had been a team, one offsetting the others' weaknesses. Mom can't see, Roy can't drive. They compromised with Mom operating the controls of her Mercury Sable and Roy navigating the course. Many bruised bumpers and near misses ensued, to the point where the Michigan DOT threatened to take away her driving privilege. Someone had to intervene and break the news that they could no longer be a Captain and First Mate team. Reluctantly, I confiscated the keys to the Sable and put it up for sale. Mom has lost her stalwart navigator, and deep in the recesses of her foggy, syrupy malfunctioning brain, she knows the painful truth—she can't steer the ship on her own.

Your cousin, Elle.

February 16, 2009

Dear Elle,

I am facing the same kinds of problems with my parents. They have moved to an assisted living facility in Gastonia, North Carolina. What can we do, other than to love and support them? It is difficult because they are unable to make their own decisions, but they don't understand that. You need to either step back and let them determine their own path or take the reins and dictate their future. What do you think is best for them? What do Roy's children add to the equation? How are they helping? You can't take this on without input from the others involved.

Love, your cuz Barby

March, 2009

Dear Barby,

Drama continues as we attempt to launch the ship taking Mom out of the house and into a senior facility.

We planned a one-day estate sale in mid-March, to begin at 8 a.m. and close at 4 p.m. It was to be a gentrified, upscale event.

The vultures flocked two hours before the announced starting time. When the doors finally opened, a tornado of shoppers nearly knocked us over to get first dibs on every towel, knick-knack, appliance, TV tray, chair, pencil, or picture frame that was up for auction. At one point, I felt the need to dial 911 because two of the attendees were going fisticuffs over a hammer. The house was eviscerated—a eunuch of its past. A house enveloped in love, laughter, wine, and music had been reduced to the skeleton of belongings we were moving to "the home".

At the end of the day, we were exhausted, spent, over it. Uncle. Mom's worldly possessions were in the hands of hucksters who paid fifty cents for priceless commodities that could never be replaced. The house—their respite for the past seventeen years, had been ransacked by a hoard of strangers. Their possessions were left in the dirty hands of greedy bargain hunters. Roy lies corpse-like in his locked wing of the "senior living facility" that Mom will move into in a couple of days. Gone are her possessions, her car, her independence, her life.

Mom bravely says: *That was then, and this is now.* I just hope that she can stay the course and adapt to apartment living. At least she will be closer to Roy.

Love, Elle.

April 3, 2009

Dear Elle,

Welcome to the world of caregivers! Now that all of the Wise sisters are in some kind of "senior care facility" (although your mom is the only one not swimming in the Alzheimer's pool – but she is dipping her toes in and testing the water) we can all commiserate on our role-reversed lives. Parent becomes child, child becomes parent. Prepare yourself for changes they will experience: mood swings, physical aggression, hysteria, and the driving force behind all of these behaviors – memory loss. It's as if there was a raging fire in your brain and all has been eviscerated – no, more like a smoldering campfire that has been doused but isn't quite extinguished. The smoke continues to cloud rational thinking and memory banks.

My mom still knows me most days, and she gets much joy from reliving her younger days. It will help your mom if you ask her to regale you with stories from her past. Be careful not to admonish when she doesn't remember. Don't take it personally. She doesn't want to forget you, but she is being ravished from within from something beyond her control. Join a support group! Read everything you can about the progression and how caregivers can cope. Most importantly, remember that all of your cousins are experiencing this right now and we are all here to lend a guiding hand.

Love, Barby.

May 14, 2009

Dear Barby,

Thank you for your words of advice. It's something that I don't want to face, but more likely than not, Mom will follow the paths of her sisters and parents down Dementia Lane. Mom has moved to Holiday Hills, a multi-functional senior living center that houses all those in their golden years ranging from the ambulatory and sharp to the listless and lifeless. It is a paradigm of elder options. Roy is housed two floors above in a locked ward, and Mom plans her day around regular visits.

Holiday Hills was the primo destination for every soon to be retiree back in the 80s. It looked so good from the outside! Activities, outings, daily healthy meals, bus rides to the local grocery store, regular physical workouts, stimulating discussion groups, libraries, book talks, and it was great on the inside, until you had to be a resident, give up your driving privileges, your freedom, your life. But be happy!

Everything was scripted. Breakfast from 7 a.m. to 9 a.m. Lunch from 11 a.m. to 1 p.m. Dinner from 5 p.m. to 6:30. This did not fit into Mom's regimen of getting up whenever, and doing whatever, whenever—usually with the company of an "inch" of Chardonnay, her constant and loyal companion (especially when one inch turns into six).

She hates living there. She spends her days pining back to thirty years ago when she was resting on the meandering shores of Grand Traverse Bay—living in a world of wine, relaxation, love, and self-indulgence. At HH, her every move is monitored, and she doesn't have a car to escape. If she could drive, she would be on the road, one-eyed, headed for her retreat in Elk Rapids.

The saddest part is, in her mind, she is still physically capable of getting around, but her mind is slipping away, like ice slowly melting from the sidewalk on a warm March day in Michigan. She is trapped and unable to release herself from this mental hold that is stopping her from continuing on with her life. Everyday tasks are becoming as confusing as the New York Times crossword.

I'm sorry to burden you with all of this family nattering, but you, my dear cousin, are my sounding board. In the event that I am formally inducted into the nuthouse, you are my witness that I tried to help her down this jagged path.

Love, love, love, Elle.

May 29, 2009

Dear Barby,

As I mentioned before, Mom hated HH from the get go. She has only been there for two months and now she announced that she wants to move to a different apartment—meaning that Jean and I have to drive 300 miles – one way- to appease her wishes. Are we enablers, or do we just want to pacify her whims? Or, is this guilt of moving away and living in neighboring states just getting the best of us?

She is becoming more irascible, impatient, and demanding. We chalk it up to her upbringing, and self-centered personality, but yet, we cave into her demands.

We moved her two doors down, just to keep the peace. We were unaware— no, we just never even considered that she no longer has full hold on her faculties. Her decision-making process has been compromised. Memories are sliding into the unusable recesses of her brain. She is impatient with all of us, and most often, I hear from her that she is bored.

I don't understand. There is a myriad of activities every day, a full library, work out facilities, day trips, and daily shopping excursions. Someone comes in weekly to clean and do laundry; it is a life I dream of for myself.

What I suspect is that she is losing the grip on life. She feels trapped, and she probably knows that her memory is fading. But we, the children, the new caregivesr of our mother, keep on in our stable, sheltered lives, denying the inevitable.

I don't know how to make her happy and comfortable. Other residents are affable, funloving, and carefree. Why isn't Mom feeling the same way?

Love you, Elle.

July 23, 2009

Dear Barby,

Mom and Roy have lived at Holiday Hills – Mom on the 1st floor (independent living) and Roy on the 3rd floor (assisted living) for four months. Roy isn't improving. Mom is impatient and irritated with her "independent living" lifestyle. She misses her freedom to come and go—to get to the liquor store, or the mall, or the gym.

But the three of us, her children—remain clueless of Mom's failings, with our blinders tightly intact. She is safe. She never cared about what we were doing, so we had learned from the best, and kept our heads firmly planted in the sand. Living six hours away makes it easy to immerse ourselves in our own lives and ignore hers.

Then the phone call came. Mom was done with her regimented, "independent" life at Holiday Hills. She was moving to Elk Rapids, the location of her summer home, and I was going to make it happen. "What about Roy?" I asked. Her reply was curt. He wasn't getting any better and she wasn't going to wait around. Please arrive in a month if possible, she instructed. We'll pack up my belongings, and you can drive me up north.

So I am doing what I have done my entire life. I am caving into the demands of my mother, not asking any questions. Next month, I am driving six hours to East Lansing, packing up my mother's possessions, and moving her three and a half hours north to her condo in Elk Rapids.

Every time I get into a situation like this, I wonder: why don't I take charge? Why don't I just tell Mom that she is in a good place, and that she shouldn't—at age eighty-five—move alone to her condo in the middle of nowhere? It makes no sense to move out of a restful, safe place, surrounded by people in similar circumstances, to a town only occupied by tourists during the summer.

Now I know that it's because I never learned to step up or to take command. I just did what I was told to do, regardless of the consequences. What the hell is wrong with me?

Guide me, oh sage one! As The Clash asked back in 1982, "Should I stay or should I go?"

Loony bin, here I come! Love, Elle.

September 6, 2009

Dear Barby,

10 p.m. on Saturday night. Mom and I arrived at the Elk Rapids condo after traveling four hours to our destination. Goodbye, Holiday Hills, the idyllic destination for the elderly. My car is bursting with her belongings, and she is determined to live alone in her bayside condominium. We decided to leave the car filled to capacity and tackle unpacking in the morning.

In the early light of morning, we unloaded the car, leaving Mom's property at her new home—devoid of any neighbors, friends, or caretakers. It is the day of my departure. Am I really doing this? Leaving a forgetful, fragile, unstable parent alone, just because it is what she says she wants?

Yes, I guess I am, because I have never defied my mother before, and I'm not ready to start now. She is insistent, and I am weak. Besides, what option do I have?

We found a couple of retirees who we hired to check in on her every other day – I guess that is the best I can do. There is no talking Mom out of this plan – she still thinks she is capable of living independently. I'd like to think what everyone who makes a poor choice claims: "I'm doing the best I can!" but somehow, those words aren't very comforting.

Your cousin, Elle.

September 15, 2009

Dear Elle,

I just can't believe how rooted you are in caving into the demands of your mother! You should have recognized years ago that this is part of the onset of Alzheimer's, yet you and your siblings have been in denial.

I'm sorry to be harsh with you, but WOMAN UP. Take the reins from this out of control horse and bring it back to pasture. Change your mindset and think of it as helping by making decisions for her, rather than allowing someone not in their right mind to call the shots. Face it – she is no longer able to make sound decisions. Step up. Take a stand and start directing her down a path of comfort and safety. She doesn't know what that is at this time.

Your bitchy (but honest) cousin, Barby.

September 25, 2009

Dear Barby,

I know how stupid is was of me to fold to Mom's demands to move from Holiday Hills to Elk Rapids. When she called me a couple of months ago and insisted that she move, I should have told her no – but when have I ever been able to say no to Mom?

As I ask myself these questions, you won't believe what happened. Apparently, as she was making dinner the other night, the sauté pan contained a simple grilled cheese sandwich. She turned the element to heat setting number 5, low enough so that the cheese would melt with parity.

She can't remember how to cook much more than putting together a sandwich or soup anymore, and grilling was a stretch. The memory of how to adjust temperature, and how long something should cook, now evades her. She is trapped in that unreachable, mysterious portion of the brain where dying thoughts go to lie dormant.

As she recants the story, she merely stepped out on the porch to take in the exquisite northern Michigan sunset, melting into the peninsula across Grand Traverse Bay. In her rendition, it couldn't have possibly been more than a minute that she stepped away.

Then the smoke detectors screamed their warnings. Mom turned around to see small flames leaping from the stovetop. She ran to the kitchen to get a pitcher of water to douse the growing inferno—but by that time, the fire department had arrived on scene. Fortunately, Mom's building is hard-wired into the fire department, and anytime a smoke detector is activated, they respond without the usual 911 call for help.

Firefighters blasted into the condo—now filled with smoke. Mom managed to move the searing pan to the sink, earning a small but painful burn in the process. The firemen grabbed the pan with the charred sandwich and threw it out the window. They brought in an industrial sized fan to clear the air of looming toxins.

Later that night, the President of the condominium association called me. Was Pat really all right to be living alone? As he regaled the details of the smoldering afternoon incident, I knew what had to be done—yet I procrastinated, halted, denied, and somehow talked myself out of taking any immediate action. Maybe it was just a fluke. In retrospect, I think I didn't want to assume the responsibility of what I knew was coming. Mom would eventually have to live near one of us, and I knew it will probably be me.

Let me know how you coped with these issues with your parents as they progressed down the same path.

Love you, Elle.

- - -

October 9, 2009

Dear Rachel,

I am up north on my Elk Rapids getaway. The girls seem to think that I can't function by myself up here! There was only that one incident where the fire department responded. I don't know why—they are overprotective and they probably need some emergency calls just to justify their existence. I just had some food boiling on the stove that put off too much smoke. It wasn't a big deal. If only Jean would come up, everything would be okay. Two people come over every now and then to see if I need anything. I can't remember their names, but they are very pleasant (although they might be taking some things from the house – I seem to be missing a set of antique pens and some clothing items).

I'm out walking every day. Neighbors give me a ride to the grocery store for my basics, and when I return, the view is incredible! What more could I want? Life is completely full, undisturbed, and peaceful. Living in Nirvana and loving it.

I do have moments of loneliness, however. Why don't you and Jean consider a drive up here? It is always lovely in the fall – nature's palette paints every niche as far as one can see.

Your sister, Patty.

October 10, 2009

Dear Barby,

It is hard to write about my daily interactions with Mom. There isn't an instant that passes when I'm not thinking about her—when do I have to visit next? What can I do to make her life more bearable? Am I doing enough? Is she happy? Should I move her in with us? Why do I have to make these monumental decisions?

Then today, it happened. Maybe it was a slight stroke, maybe a drop in blood sugar. We'll never know, since Mom didn't call for help. All we know is that she fell – flat on her face, jarring her front teeth loose, causing a black eye, and a trail of blood as she crawled from the parking lot back to her second-floor condominium. No one was around to witness the incident. The next day, she must have been in a great deal of pain, because she called Jean to confess. Jean hopped on the next flight to Traverse City, rented a car, and spent a few days with Mom. It was the beginning of the end—all of our lives were about to change because Mom was aging, and none of us wanted to face it. She has resisted all attempts to move closer to one of us. Rather, she is holding out hope that her sisters are going to come for a visit, and that will be a panacea for her loneliness and forgetfulness. Only problem with that plan is that Mom forgets that both sisters are struggling with Alzheimer's and unable to travel.

How do we deal with aging parents, especially when they want no part of our lives?

Ellen.

October 20, 2009

Dear cuz,

Forgive me for being blunt, but are you out of your once sensible, predictable mind? How can you leave that old woman to her own matters when she is showing such outward and obvious signs of needing help? Time to step up and take control of this tornado that has defined your mom's life.

Cousfriend (I just invented a new word – just like the celebrity couples merge their names, now we are doing the same! Maybe it should be cuzfriend, so that it is not misinterpreted as COOZ-FRIEND) once and again, I hate to bestow harsh words on you – I know you are doing your best (sidebar: how does anyone really know that they are doing their best?) but I'm telling you, close down that party on the lake, and put her in a home where they can keep ties and eyes on her. You have done everything to try to keep her happy, but don't you understand that she doesn't know what happy is anymore?

You are my cousfriend/cuzfriend forever, B.

October 30, 2009

Dear Barby,

Bags are packed, car loaded to the gills. Goodbye, Elk Rapids. We are selling the condo, and Mom is moving in with me. We will drive to Wisconsin tomorrow and set her up in our guest room until—?

I didn't give Dave a chance to protest. What other option did I have?

I'm moving a virtual stranger into our house, knowing that her faculties are slipping, and that she is in need of a lot of attention. Disaster must be looming for all involved. Mom is moving into our home, and I barely know her. Our guest room is in the lower level of the house. What will she do all day alone? Will she burn the place to ashes when I am at work?

Mom was happy to be taking a trip, but unknowing that this was her departure from the home that she claimed for the last fifty-five years. A new beginning, and a new ending.

Love, your cousin (okay, cousfriend) Elle.

November 2, 2009

Dear Barby,

Well, it has happened. Mom has to come to live with one of us, and it ends up to be me.

We drew verbal sticks to determine which of us would end up as the caretaker of the person we knew as "Mom". Jean and Roger are nomadic, traveling around the country, and are embracing the idea of retirement. Tim is single, with teenage boys who still need daily attention. The sarcastic congratulatory slap on my back was felt when it was apparent that there was no other stable, consistent geographical location for Pat and Roy.

It's not that we don't love Mom, it's just that she never really seemed to love us. I don't have any recollection of a sweet, kind moment with her. She wasn't abusive, or mean, she was just absent. When I ask my siblings about the memories they have of Mom, they hesitate. I remember a time while living in Bangkok during a monsoon they were hosting a cocktail party (20 inches of rain will not deter Friday night revelry!) They had my brother Dave, climb up on the garage roof, waving a spotlight as if he was a human lighthouse. The force of the storm caused the roof to collapse – Dave fell through. Fortunately, he wasn't seriously hurt, but the party went on! Family life wasn't high on the rung of the priority ladder. Outward appearances and social opportunities reigned over familial connections.

With that said, it was imperative that one of us had to take charge and become Mom's custodian. I ended up with what I perceived as drawing the short straw, but in the end, my straw was longer, and stronger, than ever anticipated. I had to take this semi-stranger into my house and welcome her because she was "family".

I wonder if you are going through the same kind of decisions and experiences in your life. Am I a horrible person, not wanting to take on the burden of caring for my parent, when I feel that she hardly cared for me?

Love, Elle.

November 17, 2009

Dear Barby,

I have reluctantly become The Mom. She is no longer able to function on her own. She is being forced to give up the only life she ever knew and become a ward of a daughter that some days she recognizes, and other days, is just a blur, a faded memory.

It is such a sad realization – children become parents, parents fade into oblivion. How do you deal with this madness? I think of cultures that embrace the elderly, and they become the revered, the honored of their community. Maybe they didn't deal with Alzheimer's? How do we get the tools to cope?

Sorry to burden you with all of this grief, but I don't know where else to turn.

Elle.

November 29, 2009

Dear Barby,

Thanksgiving has come and gone. It is wonderful to have Mom with us, but she seems to be restless – uncomfortable and sad. She is moping in the corner of the living room – unwilling to partake in family games, banter, and activities. She used to participate in games of Rummikub, Sequence, and Cribbage, but now she bows out. I know that this is not the place that she wanted to spend her final years, but what else could I do? Part of dementia is losing the capacity to socialize. She can't live alone, and no one else can take her. I have to make the best of it.

Sorry to be the bearer of depressing news but thank you for listening. Love you, Elle.

December 5, 2009

Dear Barby,

I have coerced Mom into trying to make an entry in a journal every day – it isn't going well. Here are some of her early entries:

"Ellen came to visit … also brought a large scrap book showing photos from the "Osthoff Resort", where a few of us (I'm not sure I know all of the players) will spend Christmas. Went to dinner at the main dining room. Talking with Tim – 8:30 pm. We're going to shop soon." "Golf 9:30 tomorrow."

Her mind seems to be fading from reality to fantasy. I have joined an Alzheimer's support group and they suggest that I "play along" and make it sound like her ruminations are all sensible and cohesive. It is hard to play "The Pretender", but that is what my life has become at this point. Play along and make happy.

Love, Elle.

December 30, 2009

Dear Barby,

Mom acted as if family members were people she recognized, but we knew she was mentally absent. Today she called my daughter, Erin, "Jean". She is pretty good at faking her acuity —little did we realize that most days, she no longer knows any of her children or grandchildren – she looks at them as if they were characters in a story where she is looking on from above. She is becoming a shell on the outside, and everything she used to know is buried deep within. I wish I possessed the tools to deal with this departure from her soul, and to understand that I am facing a new person that I once identified as my mom doesn't always recognize me anymore.

Elle.

Book Seven
1944-1945

1 June 1944

My darling Patty,

I am preparing to leave my training I Laredo, but I'm afraid that I have been assigned to Gunnery Instruction School once again in Yuma, Arizona. I leave on June 15th and I have a short leave before my departure. Could I be so bold to ask if I could stay with you and your folks during that time? I know it is a bit unconventional, but these are strange times, and as you know, we are all having to adapt to our circumstances.

Perhaps I should ask your father permission rather than you. He seems to have strong sentiments about our being together … I wonder if he disapproves of me.

Let me know what you think. I hope that YOU are approving of my plan!

Love always, David.

3 June 1944

Dearest little sister Patty,

While I abhor the situation going on overseas, I must admit that it fills the seats on my train! Some passengers have to stand in the aisles- it has been unbelievably busy. I'm sorry that I haven't been able to correspond much. We are constantly being called to be stewardesses for the B&O (by the way, I LOVE IT!) but it is sad to see the young men being shipped off to defend our country.

Guess what? I was the featured stewardess on the cover of the B&O magazine last month!

Love, Jeannie

7 June 1944

Dear David,

Of course, you are welcome to stay with us during your hiatus from the army! I'm afraid that all we have to offer is a couch, but if it means being together before your departure to Yuma, I'm certain that you would settle for a tent if necessary.

Life at the Emerson Plant is quite humdrum. Since Jeannie left, I am kind of an oddity there – guess I'm not very good at making friends. I'm thinking about enrolling in college! I just don't think that the routine of factory life is for me. It is too late to enroll for fall courses, but I think I will aim for a winter start at the University of Iowa. Rachel loved it there, and Daddy has a better job prospect nearby. I don't know yet what I will study, but anything is better than processing time cards as I am doing now.

I hate to think of what you are going to experience in Yuma. I believe that it is deathly hot there, and there are few items of convenience to enjoy, i.e., no clean bathrooms, limited showers, and worst of all, no escape from the heat. I know that you will be the best Gunnery Instructor, and that your troops will adore you—much like I do!

Yours, Patty.

15 June 1944

Dear Patty,

Thanks to you and yours for putting up with the big lug on the couch this week. Off to Yuma now and the Army has informed us that we will not be allowed to correspond with any of our loved ones during this six-month training. I have this one opportunity to tell you that I love you, and that I will call you on the telephone as soon as we are done with this stint. It hurts my heart that I won't be able to send you a quick note … nor will I be able to receive any communication. They are preparing us for our time overseas … it is brutal and quite inhumane. Who can survive without the loving correspondence from family and friends?

You won't hear from me again until I have plans to ship back home. There is no sense in you writing letters to me, as we are isolated and unable to have contact with anyone outside of the army.

Sending all the love in my heart, David.

7 DEC 1944

THIRD ANNIVERSARY OF PEARL HARBOR. MY HEART STILL ACHES FOR THE TRAGEDY AND LIVES LOST. DARLING PATTY, WILL BE SHIPPING OUT OF YUMA ON THE NEXT TRAIN TO ST LOUIS SCHEDULED FOR DEC 10. CAN'T WAIT TO GET BACK TO CIVILIZATION. MARRY ME?

LOVE, DAVID.

9 DEC 1944

TO: SGT DAVID HEENAN
YUMA TRAINING CENTER
YUMA AZ

DEAR DAVID, I WILL BE WAITING AT THE TRAIN STATION FOR YOUR ARRIVAL. OF COURSE I WANT TO MARRY YOU, BUT WE MUST DISCUSS IN PERSON. LOVE, PATTY. PS — I HAVE ENROLLED AT THE U OF IOWA FOR WINTER SEMESTER. DADDY STILL DISAPPROVES OF OUR MARRIAGE UNTIL YOU ARE HOME FOR GOOD. HE IS PROBABLY RIGHT. SAVE THE PROPOSAL PLEASE!

29 December 1944

Dear David,

I'm sorry that I made such a fuss upon your departure. It is really unlike me to cry, but the thought of what you are facing in the military, and not knowing when I will see you again. It brought my defenses down. I wanted to show you a brave face, and send you off with a positive feeling, and there I was, blubbering like a love-struck idiot. I hope that my unseemly display was not distressing for you—Lord knows that you are enduring enough!

I have been busy trying to get acclimated to college life—it certainly is different than working the first shift at Emerson! My roommate is a farm girl from northern Iowa … a free spirit with opinions of her own, and she smokes! You will really like her—Dorothy Solis.

Classes start tomorrow. I hope I am ready to re-enter the academic life, but I guess there is only one way to find out!

We need to talk about your marriage proposal. I love you, David, and I really hope that someday in our future, we will marry. But the hastiness and anxiety of your being home, after a respite of six months, was not the time to make such a life-changing decision. I hope you can understand my desire to wait until we have some time to get a little older and not to feel that we made a decision just because of the war.

I think of you every day and wonder what kind of exercises you will be going through to prepare for your deployment overseas. My prayers are with you.

Lovingly, Patty.

January 1, 1945

addressed c/o Mrs. H. S. Wise, 5605 Chamberlain, St. Louis

Darling Patty: I had a great time over Christmas break at your place. Good to run home to Janesville to say *au revoir* to my folks. New Year's Eve was spent with old Milton buddies and I'm afraid we got a bit out of hand. After too many brewskis, the sorority gals broke in and there was a lot of singing and dancing until the wee hours. I have the headache today to prove my misguided ways.

Dad drove me to Chicago to catch the early train. We're just ready to leave Cincinnati and everything is under control. Thanx to Jeannie's old bunkmate, Gerry, I was able to get a seat – next to a WAVE, incidentally! Slept an hour on the train this P.M. but still feel like ten lbs. of refuse in a 5 lb. sack – I also met two fellows from our "Project" here so will have some company!

Thank "Mom", Jeannie, and your pop for making my stay so pleasant – tell 'em not to worry and especially that I love them all! It was wonderful to spend the holidays with you and yours.

Work real hard at school for me, for US, and for our future – I love you very much and if the Postman reads this I hope he gets an upset stomach with all its MUSH.

David

Tuesday, January 2nd, 1945

47 months – Congratulations, Babe!

My darling Patty,

Yipe!! Prepare yourself for another series of complaints because I'm back in the Army again – and what a place! You'll be relieved to know that we arrived quite safely in Greensboro just as the last streaks of daylight yawned across the sky; at 6:15 p.m. we "dismounted" from the train and 6:17 we were packed into the back of a GI truck bumping along toward our new home! Approximately 6:29 we reported for duty and were so close to being late that it was nearly a photo finish. At any rate, everything worked out okay and by 9:00 we checked out bedding, were assigned to beds, and had partially removed the dirt and grime accumulated on the train – then piled wearily into our sacks.

The ride down was not entirely unenjoyable nor was it unprofitable – from Cincinnati to Greensboro I divided my time between sleeping and playing blackjack – the latter proved to offer more compensation as I rolled twenty-five cents up to $5.65 – not bad, no es verdad? I was terribly sorry that you were worried about my finances as everything worked out well – why, I even bought breakfast for this WAVE friend that I sat next to! Gerry was sweet and apologized all over the place for not being able to spend more time entertaining me – obviously, I knew she'd be busy and was thankful for the seat she saved – and even MORE – for getting you out to see me again while I was on the train!

When I volunteered for this thing there were several things they didn't tell me about, such as getting up at 5:30 a.m. (horrible hour, isn't it?) In fact, I had learned so many things that I had forgotten about the Army! Actually, this is no more nor less than a Basic training camp. We MARCH to lectures and chow, come to "a-tens-hut" when an officer walks by, have to learn our "general orders" (for guard duty) and recite them to the C. O. before we're eligible for a pass, and today we listened to the C. O. read "The Articles of War", etc., etc. This morning when the change of Quarters called us, I stuck an arm out of the covers to turn on the light and suffered a mild case of frostbite – yipe, it's cold up here!

One of the nicer things about this place is its location – it is situated right on the edge of town but until a later date I plan on staying pretty close to camp. With our group is a battalion of former cooks, mechanics, and gunners – most of who were forced into overseas duty and are pretty sick about it. We shall all ship out together after being here between two and three weeks – from Greensboro we'll go to a P. O. E. somewhere!

Now, honey, I want to say a few words about us!! It will be much easier to leave now that I was able to see you once more; you'll never know exactly how much it really meant to me! Please be happy with me for it is honestly what I want to do – if you're skeptical about what the future might hold for me – do not worry as our work will not, in any manner, be overly dangerous. Have faith in me as I have in you and remember that I'll always love you – love you 'til it hurts!

Goodnight, David

p.s. Your picture looks wonderful in its little holder – I love you!!

January 3, 1945

David,

I received your postcard dated 1/1/45 today, and I must admit that I was quite shocked and disappointed to learn of your behavior on New Year's Eve. I hope this is not a sign of our life in the future. I will not tolerate that kind of behavior if I am to become your wife.

It sounds as if you had a grand time on the train ride down to Greensboro. I'm glad that Gerry was there to make sure you had plenty of female companionship. Who wouldn't want their best guy to be in the able hands of a WAVE? Maybe she could contact Jo Gray and arrange for a train ride for the two of you!

I'm sorry if my jealousy is showing ... but it was so hard to leave you, and the thought of you being entertained by anyone but me is quite disconcerting.

I have selected my classes for this first semester – I hope I can keep up with the workload. Academics has never been a strong suit of mine.

I'm sorry if I overreacted (above), I just want you all to myself. Envy and possessiveness are two of my least flattering characteristics – are you sure you know what you are in for?

Your Patty.

Wednesday, January 3rd, 1945

(forwarded to Eastlawn Dorm, Iowa City, Iowa)
originally addressed to c/o Mrs. H. S. Wise, 5605 Chamberlain, St. Louis, MO

My Darling Patty:

By tomorrow you should have received my first little note since I left and Friday the first letter – then, according to my calculations, I should get your letter about Monday of next week! It does seem so lonely not to hear from you and I do miss you terribly much – each second, minute, and hour – day – week will seem like years. Gosh, Honey, when I left your Mom she said: "I'm sorry that Patty and you didn't get married – and I'll always think of you as my son-in-law while you're gone!" I don't bring that up to remind you of the fact that we didn't get married – goodness knows we both feel badly enough about it, but I do think it was very sweet and considerate – don't you?

Today we had our tooth enamel work examined and I signed up for a $50.00 bond per month for us. Since you won't have a permanent address (nor will your mom) I am having it addressed to you at 1027 Ruger!! As soon as you send your address to Mother and Dad they can forward them to you immediately – also they can inform you when I arrive at my destination, if I'm unable to cable you immediately!! What are the plans concerning the announcement of our engagement – you know that I'm all in favor of it anytime – the sooner the better!

I have your new picture sitting on a shelf next to my bed and the guys are all wondering "how I rate"!! You and I know how we rate with each other!

This marching around has just about got the best of me – just like being in the infantry and the thought of catchin' detail when we finish "processing" has added its mark. This afternoon four of us volunteered for Boxing Instruction so we might avoid KP and Guard Duty – this will entail appearing in a match in the Post Auditorium in a couple weeks – yipes! Am I desperate!! The pampering we received in Laredo has left us spoiled and rebellious against any form of discipline!!

<u>We have sheets on our bed</u> -an almost unheard of thing in the Army and I lay in bed freezing to death! Good Lord, this thing is getting just like civilian life again! There's a sign in the mess hall – "If you Accept it, EAT IT", quite unlike the signs in most places "Take all you want, but EAT all you TAKE". There's a psychological point when you eat the food here – I just ain't got no appetite!

Love you, my darling! David

Thursday, January 4, PM

(forwarded to Eastlawn Dorm, Iowa City, Iowa)
originally addressed to c/o Mrs. H. S. Wise, 5605 Chamberlain, St. Louis, MO

My dearest Patricia!!

This afternoon a letter arrived from you dated December 29 – the address was a bit peculiar but by now I have managed to get into enough trouble where the Post Commanding Officer calls me by my first name; it was only two days en route according to the postmark! It is a wonderful letter and upon reading it I felt 15,000,000,000% better. I can tell you now that I would be slightly disappointed if you didn't cry a little bit – yes, it was "HELLISH" to leave you and even now there is a funny feeling in my stomach as I write to you! You did your very best not to "put on a scene" and I really wouldn't have minded as much as I put on. Another confession – I knew all the time that I wouldn't go to the station without you! I do hope that your Dad wasn't too disappointed in me – but I do think we should have had a long talk and come to a more common understanding, don't you?? Also received a V-mail letter from Cecil (my buddy in Gunnery School) – he is APO NY and is STILL a corporal!! I think he is flying as a gunner in Italy or England. He says: "How's Patty? Fine, I hope – hope you and she are still that way". Oh, yes, there was a cute Christmas card from Suzy, too!

Babe, guess what? I'm growing another moustachio!! Isn't that awful? Anyway, a bunch of the boys decided that we should make our project notorious for something so we agreed to raise hair on our lips and get crew cuts – yipe! That should really be a combination, huh? Some of the fellows have their wives here and apparently the orders had no bearing at all – the C. O. has even gone so far as to give them special overnight passes – every night! If it weren't for your being in school we might make similar arrangements!

By now you are probably more adjusted to college and have met many new friends. I hope they are good people – 'cause you deserve only the best. Please do not mention anything to anyone about my location now, when I expect to leave here, and where we expect to be assigned. You may unload that information, if you wish, when we arrive safely at our destination. They are getting a little "touchy" about what we write and have threatened "spot censorship" – that isn't the main reason, though – I have hopes of coming back to make you Mrs. D. K. H., Jr., and to that we don't want any interruptions from A. Hitler and Company.

We have been ordered to remove all Air Corps insignias from our uniforms so people won't know what outfit is moving – also were issued a new lightweight gas mask, mess kits, steel helmets, etc.

We're still very anxious to get started and will notify you as quickly as we can! Cables, we heard today, are permitted – but only for emergency measures – it may prove rough to convince them that this is an emergency. At any rate, whatever happens, you'll know that I'm thinking of you and loving you with all my heart.

Goodnight,

David

ps – Here's a picture of me and my buddy, Max, with our new facial hair!

Friday pm, January 5, 1945

Darling Babe,

Just a wee note tonight to let you know that I'm still loving you and there's a big empty cavity in my left ventricle because you're there and I'm here.

We started our first night at pugilists today and so far the only ill-effects is a sprained left thumb. Honestly, I think it is going to do wonders for us – we shall begin roadwork, exercises, etc., in earnest as soon as our processing period is over and should get into pretty fair physical condition. I still have a guilty feeling of "beating details" aside from that, I have never felt better in my life!!

Soon I am sending a little package to you and I thought that you should be forewarned so that you'll open it in private – it won't be mailed 'til I get your address though – in case you're wondering, it will contain cigarettes!

I can't apologize enough to you for my actions that night in Janesville and I keep thinking that perhaps you don't understand. Sometimes when those hooligans tempt me with too much of the hooch, I am rendered unable to refuse. Honey, please forgive me – it won't happen again – I love you more than ever.

Honey, could you use my watch? I'll be glad to send it to you if you'll wear it!! I can find a cheap one that will suffice for my needs – please let me know right away!

Your lil' picture is smiling at me so sweetly that I'll just have to close here and give you a big kiss – I do love you so much!

Goodnight,

Dave Jr.

Saturday, January 6, 1945

postmarked Jan 7
addressed to Iowa City address

My darling Patty!

Today the mailman brought a postcard and a letter, the first with your new address!! It makes me feel so much better to know that you have overcome any fears that you may have nursed previously! I could read a distinct note of confidence in your little missive and that's exactly the way it should be – I have all the faith, confidence, trust, or whatever it takes about your abilities; you won't have a bit of trouble!

Your selection of courses really covers a huge field of study and I'm sure you'll enjoy all of 'em; especially the history and sociology phases. Do try to get something from the academics, but, on the other hand, <u>have fun</u> – that will constitute eighty-five percent of your memories!

As you have undoubtedly already noticed, there is something about school that makes the whole world revolve around it – there is the melting pot where all creeds, races, people, rich and poor, etc., gather as a group to find something that can only be found in one place in the world – college! This may sound like a frustrated old simp trying to convince you with something you already know – perhaps that's more right (sic) than either of us realize!

My regards to "Tommy" (I wonder why Dorothy doesn't go by "Dottie"?) and may she do a better job of keeping you on the beam than Kenny did for me! Your description of her makes me think that you will get along swell – and believe me, I envy her for being so fortunate in having my own Patricia for a roommate!

Honey, I have one request to make of you – read it, but use your own judgment in making a decision: Do not drink – I say this because I don't want you to hurt in any way and further, people will respect you more for it! Regarding dates – and I promise this will be the last time I shall mention it:—again, let you be the sole judge! If you are bitter about my "mistake" (J. Gray) or it's what you want, I can't say "no, you shouldn't" – but always remember this if you do: I love you, I trust you, and I want to know that you're doing the best thing for us!!

Oh, yes, we have had a little jar here today – we have been alerted, meaning probably that we'll ship from here soon! Our particular group (project) skipped over five days of processing and we finished our last day's work today! Also, they are giving our group KP and guard duty tomorrow, a procedure given usually to groups that move early! My moniker is crowning the head of the KP roster meaning that I'll have to get up approx. 3:30 a.m.

Most of the guys are in town so it is rather quiet here tonight – the big attraction being more gals than men (including GI's) in this area!! If it's all the same to you, I'm not interested – 'cause I love you too terribly much to hurt you again! Goodnight Darling,—your picture gets cuter by the minute. I love only you!

David, Jr.

ps – I have written every day and mailed them c/o your mom so this will probably reach you before some of the others!! xxxxxxxxxxxxxxxxxxxxxxxxxxxx

- -

January 7, 1945

Dearest David,

I received your letters dated January 2 and 3rd. I'm afraid that I am not as prolific of a writer as you are! I understand that correspondence is your only connection to those of us at home right now, but what I have to say seems insipid to me and would only bore you!

Once again, I apologize for being a pathetic sap upon your departure. There were so many emotions going on in my head—your abrupt and unexpected proposal—my return to academia—pressures from Daddy – rationing—the uncertainty of the world! Sometimes it is too much to absorb. I often wish that we could return to the carefree world of pre-December 7, 1941… my biggest concern was what flavor of ice cream I would be ordering at the soda fountain.

I'm adjusting to college life and making a few friends. It isn't easy being away from Momma and Daddy, but everyone has to sacrifice these days, I guess. It also isn't easy thinking of you in some flea-ridden bunk with an unknown – and dangerous – future in store. Sometimes it is easier just to put on my blinders and forget that the whole thing is happening. I pretend that you are just on a long vacation and will be returning soon.

Your Patty.

Sunday pm (January 7)

My Darling Patty!!

Remember when we agreed that we should tell each other everything about the way we feel? Well, Honey, I'm tired – dead tired and I am almost ashamed to write to you tonight … right after I finished the letter to you yesterday I climbed in bed and it seemed like ten minutes later someone was shaking me and saying that we had to get up! A week ago, exactly at 3:30 a.m. I was with you but the difference in my feeling at the same time a week apart was so different that there is no comparison! While I'm with you I felt so good – warm and cozy – but here was only a cold barracks to greet us! I only have one big regret about my furlough and that's that we weren't together day and night every second – that's the way it will be when I get back; I'll never leave you again! Patty, do you have a little different (not different) – but more intense feeling since my last leave? It is something I can't explain and this may sound terrifically funny to you and I have wanted to tell you before but I don't know exactly how to do it! I think it's even a bigger love (if that's possible) and I'm sure it isn't 'cause it was my last leave.

Before I get you all confused I had better close. Goodnight, Darling, I love you very much!

Dave

ps – please excuse the "worser" penmanship – I can't control this pen!

pps – don't tell anyone whence you received the cigarettes from – when they arrive! It's against Army regulations to buy PX merchandise for unauthorized personnel!!

January 10, 1945

Dear David,

I find you to be quite debonair with your newly grown moustache! It is dashing!

It makes me upset to think of you heading off to that war. Do we really have to help when other nations get involved? I don't understand why we don't just take care of our own. It is sickening to hear about the number of lives lost in our efforts to avert the German army.

Life at the U of I is good. I like my classes, and my roommate is wonderful! We are planning a trip to her home to an Iowa farm. She is very opinionated and quite a liberated gal. I think you will like her. She smokes cigarettes in plain view and challenges the opinions of our professors. What a rogue! I wish I had her courage and spunk.

We are deeply feeling the limitations of wartime restrictions. I can't travel home due to restrictions on gas and tires—there just isn't anything extra right now. Nor can my folks make the trip here. Maybe I will go to St. Louis on Spring Break, but if not, I'll return after winter semester is done. It must be doubly, triply, quadrupally hard for you.

I am thinking about you, and mentally thanking you for your commitment to serving our country. Your letters seem to indicate that you are comfortable but challenged by the orders that are assigned by your officers. I would not be able to march the way you describe to me—it is wise that they don't draft women. I could never be a WAC!

Please contact me as soon as you are able. I love you and miss you terribly …

Patty.

Monday, 1/8/45

Dear Dave,

Daddy reminded me that I should write. It is hard for me, given the demands of the children and the fact that I really don't know what to say.

You are a hero in my mind—I know I never paid much attention to you as we were growing up. Momma always had me tending to chores and we didn't have much of an opportunity to get to know each other. Now I don't know what to say, or what to do.

Good luck in the Army, I know you will do well and will defend our country.

Your sister, Ruth.

Tuesday, January 9, 1945

Dearest Patricia!!

Golly – things are definitely looking up! There were five letters and two packages that arrived here today: naturally, the most important being yours – one from your mom, another from my mother, a cute letter from Mona, and a forwarded letter from sister Harriette! Mom Wise was received my letters for you and says they are being sent out to you as quickly as they reach St. Looey – I should have wired my address as soon as we knew but, as usual, my negligence is only outdone by my stupidity!

You are apparently in a big maze of fog yet and I think your letters are so cute! I do sympathize with your problems and don't think that I'm belittling them – it is most natural and things will clear up considerably soon! You will come through with flying colors – I just know!

Your mom's letter was real swell but evidently I conveyed the wrong impression to her somewhere along the line: what I want to tell her was that what we'd be doing "across" would be dangerous only to the extent that we might slip on the latrine floor and crack a "funny bone" – but her letter seemed to express that I was worried about leaving. Please reassure her, Honey!

Mother was anxious to know if we still love each other as much as always so I must write and tell them that I love you even more!! Mona was primarily concerned with the fact that Kenny will be home soon – he has finished his missions! Lucky sot!

Yesterday at noon we were given passes on account of being on KP on Sunday. Several of us went into town (my first trip) and I was able to mail the little parcel to you! The rest of the time we spent in the USO playing classical records – boogey-woogey and the like! We climaxed the evening by taking a "senior hostess" out for a hamburger, then she drove us back to camp. She was a very nice lady – Ava Baumgartner by name – a teacher in the fifth grade – an ardent Bridge fiend – and about fifty or fifty-five years old! This place is a soldier's paradise as far as the female situation goes with three women's colleges within a twenty-five mile radius! Greensboro boasts the North Carolina University for Women which has an enrollment of 3000 to 4000 females. They are running loose trying to pick up soldiers (and doing quite well) – women "cut in" dances around here! The pathetic thing is that I'm just not interested – and I don't plan on getting interested in anyone 'til I see YOU again!! You can trust me and believe that as I have never been more sincere than I am now!

Another thing, Babe, today's letter – and I quote – says: "I'm quite positive you love me" – don't say that – <u>be positive</u> – I am that sure of you!!

We managed to get in bed shortly after 11:00 p.m. – tired but satisfied that we had seen some of Greensboro before leaving.

I must write to Jeannie and Gerry as I promised – maybe it will be a V-mail!

I love you tonight more than last night – it's good that love isn't measured in pounds or I would have to join a circus as the world's biggest man – 1,000,000,000,000,000,000,000,000, 000,000,000,000, 000,000 lbs!! Goodnight, sweet,

Dave Jr.

Wednesday, January 10, 1945

My Darling!!

I have just completed my laundry – fourteen pair of socks, one set of fatigues, a field jacket, and several "unmentionables" – reason: we are through with our "processing period" and one can never tell how badly I might need those things 'ere too long! Honey, when we get married all you'll have to do is suggest that we send our laundry out 'cause I know it's a whale of a job – perhaps with a machine it would be much easier!

Your first letter with my correct Greensboro address arrived today – you wanted to know how long air-mail took, well, this one took three days!! What

I meant when I said we'd have to send air mail was when I got out of the states! Anyway, I'm glad that you're getting my mail again 'cause if it means 1/16th as much to you as it does me it is kinda nauseating not to get letters!

There is one thing on my mind but I'm unable to discuss it in the mail! For that reason I can't find much to write about tonight. There is always a bigger, more important subject on my brain but you'd get pretty tired of reading I love you – I love you – I love you – for ten pages! You know it already so I'll say goodnight and climb into bed – please excuse this feeble attempt to dash a line to you…

I love you again!

David Jr.

Friday, January 12, 1945

Dearest Patty!

After a spell of three days and no mail, things showed definite improvement when two of yours plus one from Dad and another from Ruth arrived!

You seemed so blue, and although I should hate myself for saying it, I was almost thrilled – honestly happy – that you missed me so much! Right now, I'm sweatin' out a call to Iowa City and every time I hear the phone ring, my torso lifts about sixteen feet out of my chair! I need to talk to you to kinda settle my nerves!

Yesterday we moved from Section K to the Shipping and Receiving Area but my mailing address remains the same! We worked like fiends from about 3 p.m. to 10 p.m. getting our equipment sorted. Your dorm attendant just called and said that you weren't in and didn't expect you 'til 12:30 a.m. – that's 1:30 a.m. our time and since we're going on KP again tomorrow I'll have to get up at 3 a.m. and so I'll not attempt to get the call through! I told her that I'd call tomorrow afternoon but my duties will no doubt prevent it – we won't be off 'til 8 p.m. or later!

For some strange reason I'm even more shaky than before and I try awfully hard not to think things that seem to pop in my mind! There is one thing that I beg of you and that is: if you are dating I'd like to know about it – since we're still engaged that should be my business! Never hold back for fear of worrying me or causing an uncontrollable urge to do something drastic!

In a few days you will receive a card with a temporary A.P.O. mailing address – this you can use to write to me while I'm enroute – this will be an indication that we're heading out as it is being mailed after we've cleared the field by ONE HOUR. You will also know if more than two or three days pass without you getting any mail from me!

There are parts of this letter that may not sound like me and as I re-read it perhaps it should be scrapped! Don't get the wrong impression, I do trust you and I want you to get clear in your mind one thing! You may interpret our engagement any way you feel is the best way! If there is a remote feeling between us while I am gone perhaps it would be well for you to partake of parties and other things – I don't want you to sit around and brood – but at the same time there must be a relationship of real, honest-to-goodness love that cannot be dimmed by outside elements! Right now, I am kicking my fanny for not having married you while at home – I'd feel much better to know that you'd be waiting for certain!

This is not the way I intended to write tonight and I hope you pass over the contents with a shrug!

I do love you with all my heart –

Your guy, Dave Jr.

Sunday, January 14, 1945

My dearest Patricia,

After a good night's rest – a good meal – a couple o' brews and some free time, I feel much, much better. Right about this time you are probably pondering over a Botany problem or "ripping off" a few chapters of history – and my heart's with you! Things have apparently mounted to a height where you can't possibly imagine that you'll ever catch up, but by the end of the week you'll realize that you've, by some way or another, been able to erase a lot of back work even though you'll be still behind in one or two subjects. Through some miraculous force, things just seem to align themselves and before you know it, you'll be wondering how you manage to have so much free time! Naturally, I'm not acquainted with the activities of "big schools" but I'm certain that your schedule will work out okay! Your little troubles remind me so much of the "adjustment period" I had in school that I can almost feel every emotion that you are having! So don't worry, Babe, they've (the troubles) been experienced by every person who ever attended a college or university – if you ever reach a point of mental depression so low that you feel hopeless, go to your advisor and he or she will be able to understand and offer better consultation than I can give!

Yesterday's letter told me all about your "roomie", Tommy, being in Washington – that's only a seven hour ride from Greensboro; perhaps you should have gone with her! Our time is so allotted that we're unable to stray too far away or I might have made arrangements to see Jeannie during her stay in the Capitol – but, since our time at this place is most uncertain, it would be difficult to make plans.

This little morsel of news is being written at the USO in town; we came in to buy a decent meal and decided to write a few letters!

Enclosed you will find a photo of one of my buddies, Bob Maxwell of Idaho, and myself with all the gruesome accessories attached – we had this "pic" taken as a last reminder of our moustaches as they are being removed tonight! He is the fellow that I mentioned to you as being married and his wife is some six or seven months expectant! If the sight is unbearable you have my full permission to burn, tear, or subject any other drastic fate to it!

Now my darling one, I shall have to write to me mater and pater – I love you so much!

David

15 JAN 1945

DAVID, I HAVE CHANGED MY MIND AND WILL ACCEPT YOUR PROPOSAL. YOU ARE THE ONLY GUY FOR ME. WILL BE ANXIOUSLY AWAITING YOUR RETURN, AND IT WON'T BE TOO LONG UNTIL THIS WAR IS OVER. WE CAN WAIT. MUCH LOVE, PATTY.

Book Eight
2011

March 1, 2011

Dear Barby,

Mom has been in her own apartment now for a year at Fairhills – a progressive senior facility housing all levels of care. Her little one bedroom apartment allows her all of the freedom that she can handle at this point. There are daily activities, bus trips, grocery runs, even transportation to appointments. Every meal is served in the dining room which has allowed her to become acquainted with the other residents. It is a lovely campus and she seems quite happy (as long as I keep a plentiful supply of Chardonnay cooling in the refrigerator). I stop by every other day just to check in and visit for awhile.

Most days, she seems to recognize me (or else she is a really good faker!) but more often than not, she doesn't recognize her surroundings ("Where am I? What city is this?") Tim is planning on coming up this spring to help her plant a small garden (she and Roy used to do this every year). In the fall, Jean and I are going to take her on a trip back to Elk Rapids (perhaps her last? It's a 10-hour car ride) to look at familiar sites and take in that famous Grand Traverse sunset that she enjoyed so fervently.

Hope all is well with you and your family! Love you, Elle.

October 16, 2011

Dear Barby,

I was on vacation with Mom in northern Michigan when the call came in. We were spending a few days at her condo in Elk Rapids, enjoying the change of seasons from summer to fall—having a glass of wine on the porch.

"Fairhills calling. We have an opening in the Assisted Living section of our building, and we think that you should consider moving your mom there".

I was acidic with my retort: "Why does she need to move? Isn't she doing well in the independent living section?"

Their reply was curt. "No, she's not. You need to accept the fact that she is declining and needs more help. The room will only be available for the next forty-eight hours, then we're going to offer it to someone else."

I guess I have to move Mom – again. How did you and your sibs decide to move your mom and dad to assisted living from independent living? Or did they make the decision for themselves proactively? I just thought she was doing so well on her own in her little apartment, but once again, my head must have been deep down in the sand.

Love, Elle.

October 20, 2011

Dear Elle,

It is a process. Unfortunately, I can't tell you how to fix your situation, but I can tell you some ideas about how to deal with this experience. Your mom is on a path toward the end of her life. You and your siblings are going to have to guide her down that rocky, tumultuous road.

Engage the help of all family and friends that are willing to help. That may include people who are eager to sit and talk to her about her past, or people who will write letters, or to give her a phone call every now and then. It's good that you have gotten in touch with the Alzheimer's Foundation – they offer awesome support. Reach out to anyone you can think of that might take an interest of being a part of those early memories of her life. It will help her to depart into the next world with a sense of calm and relief that she has accomplished what God has sent her into the world to complete, and once she knows that, she will be able to let go, and let God.

Your meddling (but honest) cousin, Barby.

. . . .

October 29, 2011

Dear Barby,

I parlayed the move to Building "C" – assisted living—as an upgrade. Mom is getting the "penthouse"—a corner unit with a living room and bedroom with much more space than the other residents were given. The fourth floor boasted a sun-kissed *pied a terre* right next to her new digs, boasting large planters and a seating area. What is not to be liked?

Another loss of freedom. Nurses coming in every couple of hours to check blood pressure, instill eyedrops, help her go to the bathroom. Showers have to be monitored. Another loss of dignity, of self-dependence, of living life on one's own terms. At least she still has her one stronghold on her independence—a dorm-sized refrigerator, full of her favorite beverage, Woodbridge Chardonnay.

She seems to be okay with the move, but I know that it is one step closer to her lack of independence. I know you are right when you tell me to step away from the situation and to look at it from a safety and comfort perspective. It is hard.

Cousins and friends forever, Elle.

Book Nine
1945

Monday, January 15, 1945

Dearest Patty!

Your telegram arrived today – right after lunch – I am over the top with happiness! Upon receiving the notice, I ran like a bunny to the Message Center; since I had had no letter from you for two days I was a bit puzzled – you have almost spoiled me. You're right, it won't be too long – perhaps much sooner than either of us dare to think! There is one little item I think we should positively clear for you and all parties concerned – when I get home next time, in a month or four years, I'm going to claim one Patricia Marie Wise and there'll be no mistake then! I let you slip by once but another time will portray a different story – if there is any question in your mind now, you had better get it solved and get used to the idea that <u>you're going to marry me</u> – that will shorten our post-war engagement by at least fifteen minutes. I figure it shouldn't take longer than that to convince you that I love you so much if couldn't be any other way – and I'm sure you feel that way, too!

When I left you that Sunday a.m. in St. Louis, you asked about having our "marital intentions" publicly declared via the newspaper – however, since that time it has been a purely a one-sided conversation – your letters even fail to mention it! Your decision will have to be the final one as I can't do any more than I say: "I'm all for it!" Besides, it's only fair that people know how fortunate I am!

It has been a cold, damp, drizzling day in Greensboro – the kind of day that make you feel all "icky-pooh" inside. I have been nursing a slight cold and this weather doesn't help a bit! We had our little gab-fest with the Post Athletic Officer this p.m. regarding the proposed boxing exhibition – he is hoping to stage a match in the arena on Wed. night but is holding back for want of participants – he'll get a show, a show like he's never seen before if they only stage one bout; with my knowledge of pugilistic technique (negligible) and Keebler's condition (my opponent) we should be able to produce nine minutes of fun and entertainment for one and all!

The little picture with the 'stache that was enclosed last week would look entirely different now as both Max and I have subjected the upper lip to the razor! If I do say so myself – the difference is striking and perhaps even for the better!

This stationery is compliments of our Camp Service Club – a neat little haven for writing letters – especially to my best gal. I love you, Babe!

Your guy, David.

Thursday, January 18, 1945

Dearest David,

I received your latest letters that have been forwarded from our St. Louis address. My new location is: Eastlawn Dorm, Iowa City, IA.

College life is quite different than what I was doing working in a factory in St. Louis. I really like the studies, but I feel as if I am shirking my responsibilities as an American citizen by not working in an armament factory.

I have no reservations about our engagement status, and I don't think that I will be sitting around and brooding! I have met some new friends here in Iowa City and I hope to be able to send you upbeat news about what is going on here. Mind you, I am not seeking out other relationships—I am making it well known that I have a guy in the Army overseas, so the few men that are on campus will certainly keep their distance. So, I WILL be waiting for certain!

Dorothy has invited me to spend the weekend at her home. I'm not much of a country girl, so I don't know how that is going to go, but I accepted! I am a bit homesick for my parents, so maybe it will help to be with a real family.

U of I is a bit overwhelming. I hope I am making the right choices when it comes to classes and a degree. I think I am well suited for a Home Economics specialty, don't you? My first classes will be the "basics" such as math, English, and humanities, but soon I will be able to delve into my chosen path.

Must go! I'm meeting a few friends down at the local tavern. I wish you could be there with us.

Sending love, Patty.

Note: you have to remember that the replies are not immediate…there is a three or four day lag between letters.

January 20, 1945 Saturday P.M.

My Darling Patty!

It is rather a problem how to start this letter tonight – I'm downright ashamed, honestly astonished at my own stupidity for even letting myself imagine that you were steppin' out already! I feel so low that if you'd ask I'd get on my knees and apologize!! I'd do it!! Please, please forgive me this once and I'll do my utmost to see it doesn't happen again.

When I called this afternoon, I had a dozen things to ask and tell you – perhaps offer a little moral support in your present difficulty – but for some reason all those things were unimportant; just to hear you say that you loved me and will marry me is well worth a month's pay! Everything happened so suddenly that I won't really be able to appreciate it until it registers completely in my brain! I have heard that real-honest love is similar to a sickness and, Babe, mine's almost fatal! Right now – tonight – I could walk into you in Iowa City and not even notice! Shameful!

Today, after we came "home" from the mess hall, there was a letter mailed only two days ago and as I read it I felt almost like I was really hearing you speak to me! I love writing to you every day – mainly 'cause it affords a chance to "talk" to you and I want that as often as possible! You tell me of your little troubles and I give you a long story of my woes – it's kinda like we can solve things so much easier together!

Your mom sent my "personalized" matches and a big box of pecans – gee, she's sweet. I think that I could have fallen in love with her if I hadn't met you first! It's little things like that that make a guy feel wonderful – to know that someone is thinking just a little extra special about you stirs up an ego that "builds you up"!

Our setto (you may not be familiar with this word – it is Army speak for fight or sparring) with the Mess Sergeant proved to pass without too many ill-effects! For the most part we didn't even have reason to cuss him out properly! I was assigned to cleaning the kitchen floor and the one beautiful part of KP here is that as soon as you finish your job, you're permitted to sleep – take off – or make entertainment! The latter we stretched to an extreme and sang such old favorites as "Dirty Lil" – "Fisherman, Fisherman", etc. Even the Mess Officer smiled graciously as we ripped those melodies apart. Our project doesn't have too much to offer in the line of crooners or harmony makers, but we struggle along!

Honey, the stretch from 3a.m. 'til 9:30 p.m. is beginning to have its effect and my sack is screaming for company!

I miss you and love you so much that it hurts. Goodnight, sweets.

David

Wednesday, January 24 PM

DEAREST Darling Patty!

This is the scheduled night for our bout – but, as you can see, I'm spending the night writing letters! Up 'til 2 p.m. we thought that our judgment day had come and I must confess, I began wondering if I had chosen the right path- boxing in lieu of labor– perhaps a little detail wouldn't have been so bad after all. However, at about 2 o'clock our poker game was interrupted by one of the boxing instructors – at the last minute they decided that we will postpone the match. Things are stirring here and we are expected the "all aboard" call to go out any day now.

We had a final dental check today – the second since we've been here! There were several fellows ahead of me and each were required to get some type of work – in fact, there were only three or four out of forty men that didn't have to stay! By the time my time came up I was "fit to be tied" – shaking like a leaf as I listened to: "cross 18, 16 DO-MO, 15 MO, 6 silicate", etc. This continued for some three or four minutes as he probed around my teeth trying vainly to dig a hole if there wasn't one there already! After he said, "Okay, next," I asked the results and the nurse (kinda cute) said there was a facial filling that had to be re-drilled and re-filled – plus cleaning if I wanted it. The idea of the extra-special check was to correct any defects prior to combat duty! A lot of guys had "wisdom teeth" pulled but he didn't even mention it to me – thank God!

Babe, this is Wed. and still my mail box is empty (Sat., I think was the last letter from you) – gosh, I hope nothing is wrong! Today the brilliant thought hit me that your telegram was sent kinda sudden like to cover your failure to write – right? You're cute. I'd undoubtedly do the same thing! I do realize that you are very busy and it's hard to find time to write.

In approx. two weeks we shall be celebrating our 48th anniversary – four long, but wonderful and beautiful years. There doesn't seem to be much I can do to show you how much I appreciate the fact you are so swell and too, in a small way, repay you for everything you've done for me! Sometimes I wonder how I could bear all this crap if there wasn't the big reward waiting when it's over. So, enclosed you will find a couple bucks that is for you! Please know that I'm not trying to cheapen the immense valuation I hold for you and believe me, a million dollars would never one-half show you what I think of you or pay, in any part, the debt I owe you! Know that I love you with all my heart and I'm thinking of you twenty-four hours a day.

Four years' worth plus the rest of my life!

Please write!! Goodnight my darling,

David Jr.

Book Ten
2012

April 12, 2012

Dear Barby,

Fairhill was right in their assessment of Mom. Every day I see scant changes in her behavior and cognitive abilities. I keep trying to remind myself – she IS 88 years old!

Last summer, I hired an aide to spend the summer with Mom for one last time in Elk Rapids. I wanted her to spend one last summer on the beaches of Grand Traverse Bay, soaking in the sunshine, the beautiful sunsets, the gin and tonics imbibed while lounging on the pristine beach. Then I knew it was time to sell.

Recently, I received an offer on Mom's condo. It was the last of her belongings to part with, and perhaps the most painful, but it is a ten-hour drive from here, and the aide is expensive! I had to make the decision to sell the place that she loved for the past twenty years.

I had it on the market for $229,000. The offer came in at $205K. I countered at $210,000. The buyer told the realtor that he had a bad day on the golf course, and that he wouldn't budge. I suggested that he take up tennis.

We closed at $210,000. Goodbye to our Michigan ties, but we are so thankful for the many blessings having a place to visit in beautiful Elk Rapids!

Elle.

May, 2012

Dear Barby,

Today I took Mom to UW-Madison Geriatric Unit for some testing. Here is a synopsis of how things went:

"Pat, I'm Dr. Waters. I just want to run you through a couple of tests to see how I can help you—is that okay?"

"Sure, okay."

"Pat, do you know what year it is?"

"1998".

"Do you know the month and the day?"

"No".

"I'm going to give you three words to remember, and I'll ask you about them in the next few minutes. The words are turtle, sink, and vase. Can you repeat those words for me?"

"Turtle, sink, vase".

"Okay. What are you doing here today?"

"I don't know".

"How many items are in a dozen?"

"I don't know—20?"

"Okay. What are the names of your children?"

"Jean." She paused as she searched those holes inside her where she knew the information lived. "Ellen." More searching, more struggling. "There is another, and I think one has passed away".

What are the three words I asked you to remember?"

Silence.

Well, at least she remembered my name! I hope I don't cause her trauma when I put her in situations like this – I'm trying to help and to get her the best care possible, but more often than not, she resists going out – even conversation is getting more difficult.

Love you, Elle.

May 2012

Dear Jean,

I don't really know where I am, or what time it is. My memory is a fog. I don't feel like talking anymore, there just isn't much to say. Sitting around, looking at pictures in an album, most of the people I don't recognize. There is a book here that says I should write down daily activities and thoughts, my mind doesn't want to put pen to paper. I asked my nurse, Julie, to write this letter to you on my behalf.

I am talking with Tim at 8:30 p.m. Otherwise I don't know what is going on. Ellen has me in this place and I don't know why I can't go back home. What has she done to me? Help me to go back to where I belong.

Your mother.

August 2012

Dear Roy,

(This is Pat's nurse, Julie writing this note for her) Won't you come and visit me soon? Maybe your family could come, too, and they could spend a couple of days at Wisconsin Dells. I can't write very well anymore (guess I'm getting old!) so I will close this. Maybe we could go to Elk Rapids? Once again for auld lang syne? You could play tennis, and I'll wait for you on the beach.

Your Trish.

September 2, 2012

Dear Barby,

I was spending a quiet, pleasant weekend with Mom and Jean when I received the following message: *"Fairhill calling ... we have come to the conclusion that your mom can no longer function on her own and needs to be moved to the Memory Care section of our facility. Please contact us at your earliest convenience so that we can plan this transition".* Now this mirage, this myopic dream world in which I have been resting so comfortably in the arms of denial, is crumbling like an imploded building. Mom is no longer part of the world as she has known it, and I need to prepare for upcoming downhill descent into the mental waterspout that awaits.

Love you always, Elle.

September 4, 2012

Dear Barby,

I feel like the opposite of a superhero – more like the devious villain taking part in a nefarious plan to oust Mom and secretly remove her from the place she has called home for almost a year. Unbeknownst to her, we are taking all of her belongings and moving her to a new residence at the memory care facility. Tim took Mom out for breakfast, and a team of Fairhill employees descended upon Mom's penthouse to clear things out and move them to her new residence. We arrived at 8 a.m. I hid in the shadows of the Community Room as Tim escorted Mom out for a meal. Little did she know that when she returned, her life would once again be a hurricane—she no longer lives in the place that she has called home for as long as she could remember (which isn't long). Now a new home, new caregivers, and new restrictions await her in a locked facility with limited mobility and access to the outside world. Her brain is malfunctioning, and I am in denial. She needs more help than I can provide.

The defiant quadrant of my brain screams: "No way has Mom gotten that forgetful, unable to care for herself that she needs to move to the Alzheimer's unit! She is eighty-eight years young and functioning fairly well on her own, with some assistance, right?" When did she tumble from having an aide stop by a couple of times a day to administer medications to this level of dysfunction? How did I not see it happening?

But I trusted their judgment and succumbed to the recommendation that she be moved.

The staff has obviously carried out this regimen before. They marched into Mom's room, and ruthlessly began stripping every one of her belongings into a waiting cart. Without remorse, they opened every drawer, and dumped her precious belongings into a heap of stuff. The entire contents of her closet were shoved into a mobile piece of luggage – no regard for her personal attachment to any item. It seemed cruel to me as I watched this band of strangers ransacking the last vestiges of Mom's life – callously throwing her life's remaining possessions into an awaiting cartage bin and prepared to shove them into her new destination: Hartstone. She will have her own bedroom and half bath, with an attached community living and dining area. Kind of an open concept floorplan. Gone are her private moments—her independence, and her life, as it existed a mere few hours ago. Now she is a member of a community of lost souls, who endure their days trying to remember who they are—straining to recall their family members, their daily activities, and just coping to get through every agonizing, crippling, humiliating day. And it all fell on my shoulders to make the call that it was time.

Sorry to burden you with all of this sadness, but I don't have anyone else to turn to.

Your cousin, Elle.

September 14, 2012

Dear Barby,

I have been visiting Mom nearly every day since her transition to the memory care unit. For the most part, she is kind and calm (she refers to all staff members as "my angel") but I know that there are demons and fireworks that are festering within. Her frustrations lie in not knowing where she is and why she is here. She is also painfully missing her daily dose of Chardonnay, but staff has assured me that it is available upon request.

When encouraged to tell stories, Mom talks about the years in Bangkok, the summers on Grand Traverse Bay, travels to Italy and Spain, and her years with Dad and Roy. What a blessing that she is not harboring ill will and anger, but swimming in a sea of fond, warm memories? My plan is to encourage that by focusing on thoughts she seems to be attached to now – events from the 1940's through the 1990's. The rest I will have to put in my memory bank, as I find that for her, the oldest recollections seem to hold on the longest.

Love you dearly (you're my angel!), Elle.

Book Eleven
1945

Thursday AM January 25th

Darling Patty!

Well, this is it – I think! Our packing is finished and we're waiting in the barrack for official word. It may be sometime before you receive another letter and that will be censored – but I'll write at every possible chance: probably every day and mail 'em all at once.

Right now I'm more in the mood to talk about us – soooo, here goes – we have so much to look forward to and every minute, hon, and day I'll be thinking of that one thing – primarily! If I could only find the right words; or if I were a musician I'd write a sonata. If I could be an artist I'd paint a picture; but since I'm not any of these things, I'll have to be content to tell you from my heart that I love you!

Please don't worry about me – I'll be okay! As soon as I can write to you again we'll be able to straighten out things considerably. Please tell your mom and dad that I'm sorry that I couldn't write a last minute letter to them – we've been pressed no-end for the last few days.

This was originally intended to be a long, more explanatory missive but time is getting short. Please believe me when I say that I'll miss you so very much and love you with all my capacity – plus. Bye, honey.

D. Kyle Jr.

Ps – here is a little picture of how I see us after the war is over – will you be able to handle my foibles? I have been told that I snore and I talk in my sleep. My bunkmates are able to throw a boot in my direction to get me to shut down – what will you do? A slipper probably won't be as effective as a good shove in the arse, if you pardon my expletives. This war is grinding on me, and I'm afraid that I have lost the social graces that I once knew when I was stateside. Love you again and again and again.

Thursday PM – January 25, 1945

My dearest one!

Well, that wasn't so bad – the dreaded thought of going to the dentist has become a memory and we're 100% pure – ready to leave! All that happened was approx. five minutes of drilling and picking – and it was all set to be filled; I went downstairs where a nurse re-examined me again and pronounced me okay – believe me, it's a big relief!

You must be wondering why you are getting these twice-day letters – kind of like a hog feeding schedule! We are ordered to our quarters in the a.m. and p.m. and told, "Write a letter to your mama – if you don't have a mama, write to someone else!"

Another letter came today and it's so encouraging to know that you hadn't forgotten about having our engagement announced (I knew you hadn't). Honey, I hope this means as much to you as it does me; like I said 1000 times before – that builds me up to heights higher than I've ever experienced since joining the ranks! You make me so happy – honestly!

I was wondering how my moustache would effect (sic) you – and I think (candid-like) that you rather appreciated the novelty – although I didn't expect you to acknowledge it. Now you have in your possession another "monstrosity" maybe you'll want me to grow one again! I wasn't trying to tell you "when we expect to leave" in any of the past missives but you might get prepared for the "D. Kyle" any day now ... encouraging news this p.m.!

For some strange reason, we have been notified not to report to the gym for further boxing instruction, so aside from the dental appointment, we were permitted to remain in our sacks all day. Tomorrow we report to a "Lt. Greenley" for warehouse duty – meaning absolutely nothing excepting that we'll be working our "rooneys" to the bone! Without the daily road-runs, exercise, and sparring, I'm afraid that soon I'll slip back into a groove of laxness. Me, what was in such fine condition, too.

Darling, please don't ever think twice about thanking me for any little (and I do mean little) gifts which might come your way. It is so small in proportion to what I'd like to give you – and what you really deserve!

If at any time, I may give you a little mazuma ... please, please tell me! Things like that make me very happy and perhaps a little proud that I can do something to help – honestly, it would mean an awful lot to me and I want you to feel that we're so close that you won't hesitate a bit.

I love you so very, very much!

Your guy, David Jr.

January 24, 1945

Dear David,

I hope you accepted my telegram with a sense of relief ... I'll be waiting for you when this war is over!

Getting back into academic life has been quite an adjustment. The U of I requires that all students take a physical examination, which includes agility and endurance testing, intelligence quizzes, and a very personal medical examination. It was humiliating and exhausting, but I guess it is a measure of one's stamina and dedication to higher education.

I worry about your boxing encounters—it just doesn't seem to be a sport that suits you. I'm not sure if I want to hear anything more about it or not. It does sound like they keep you busy with preparations (not only for overseas, but food, cleaning, and visits to the dentist).

Classes are in high gear here. I'm finding it hard to juggle all of my obligations! I hope college was the right choice for me. Maybe I should have stayed at Emerson and helped with the war effort.

I look forward to hearing from you soon, love, Patty.

Dear David, I am loving you and missing you ... it is so hard to be apart, but we will be together again soon!

Love, Patty.

Friday PM

postmarked January 28

My beloved Patricia!

I'm so glad that you wrote, and for the past three or four days your letters have come very regularly – the reason I'm especially glad is because I have <u>really needed them</u> like I've never needed anything before! As you may have surmised, our time is getting more limited in the place and, therefore, we are subject to twenty-four-hour duty – we haven't missed the full day of work by too far since yesterday morning! We were so busy that I couldn't even write a wee note last p.m. "Security" stops the urge to tell all that is happening but I think it's okay to say that we've been alerted and prepared to move on ten minute's notice.

For the first time in my Army career I have noticed a genuine efficiency, most uncommon in GI circles. Everyone is keyed up – waiting, lest any minute we are told to shove off. The normally "big-mouthy" guys have lost all their boisterousness and everyone is either writing last minute letters or scanning the news. I'm sure that at least fifty percent of us can't visualize what's coming so, naturally, are more concerned with whether or not they'll get a letter, etc. I want to get out of here in the worst way and so anything that sounds encouraging bolsters morale.

Golly, Babe, the "physical exam" they subjected you to sounded horrible! I don't understand why they insist on having girls (especially mine) run obstacle courses, etc., not being used to having your photo taken – less wearing apparel (thank God for that) your reaction was certainly not unusual! They should be a little more discreet and allow for the fact that there are a few decent and modest souls in the world – however, don't let it throw you, Babe, I'm sure you won't have to endure it again! Besides, no one will ever see you in that situation (without clothes) except your family and your husband (AHEM! meaning ME, of course) and I'm certain none of us will care a bit if your head does tilt just a little! I'd grade you A-1 – one hundred percent wonderfully okay!

Already there is a slight hint that you are becoming thoroughly acclimated to your new "work" – I'm glad, Patty, you can do it so easily and there is so much good to be had from school. Wouldn't it be great if we could finish our last year together – but perhaps we'd just better wait to see each other to make plans for that.

I look forward to that day with as much zest as humanly possible. I love you so very much.

David.

Sunday, January 28th

new return address: Squadron B-1, APO NY

My darling Patty,

Another "two a day" letter – I hope you enjoy reading them as much as I like writing! As you may have guessed, during the past few days we have been hopping around like a one-legged ballet dancer with the seven-year itch. Due to our precarious situation, our mail is being subject to certain restrictions – soooo, I'll try to surmount some of the weaker barriers of censorship and let you know in a vague way what we're doing; what we have done and expect to do needs no further discussion.

After listening to at least a dozen different individuals discuss "security measures" I have come to the conclusion that I have one of two alternatives [word cut out by censors]: 1: write a form postcard "Am fine – miss you – love you, etc.; 2: "Got up at 6 a.m., ate 3 meals, went to bed at 10 p.m." Obviously, both of us would suffer from nervous repercussions so 'til we are better informed on what to write or what not to write, you'll have to bear with me [censored].

By this time you should have received a card with my new address and, if not, you will use the one enclosed hereon [censored]. This is a temporary A.P.O. number – a permanent address will come at a later date, as soon as we're more permanently affixed [censored]. Right now I am not at liberty to disclose our location.

I received your very sweet and appropriate valentine – letter while at my last post, thanx Honey. Please keep writing. I need 'em very much! The folks have said that they'd keep you informed on any reports via the War Department regarding your No. 1 guy – I think they already have your address but I'll send it again to make sure. Probably you have written to them by now [censored]. Well, Babe, I must clamp the finale on this epistle. I love you so very much [censored].

Dave Jr.

January 29, 1945

Tuesday PM

My darling Patty:

Well, here we are back playing "USO Commando" in the Service Club – the main reason is that the noise in the barrack is so terrific that I can't think of real nice things to say to you! For some strange reason, there are certain days that I get so lonely for you that there is no escape – any place; tonight is "one of those days" so if this seems a little moody – please try not to think badly of me if I get a bit "super-mushy". Whenever I get particularly blue I just lay on my sack like a sentimental old Billy, look at your picture, and say "Gosh, wouldn't it be shameful if Patty could see how sick you look? ANSWER: no, I think she'd be "tickled pink" 'cause she'd be able to coo and besides, it would do her good to know that I miss her that much. It does, however, give me a little boost jut to know you must be lonely, too. Do you understand what I mean?

I finally got around to answering your mom's letter and thanking her for sending the packages. I had planned to write a dozen letters to catch up on my back correspondence but, on second thought, decided to save them 'til I get overseas and then they'll be able to answer it with the correct mailing address. It really doesn't matter if I ever get any mail just so long as there's a letter from you waiting when I'm through working. Do you understand that?

Gosh, Darling, I love you so much! Please love me too – real much!

Goodnight, David

January 30th, 1945

My Darling Patty,

We have just been entertained by an orchestra here in the Service Club comprised of fellows from all the "name" bands we knew as civilians and believe me, they were terrific [censored]. Each individual was introduced and the name of the outfit he was with before coming to the Army [censored]. Kay Kyser, Bennie Goodman, Les Brown, Andre Kastelanetz, The Chicago Civic Symphony, Jimmie Dorsey, and several others made up the list [censored]. I have never heard anything better in all my life; the pianist was recently recognized as the outstanding "boogie-woogie" artist in the nation. Along with the program (incidentally, the orchestra is governed under the name of Johnny Messner [censored], you might remember him with the addition: [censored] and his Toy Piano. He's a Sgt. now [censored], rough, huh? Was a character the likes which you have never seen [censored]. We were seated alongside of some "Limies" (Englishmen to you, Darling) and their enthusiasm is incomparable with anything you might imagine – we sat there ready to split a gut as it were, and those ungrateful blokes wouldn't so much as twitch a facial muscle [censored]. I marvel at their self-control and would like to swat each one to liven them up a bit [censored].

I was the Barracks Guard today; my duties consisting of logging a little lost "sack time" so, naturally, I feel pretty good tonight [censored]. Max is brooding quite a bit worrying about his wife, [censored], she's expecting in about a month or so…gosh, I'd be scared silly [censored].

Gee, Hon, I'd give anything to see you again [censored] and I'm counting every day 'til that little dream comes true [censored]. I love you so very much and can hardly wait until a letter arrives. I hope you continue to write to my Greensboro address 'cause the boys are getting mail from there regularly … perhaps one tomorrow?

Now Darling, Max is getting ready to go back to the barracks so [censored] this short. Goodnight, Honey, [censored] write again tomorrow.

Dave Jr.

ps – As I re-read this missive it is very distracting to see all those [censored].

Wednesday, February 1, 1945

DEAREST Patty!

Yesterday your first letter since last Thurs. arrived from Greensboro. I'm just wondering what it will be like when I don't get a letter for perhaps a month or so if I sweat it out like I did those last six days! Anyway, they were two beautiful messages – I guess that your re-assurance was all I needed.

Everything that happens to us now is completely surrounded by uncertainty – naturally! We're waiting for shipping orders and when things don't go exactly as we expect them to there is usually a flare of temper! Arguments are frequent and even an occasional fight is not unusual. It will be good for us to get moving – I have never seen men so "touchy". Tonight we are having a big party for the Project men – dinner and the like – perhaps that will help to encourage more friendliness and relaxation. But I shouldn't bother you with all this tripe – perhaps I'm still looking for an excuse for writing poor letters!

Last night we went to a USO show "You Said It" – just to see what they're like! To tell the honest truth, I wasn't too much impressed with the whole thing. Some woman, who couldn't carry a tune in a beer vat, sang several selections to the rhythm of wolf-calls, hoots, and hollers. She was stacked like a red brick privy and that was the main attraction as far as she was concerned! A juggler, mind-reader, trio of feminine tap dancers, comedians and comediennes, plus a band completed the program. It was an hour and a half of "different humor" – and we needed a little "different" monkey business!

Bright and early Monday Ayem I report to have my "facial MO" repaired. For some peculiar reason I have no yen to get into that dentist chair – they scare the HELL out of me – and I'm not making jokes! Those guys are strongly reminiscent of "missing links" – especially that major that checked me the other day. Their Neanderthal ways are just a step above their sadistic need to yank the teeth out of a soldier's mouth!

Love to you, David.

1 February 1945

David dear,

I recently received your note about being put in the boxing ring! I hate the thought of fighting—aren't you in enough danger?

School is going well, but I haven't yet found an area of study that I would like to focus on. Rationing keeps us from doing much of anything- no travel, not much of a social life, but that is okay! We are all just praying for our boys overseas, and especially MY boy, on his way!

Please send more cartoon images of my family … it boosts my spirits! In the meantime, I hope that you are enduring your enlisted time, and I can't wait for your return.

All my love, Patty.

postmarked Feb 19, 1945

return address is an APO NY
censored/passed army examiner (stamp)

My darling Patty!

It seems like such a long time since I have written a letter, 'though actually, it has only been a few days – so I shall try to divulge a few little items while we are still at sea and this missive can be mailed as soon as we reach our destination! Perhaps I had better explain my plight in regard to this horrible example of Palmer Method Penmanship: it is quite a feat (now I'm boasting) to make any semblance of legible writing while sitting on a canvas bunk, using a life jacket for a desk, and attempting to overcome the slow, irregular rocking movement of this ship. Ne comprendais pas?

To make this letter follow a half-way chronological order, I suppose the proper place to begin would be where the last chapter stopped … after we left our last station! It was one of those nights a person would associate with a murder: cold, bleak and damp. We were carried on the loading docks by the trucks and were left in formation for our turn to board the vessel; while we were waiting, Red Cross ladies wandered through the mew with coffee, doughnuts, candy, etc. Needless to say, a relief from the chilled night air. The hour our shipping number was called – each man, loaded to the hilt with clothing and equipment, started up the gangplank and ultimately to our compartment. If I can think of one good thing to say for the Navy, it would be that they are masters in the art of conserving space; every man is allotted approx. twenty cubic feet for his bed and all equipment. It was the first time I could sympathize with a sardine!

Anyway, we finally embarked about ninety-nine percent of the men on deck to bid adieu to the "old lady with a torch" and we were really coming to realize for the first time, that we were GOING.

Life on board ship is neither exciting nor dull – but kinda interesting! The primary thought of nearly everyone was "seasickness". Fortunately, I did not join the ranks of the "railbirds". It was not at all unusual to see some negro's pigment change to a pure white or a white man turn a little green. As one fellow explained, "At first I thought I'd die – then I was afraid I wouldn't!"

They just about "broke their backs" trying to keep us entertained with movies, books, church services, and the like. They even sponsored Army-Navy basketball games, in which the army officers were losers (couldn't get their sea legs) and enlisted men winners! My main duty on the team was "guard" duty – very simple work. The biggest problem connected with it being to refuse entrance to any troops who want to come into their compartment during inspection and chasing obstinate characters out of their sacks during boat drill. Once I ran into a fellow who was evidently worried about being in the middle of the ocean, so, in an effort to cheer him somewhat, I asked a passing sailor how far we were from the closest land. He replied: "Oh, about two miles". This despondent lad lit up and inquired the name of the island. "Island?" says the tar, "the only land around here is straight down!" Since then I have become a rank atheist to being a "spreader of good will".

Gosh, Honey, it will seem so good to start sending and receiving letters everyday again – as often as they permit, or as often as planes will carry it – I shall be writing to you! Naturally, I miss you very much! The day before we left I received the article from Dad and your picture is wonderful. I am carrying it in with the picture in the folder. Now Honey, I shall submit this epistle to the censor and ring down the curtain. I love you so very much.

David Jr.

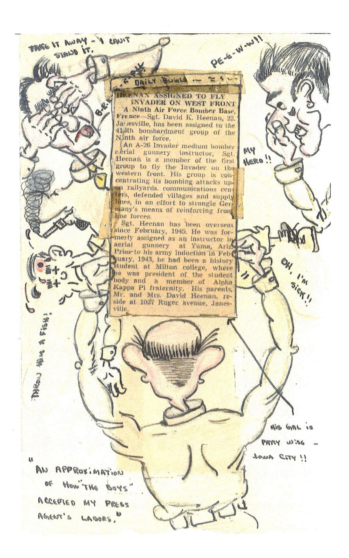

Sunday PM February 20, 1945

My Darling Patty:

Received another letter last night (supposed to get it today but a buddy brought it over for me), the one introducing all your little friends. You may tell them that I am very happy to "know" them and make the rounds saying

"Howdyadew". There is only one little thing that needs correction in your letter: "Patty's a cute, sweet little girl, not too fond of studying." Honey, I know loads and loads of people who like to study and one, especially, who had better like to indulge in academics – meaning YOU, sweetheart!

Last night we had our party, as scheduled, consisting of spaghetti, chicken, and beer! It was quite a cusses – most of the guys brought along special brew! I guess that I owe an apology to you for having had "a few" – but it is the first and final time! I won't ask you to refrain without stopping too, okay?

Max got a little "plowed" and the first thing he wanted to do was get a picture of US so he can show his wife how we look without moustachios! The horrid thing is enclosed for your enjoyment – yipe, ain't it awful? Max used to be a teacher in civilian life and is a very intelligent boy – so if in my future letters I refer to "Bob", "Max", "Tex", or any other similar or close facsimile, you'll know who I mean. The name Tex being applied 'cause he despises all inhabitants of the place.

Apparently, there was more reason for having the get together than any of us visualized. I shall write every day 'til we leave and then as often as they permit thereafter! Your letters might come through faster to me than mine will to you while en route so please don't quit writing.

I am writing to Mom and Dad yet tonight after this letter so I'll cut this short. We slept all morning and part of the afternoon so didn't accomplish much. I do love you and I miss you very much … goodnight, my darling …

David Jr.

February 25, 1945

David dear,

I understand that someone is reading your letters before they arrive in my hands! But I'm sure there is good reason for this practice … I can't wait for the time that we are back together and can have a normal conversation!

How are you doing, dear? It sounds as if the Army is providing you with some entertainment to lessen the monotony of the daily grind, and I am happy for that!

Classes continue to be interesting. I'm not the best student, but it is better than factory life! However, I still feel that I should be doing something to help with the cause—I just don't know what that might be. Do we really want to be fighting a war? I don't want to sound unpatriotic, but really, what are we fighting for? I just don't understand. Let's all get along and just be a world of people that can be friends. Does that sound too simplistic?

I love your letters, and even though I'm not the best correspondent, I think of you daily and wish you were by my side!

With love, Patty.

February 1945

David dear,

Many of my classmates think that I have "invented" you because you sound too good to be true! They wonder what a simpleton like me could do to catch your eye. So this letter, I am going to introduce you to some of my friends, who I hope you can meet in person in the NEAR future!

Dorothy (Tommy) writes: "Hello, David! Thank you for your service to our country. We are keeping a close eye on your beloved Patty! She is spirited and always ready for a good time. We make a good team! Good luck to you as you shove off to Europe".

"David, we just love your girl! We'll take good care of her while you are away. I hope to meet you in person soon—we accuse her of making you up! Your new friend, Helen".

"Hello, David: according to Patty, you walk on water—is that true? Patty's a cute, sweet little girl, not too fond of studying, but always ready for a good time. We love her and will watch over her while you are away. Be safe! Charlene (my friends call me Charlie)"

Okay, now you have a taste of some of the gals that I am getting to know. I hope they painted a good picture for you of my life here at the U of I. I'm not anywhere as naughty as they suggest. I am attending classes and doing what is expected of me.

I miss you terribly. My heart feels stomped upon when I think of the hardship you are having to endure. Return home soon! My future (and the future of our children) depends upon it!

Sending love, Patty.

Book Twelve
2014

February 3, 2014

Dear Barby,

Every time I go to visit Mom, I think about you and your parents. If there is a way that we can avoid what they are going through, are you up for it? I'm thinking OREGON! One pill and our aches, our confusion, our frustration, our boredom – OVER. FINIS. NADA.

I don't mean to make light of us morphing into taking on the role of parents for our parents, but really, do you want your children to have to endure the daily worries and sadness that rides piggyback on our lives? While there are occasional moments of lucidity and laughter, the cloud in which they exist must be more painful than the frustration we feel living in it.

I don't want that for anyone. Let's all live a good life, focus on the positive, and love, love, love. That's what I'm sending to you. E.

March 11, 2014

Dear Elle,

I'm not sure that I agree with you on the Oregon trip, but I feel your frustration. It's kind of like traveling down the highway, and we hit something and the tire blows. We don't know how to change a tire! Even if we did, we have places to go and this annoyance is just getting in the way.

The difference is that a car can be fixed, and our anger and frustration is going away once the tire is replaced. I think you need to change your outlook on the big picture here. Rather than lament about times gone by, why not figure out how to deal with the situation at hand? Your mom's memory is shot. If you tell her that today is Friday, she will ask you 30 seconds from now what day it is. 30 seconds later, she will ask again. Then again. Then once again. You need a coping mechanism to alleviate the frustration and anger. Your initial reaction is "Friday, FRIDAY, FRIDAY!!!!!!" but instead, why not throw it back at her and say, "What was the best day of your life?" and have her reminisce about times gone by? Deflect and redirect. It has been the best solution that I have been able to cope with the failing synapses in their brains. Just remember that they can't help it – they aren't asking the incessant questions over and over again because they want to, but their brains aren't functioning like the well-oiled machine they possessed a few years ago.

Some guitar crooner told us that we need to "roll with the punches". Honey, I just think that you need to take a roll – punch it out, and in the infamous words of John Lennon, "Let it Be". This is out of your hands to control, just "roll with the flow".

Enough with the lyrical advice. My final words: this is out of your hands. Try to divert and redirect conversations.

Your cousin, and your muse (? Or maybe your conscience) Barby.

May 2, 2014

Dear Barby,

The home called. Mom fell (again) and injured her hip. They are transporting her to the nearby hospital. Nothing seems to be broken, but they are keeping her overnight for tests. All she wants is to get back home—home to Janesville, to Milton, to East Lansing, to Okemos, to Elk Rapids, to Delavan. That is all she remembers. Every day is filled with angst, anger, and anxiety – but I don't know what I could have done differently.

Cousin Elle.

May 15, 2014

Dear Barby,

Today I received this desperate phone call – the nursing staff put Mom on the line: "Call my daughter!" Mom screamed at the nurses as her hands shook with the newspaper being held prisoner. "Call her now!"

"This is Hartstone calling. Your mom believes that her husband is on the missing Malaysian flight 370. We can't console her—could you come to visit?" I drove like a person possessed to be by her side. She was empty of passion when I arrived. Roy was forgotten, a mere image in her brain that couldn't release. Apparently she saw a picture in the paper of the search efforts and it glued in her brain to a person missing from her life.

Roy died two years ago. I don't know what to do to console her. There aren't enough drugs or bottles of Chardonnay available to right this ship.

Cousin and confidante, Elle.

May 27, 2014

Dear Cousin Elle,

You have to stop worrying about your mom. Just remember that she had a blessed life with a great husband (not one, but two!) traveled around the world, and enjoyed love from her sisters and cousins. Focus on the good, not the bad! Again, it's time to let go. Be cheerful and positive during your visits, but the rest of it is out of your hands.

Love always, Barby

June 7, 2014

Dear Barby,

I'm just leaving from a visit with Mom, and I am shaken – using that word, perhaps I need a martini! (although I've never tasted a martini in my life, maybe now is the time). Mom thought that it was 1998, and she didn't know who I was. We had a nice lunch together, but her mind kept wandering back to 1941 when she was in love with Dad, and the rest of the world was on the brink of love and turmoil – a 16 year old didn't know the path to take. She kept asking me to take her back to Janesville to see her parents! I agreed to do that, yet felt terrible when my car steered back to the memory care facility. Am I doing wrong by deluding her into a life that she can no longer experience?

Hearing her stories gives me a greater appreciation for the growth of their love – perhaps in my earlier judgments of their actions and love, I misinterpreted the overall picture. They were two kids in love, struggling with the hardships of war. When it was over, they quickly married – really only knowing each other through the mail. How could they learn to be parents? For Dad, when you grow up in a home where love is absent, how do you learn to love?

I think I have been harsh in my previous assessments of their lives. Think I'm going to try to back off a bit, and relish the privilege of being their daughter.

Love, your cousin, Elle.

June 30, 2014

Dear Barby,

I have tried for the past couple of years to encourage Mom to write down events of interest or significance. Unfortunately, I noticed when she first moved here that she had lost her ability to write. It is sad, because she was always a journalist – I have scores of books where she kept notes on their everyday "doings". Now that I review them, I see the entries fading, and her ability to put pen to paper diminishing. I now feel a bit ashamed to have admonished her for not making journal entries because I realize she was not able to do so.

However, when I looked over the "journal" she has attempted to keep – illegible, nonsensical scribblings really – a sheath of paper fell out from the back of the book. Here is what she wrote:

December, 2009

Dear Family,

I hope that my deteriorating condition has not caused you much hardship or sadness. It's just a part of life's journey – remember that I have lived a blessed life, full of adventure and love! Each one of you played a unique role in shaping the design of how our story plays out, and I cherish the fun and laughter we have shared.

Unfortunately, my mind (and my pen) are becoming clouded by something that is overtaking me without my permission. I suppose it is old age, but I still like to think of myself as young, vibrant, and capable. I'm lucky to enjoy a few lucid moments – such as this one – to tell you all how much I love you and feel so much joy and thanks that you are my child, my spouse, my sister, my friend.

God Bless you all. My pen is now taking its final bow.

Love, love, love, Pat (Mom)

Isn't that magical? It gives me peace to know that she loved her life, and most importantly, that she loved and appreciated each one of us, despite our shortcomings.

Love always (and thinking of your parents – let me know what is going on with them) E.

September 15, 2014

Dear Barby,

Today Mom asked me where Dad was. It's always such a dilemma as to what to answer – "He went to the store, he'll be right back" or "He's in Heaven". I went with the latter. Then she drifted back to that train platform – I think it was in 1944, when she said goodbye to Dad before he left for overseas. What a daunting, paralyzing feeling it must have been to watch your beloved head out to God only knows where – out of the safety of the states, and into the arms of constant danger! I can't even imagine what they endured.

Love, Elle.

Book Thirteen
1945

Telegram – February 20, 1945

DARLING. ALL WELL AND SAFE. ALL MY LOVE, DAVID HEENAN.

---

23 Feb 1945

My Darling Patricia!

Today represents my second anniversary on active duty in the Army – gosh, only two lousy little años and I'd swear it doesn't seem like more than twenty – isn't that awful? Actually, from my enlistment period (that includes the time with the Reserve) I have nearly three years service – and that's the baby that really counts!

I had intended to write to your Mom and Dad today but we started some laundry and it almost proved to be too much for us! You should have received my cable by this time – at least you'll not be worrying. Some of the boys have started to receive mail – one of my roommates was top man with two letters.

Well, as we expected, Max and I have separated – he's off to some base leaving just a few of us awaiting assignment. He reminded me so much of your pop – whenever anyone would err grammatically he would either grit his teeth and mumble to himself or deliberately cuss the guy out. He swears that he'll never go back to school teaching – but I think the "bug" has him. I was sorry to see the old devil leave but it happens every day to fellows and soon we'll meet new friends and, perhaps, even become better buddies. I guess I'm not quite my usual self tonight – tomorrow I should write a more precise letter – this unreasonable facsimile is hardly worthy of its postage.

Perhaps, though, I can make it justifiable by saying that I love you – that's the main message I'll ever have to impart. I do love you very much.

Goodnight, Babe.

David

postmarked Mar 1, 1945

return address is APO NY
censored/passed army examiner (stamp)
26 Feb 1945

Darling:

Another letter arrived today – mailed eleven days after the first three that came two days ago! Gosh, Honey, I know the anxiety and feeling of being despondent that arises from not receiving frequent messages – I do hope that soon you'll be getting these letters and I'll be getting yours; then we'll be much happier and less inclined to conceive that "blue feeling". You didn't say anything about mail coming during the first few days after leaving No. Carolina – several letters, valentine, etc., should have reached you!

Babe, I'm a little bit worried about the "job" you referred to – does it mean that you're working part time for board, a job that pays money, or what? Naturally, I'm in no position to criticize or commend your actions, but it sounds as though it is an "under cover", secret affair that you're not letting your folks know about. Your judgment is A-1 excellent as far as I'm concerned and can better tell what you can or can't do. Only please, don't let your work interfere with your primary objective of attending school.

Each day our stay here begins to look more like a permanent status – after waiting all this time we are more than anxious to start whatever they plan for us to do. Definitely, I'm not trying to suggest the proper way for the "wheels" to run the war, but I do wish they'd find the place we're to fit in to help pay the government for the ride over here. I might even say we're a mite impatient.

I did manage to write to your mom, and your dad has top priority for my next letter. A nice valentine from sister Ruth also came today – she was gracious enough to sign it "Love, Ruth". That was the complete text of her personal message! Yipe, and to think a big, long letter could have been enclosed for the same postage. All day today Bill and I sat around the room gravely expecting an assignment to some form of work, only to find that we could have been sleeping, reading or writing without interruption. That is the most disillusioning thing in the world.

Patty darling, take very good care of yourself and remember I'm thinking of you constantly – I love you very, very much.

David.

March 1, 1945

Dear David,

We are receiving news of much activity in Europe. It is pure hell (sorry for the expletive) not knowing where you are, or whether you are in danger. The most reported story is the bombing of Dresden … I know you are part of the aircraft bomb squad. Where are you? What is going on? I am sick with worry. It is hard to concentrate on my studies when I know you are in the face of peril.

I don't have much to report here, other than a heavy heart waiting to hear some good news from your location.

Sending love, Patty.

March 10, 1945

Dear David,

I am nearly crawling out of my skin, not knowing of your whereabouts or condition. Couldn't the army be a little decent, and allow you to contact us? It is also quite a mystery as to the whereabouts of President Roosevelt. Apparently he is resting in Georgia but there is very little news of his whereabouts. This is disturbing to the country as we are anxiously waiting for word of progress in the European aggressions.
Please write soon!

All my love, Patty.

March 17, 1945 – Happy St. Pat's Day!

Patty dear,

Just a quick note to let you know that we are safe and awaiting deployment to France. I can't tell you any of the details about our assignment … as a matter of fact, we really don't know what the future holds for us. For now, we are safe and sound in England. It appears that the Allies are making some headway in controlling the Germans and the Japs. We are ready to report to duty when needed! Let's get this war over with!
As much as I would like to hear from you, we aren't getting any mail delivery here, so save your missives until I have a permanent (well, hopefully semi-permanent) address.

Your loving fiancé, David.

April 13, 1945

Darling David,

You must have heard by now that our President has died, and Vice President Truman has taken over. I know you said that I shouldn't try to contact you, but this news is too great to leave unacknowledged. I have no idea what this change of leadership will do to the war efforts. I just pray that you will be safe and out of harm's way.

Please let me know as soon as possible where you are, and what your situation is. Every day I pine over your safety.

Lovingly, Patty.

TELEGRAM – 17 APRIL 1945

SHIPPING OVER TO FRANCE TONIGHT ... UNKNOWN DESTINATION. PLEASE PRAY FOR US ... ALL WE HAVE AT THIS TIME IS OUR FAITH. WILL CONTACT YOU ASAP.

DAVID.

21 April 1945

Dearest Sis,

I am about mad with worry not knowing David's whereabouts or condition! How did you ever survive these past few years with Merlin being overseas? Not a moment passes when I am not imagining the most barbaric endeavors he must be facing. With what the press is reporting, emotions seem to be coming to a head in France and Germany. To think my David is in the midst of all of this hardly allows me a minute of peace. I can't concentrate on my studies—I am losing weight with all of the anxiety. How did you cope?

My selfishness is showing through! I have not even inquired about your family—how is little Susie? It must be wonderful to be a mother! At this point, I can't even imagine!

Here is what I am learning about what Walter Murrow experienced as he watched the Buchenwald Concentration Camp liberated, and I paraphrase the horror ...

During the last week, I have driven more than a few hundred miles through Germany, now is a good time to switch off the radio for I propose to tell you of Buchenwald. It is on a small hill about four miles outside Weimar, and it was one of the largest concentration camps in Germany, and it was built to last . . .

There surged around me an evil-smelling stink, men and boys reached out to touch me. They were in rags and the remnants of uniforms. Death already had marked many of them, but they were smiling with their eyes

I asked to see one of the barracks. It happened to be occupied by Czechoslovakians. When I entered, men crowded around, tried to lift me to their shoulders. They were too weak. Many of them could not get out of bed. I was told that this building had once stabled 80 horses. There were 1200 men in it, five to a bunk. The stink was beyond all description.

They called the doctor. We inspected his records. There were only names in the little black book—nothing more—nothing about who had been where, what he had done or hoped. Behind the names of those who had died, there was a cross. I counted them. They totaled 242—242 out of 1200, in one month.

As I walked down to the end of the barracks, there was applause from the men too weak to get out of bed. It sounded like the hand clapping of babies. The doctor's name was Paul Heller. He had been there since 1938.

As we walked out into the courtyard, a man fell dead. Two others, they must have been over 60, were crawling toward the latrine. I saw it but will not describe it.

We must hold steadfast to the faith that President Truman will continue affirmative steps to bring an end of this cruel war. I understand that we all have to pay a price for the freedoms that we enjoy, but haven't we had enough pain and suffering? I hate to sound selfish and exhausted, but please! Bring our boys (and WAC's) home!

Your loving sister, Patty

May 1st, 1945

My dearest David,

I am trying to find items of interest to arouse your amusement, but it is difficult at this time. We are all sacrificing our basic needs (I'm not complaining, I am totally understanding of what is going on). Enclosed you will find some cigarettes, and some candy … it's all I can muster at this time.

Life at the U of I is tolerable, but again, I'm just hanging on until your return. It's hard for me to think of anything else.

I love you! Your Patty.

Book Fourteen
2015

April 7, 2015

Dear Barby,

Mom's downward descent is agonizing to watch. I find myself inventing excuses to avoid visits – I might be sick, or there are too many other things to do, like walking the dog or cleaning the house. When I do go to visit, it is tragic – heartbreaking – to see the many that sit idle – some have never had visitors, friends or relatives checking on their well-being. Family assumes that the residents of memory care don't know because they don't respond, but internally, they know. It is all trapped inside, like a bomb waiting to detonate. They have simply lost the ability to express their emotions outwardly. So sad.

Love, your cousin Elle.

June 2, 2015

Dear Barby,

Here is the call that I received today: "Ellen, it's Hartstone calling. Could you come here and help us with your mom?" This is a request that I was to hear with increased frequency. Alzheimer's disease is irreverent – unpredictable—cold, but uncalculating. There can be months of calm, of acceptance, then one small trigger can send her into a tailspin that is difficult to unravel.

Today Mom thought she learned that Roy passed away, and she is inconsolable. Roy died three years ago.

I picked her up and we drove to WalMart. There, we made fun of the iconic WalMart shoppers and the crap they try to sell to the unsuspecting public—plastic lawn ornaments, singing mounted fish (he does a great rendition of "Take Me to the River"), obscenely banked shoes with cork-filled heels, and eighty percent off books that nobody wants to read. We laughed as we shuffled through the myriad aisles and seemingly endless, meaningless stuff that lines their narrow, junk filled aisles.

She forgot about Roy's passing. Actually, I think she has forgotten Roy altogether.

Your cousin, Elle.

October 17, 2015

Dear Barby,

Mom seems to be progressively less and less interested in outside activities and any kind of social interaction. She holes up in her room and only emerges for meals. The staff is worried. I don't know what to do to lift her spirits—it is difficult to summons the energy to present a positive front when you know, deep down, that any effort will be only remembered for a split second, then disappear. What I have to keep in mind is that I am providing some type of joy, if only for the moment that it is experienced.

I just hope that deep in the depths of what memory is left that she knows she had a rich, full life, and that she is loved and cared for.

Your cousin, Elle.

Ps. I'm sorry that I only write about Mom's condition – there must be other good news to share! Unfortunately, I'm a bit obsessed with her, and I know that you understand my situation, having gone through it with your own mother recently.

October 15, 2015

Dear Barby,

I just got back from a visit with Mom. She said that someone named "Tim" called, but she couldn't remember who that was! It is funny that she remembers Jean, but her recollection of me and Tim has faded away. Maybe it is the name – her sister was Jean – and that just rings true in her clouded memory.
As always, she recognized my dog, Ike! She loves her canine companion, but is ready to release her human links.

Love you, Elle.

November 22, 2015

Dear Barby,

I picked up Mom today to go visit Tim. When I arrived, she was in a Rainmanesque state of mind—rocking on the bed, telling herself, "Ellen is coming, and we are going to visit Tim", ad infinitum. The hour drive to Tim's apartment was quite upsetting for her. The rocking and mantra continued for the entire trip.

It seems to do more harm than good to disrupt her daily routine.

Your cousin, Elle.

November 13, 2015

Dear Barby,

Mom asked me today if she was ever married, and if so, to whom? She asked if she had children, and asked about her sisters. She also wants to take a dip in Grand Traverse Bay! If I could arrange that, I would! Her mind is a fog of things that happened in the past, and I don't know how to sort them out for her.

I hope that you aren't experiencing this with your folks. Love and kisses to them!

e.

December 1, 2015

Dear Elle,

I'm sorry that I don't write back as often as I should. I know you need a sounding board but I just don't know what to tell you! I get so sad when I think of the plight of the Alzheimer's victim. They are trapped in an outer shell, begging to be released, but unable to figure out an escape. You just have to get in your mind that, even though your mom doesn't respond to you, she knows you are there and she appreciates the visits. Talk about "old times" with her – read her old letters and cards. Talk about your dad and some of his crazy antics. Hold her hand and tell her she is loved.

One strategy I used with my mom is I started calling her "Rachel" rather than "Mom". That way I could separate the memories between the person she was and the person she has unwillingly become. If you can create that chasm, it may help you to cope with the devastation and sorrow that rides on the back of family members. Remember her how she was in her heyday. House those happy memories in a special place in your heart and take care of the new Patty.

Your cousin, Barby.

Book Fifteen
1945

May 6, 1945

>669th Bomb Squadron
>416th Bomb Gp (L)

>My Darling Patty!

>Gosh, whatta time we had here last night. Word came that hostilities had ceased and within fifteen minutes the air was filled with rocket's tracer bullets, and "distress signal" flares. Streaks of red, white, yellow, blue, green, and orange raced over our heads and it looked very much like a pre-mature 4th of July at Riverside Park. Officers and enlisted men went about "back slapping" and congratulating each other. A lot of the fellows got out in front of the row of tents and began singing, hollering, and raising as much Hell as their voices would permit. Some of the Officers had saved their liquor rations for the occasion and it wasn't long 'til half the guys were reeling all over the place. It wasn't all havoc-raising though; some of the fellows had some pretty grim

experiences that remained in their minds and they just couldn't forget them with the war finished – there's much more than a celebration necessary to complete their "mental conflict".

Our work has been pretty well outlined for us – an increased gunnery program and beaucoup work in store. I was trying to "swing a little deal" whereby I could go to the University of Paris to attend a few courses as a review. They have an extensive program organized for GI education but with a tentative expansion of our department it is nearly asinine to think I'd be able to participate.

I sent the money home and next month will forward a money order to Iowa City – I think I told you what the procedure is to send money home. It's really terrific.

Must climb into a very neglected sack! Work tomorrow a.m. I love you and miss you very much.

David.

8th of May 1945

David dear...

The news is buzzing with the German surrender—surely you will be coming home soon! Here in the States, we are elated! Parades and celebrations are going on all over. That must mean that your tour of duty will come to an end, and we will be able to go on with our lives.

Time Magazine published a picture of Adolf Hitler on its' cover with an "X" drawn over the image ... all of us here are heaving a sigh of relief as we understand that there will be a new world order ... one not dictated by a man trying to shape the course of our future. What a wonderful world is ahead of us! The sky is the limit!

We were able to see Winston Churchill's declaration of Victory in Europe Day, declaring at 12:01 am, we were officially at a truce. God Bless America!

Now the important part of this scenario is getting you home. Please keep me posted on your orders ... it could be just days from now! I can't wait!

I'm so proud of you for serving your country ... you will arrive home as a hero!

Love, Patty.

- -

June 1, 1945

David dear,

What is the delay? After V-E Day, we all expected our guys to return victoriously, yet none of my friends with boys overseas have yet to hear a word. Are you even getting our mail? We are anguished with worry over your plight—despite the end of the fighting, I'm sure there are still perils that surround you daily. Is there any way you can get word to me that you are okay?

Your safety is my only concern. Please contact me as soon as possible.

Love always, Patty.

- -

7 June 1945

Darling Patty,

So sorry that I have been incommunicado during the last month ... as I'm sure you can understand, it has been a time of celebration, confusion, and more celebration! We're still standing by in case something goes awry and we need to be called on for action. So far, it has been a whole lot of nothin'.

I'll let you know when we receive our new orders ... right now it is status quo. Not much news to report, other than we are surviving day to day in our bunks with the occasional whisky drop ... that makes the days pass a little faster.

What I'm really looking forward to is being able to sweep you off your feet, claim you as my wife, and starting a new life!

David.

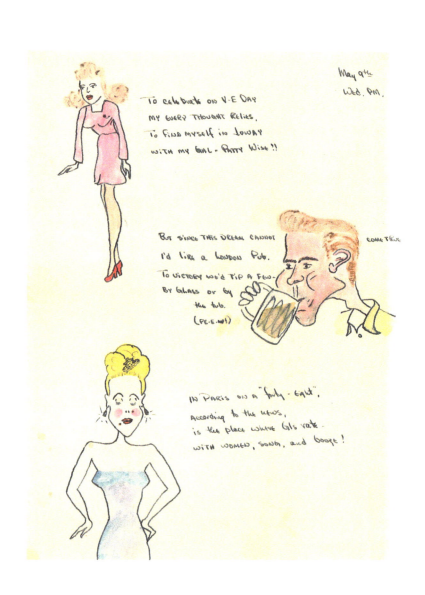

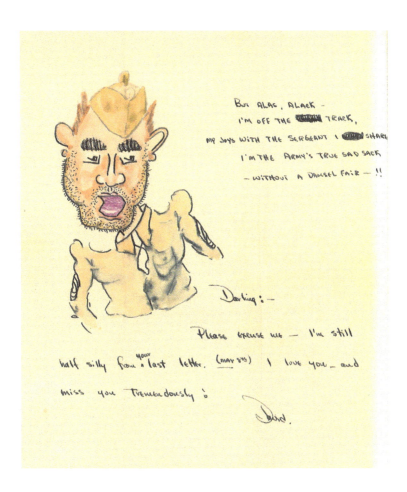

10 June 1945 – letter from Harry

David,

Well, I'm sure that you must know how relieved we are to learn that tensions in Europe have subsided, and that soon you will be out of harm's way.

I apologize for questioning your dedication to our Patty prior to your departure. Now I know that, upon your return, you will create a loving family, and that we will be able to nurture some new grandchildren of our own.

We will be awaiting your train, whenever it arrives, with open arms and, most importantly, open hearts. I know I send love from Zella as well.

Sending love to you, your Pops, Mom, Jeannie, Rachel, and Merlin.

9 June 1945 – written from the University of Iowa

Dear Momma and Daddy,

I am just sick with worry about David's well-being. It is so unlike him to pause in his correspondence, especially after V-E Day … what could take so long?

I haven't heard anything since May 8th… it's driving me crazy!

I hope that all is well at home. I plan on coming back to St. Louis in a couple of weeks, once school is done.

Your Patty.

10 JUNE 1945

Telegram to: SGT David Heenan, 669th Bomb Squadron

Your family needs to know where you are, and whether you are still intact. Call us, telegraph us, SOMETHING—please do something to let us know you are okay.

Father.

21 June 1945

Dear David,

Patty has informed us that she hasn't heard from you for a month now. This is quite unlike you! Given the news this conflagration has ceased between the allied forces and Germany, can't you please give us a sign that you are safe, and on a route back home?

Yours, Harry Wise

29 June 1945

Still holed up in our barracks … the Army keeps promising us that we will be sent home soon. We are despondent … hope is diminishing … it is hard to send you notes that we will be returning soon.

Love, DKH Jr.

July 19, 1945

My dearest David,

Life back here in St. Louis for the summer is drudgery. Every day crawls by as I await word that you have been placed on a ship and are enroute back home. The only things that keeps me afloat in this sea of despair are my thoughts and dreams about our wedding and eventual life together! After a quick (and small) wedding upon your return, I think that we should go back to Milton in the fall for your final lap (you'll return as a senior, right?). We can both take classes and make a home in a small apartment. I don't need much in the way of possessions, and I am watching for inexpensive ways to decorate a small space. All I really need, though, is YOU.
Come home, soldier! Your new life awaits impatiently.

Lovingly, your Patty.

Wednesday pm Tuesday night, July 31st

My Darling!

Had two letters today – one from Pop and the other from sister Harriette & Hooks. Things at home seem to be progressing in a normal vein but the Klanns are still "sweatin' out" Uncle Sam's decision whether Hooks will get overseas duty or not. They think that if he were to leave now they wouldn't have to worry about him being detailed for the occupation forces – oh, little do they know!

White on the subject of militarism, I noticed in a letter sometime back that Bud is already realizing the effects of the war-time army! Perhaps they aren't as well off financially, but at least they can be together and happy; in that case money doesn't account for much.

Among other things, we have some negro outfit here with one fellow who claims to be second only (in his particular style of playing) to one Count Basie. Whether his claims can be substantiated, I don't know – but he is GOOD. Every night hundreds of guys congregate down at the mess hall or Red Cross to hear him "give out". I have heard him once and can vouch for his unique ability!

The 416th Bomb Group officially received a Presidential citation for a particular bombing against Germany. This award has been given to a great many outfits for some heroic action or other but does not warrant any discharge points. According to the report, I am entitled to wear the citation (blue ribbon with a gold metal outline) – 'til I leave this Group!

Saw Capt. Fountaine today for the first time in weeks. Boy, I hope that he stays with us – there isn't a better fellow in the Army today. Tomorrow I must report to the dental clinic for a checkup. I don't know what they could find wrong – I had 'em checked about six weeks ago.

I must leave now, Darling! I miss you and love you so much!

David.

Or something to that effect. My Darling, I love you!! Your letters were such a major part of my life that I'm twice as lonely for you. Please love me like I love you — always!! David

· ·

1 August 1945

Dearest Patty:

Oh, my achin' back. Today they pulled us out for detail – the first I've pulled in sometime and my bones and muscles had a hard time reconciling this abrupt exercise. Now tonight there is a big Air Force band playing at the Red Cross but we're too tired to move much beyond the boundaries of the tent.

Babe, I expect to leave this theater in the near future and this may mean an unexplainable delay in the mail reaching you. There is absolutely no cause to worry and I shall write as often as possible – keeping you informed of my activities. I just thought you'd like to know and any absence of letters will not represent any loss of affections or desire to write. God knows that I love you and I feel certain that nothing could ever change those sentiments – ever!

Today being the anniversary of the Army Air Forces – a sort of celebration was held tonight with a gala assortment of GI entertainment. This negro pianist I wrote about before was on the program with one of our fellows, a singer, and a miscellaneous selection of other artists. They certainly have a wealth of material in this place for such an occasion.

Gosh, Honey, I guess that I'll never be able to sleep any more without some thinking about our future – it has come to be a regular habit for me to lay aside an hour or so every evening for the expressed purpose of organizing and scheming for us! I would be ashamed that I was homesick, 'cause that's for children – but I'm proud to say that I miss you almost too much.

Goodnight, David.

Tuesday pm

No postmark
US Army Service Club letterhead

My Darling Patty,

I found this little typewriter up in the service club and decided to write another letter that you might be able to read … nice, eh? Excitement is just about as prevalent as a three-legged race in a Sunday School picnic so therefore I can't find much to write about. We have been thoroughly schooled on the things we might expect to see in the next few weeks and again it is just a repetition of all the past couple of years, however, there is one consolation that this may be the last time we are subjected to this crap for some time to come … naturally, I can't be too specific on any subject lest I trample on the toes of the censor and he happens to be my C.O. You just don't do things like that in the army.

The most beautiful thing about this whole set up is the fact that we have no reveille … if we choose (and obviously I do) we may lay in our sacks 'til 0830. We have passes but again we're restricted from saying what we saw, etc. Remind me to give you the whole story when I get back. It's unique for me. No "PT", no details (yet) and so far I have managed to avoid getting into any trouble.

Gosh, Honey, I certainly miss not hearing from you and I hope that soon our mail will start coming in again … it's good though, that we are allowed to write from here so that the time will not be too long between letters. I honestly try not to get sentimental 'cause people always get the wrong idea … believe me, I am not sorry that I got into this deal … we have a pretty swell bunch of guys and a good organization. If things stay as friendly as they are right now we won't have a single thing to complain about. At least the fellows are all working together and to my knowledge no one is trying to "beat his buddy" out of anything. Our No. 1 soldier is a lad from Milwaukee – a wonderful guy – later we shall undoubtedly be broken up into smaller units to oversee the post-war adjustments, and the peculiar thing is that I have very little doubt that this will work out even better than we planned.

Babe, I miss you very much and I hope that you are missing me just as much. It's kinda' miserable to think about it but somehow it gives one more satisfaction than anything else … soon we'll be able to resume exactly where we left off – 'til then remember that I love you and you'll always be my number one thought.

David Jr.

Ps – you only need six cent stamps for letters now!

Thursday, August 2, 1945

My dearest Patty!

It seems that a month ago you wrote that we were celebrating our four-and-a-half year anniversary on July 2nd. Count again, Darling. August 2nd really marks the six-month mark. Not that it matters – it isn't the number so much as the sentiment behind these dates! HAPPY ANNIVERSARY!

Received a letter from you postmarked July 19th today oh, whatta swell letter. I can't think of anyplace I'd rather spend the first days of our honeymoon than in your little apartment. Frankly, I must admit that I was extremely puzzled where we might go to be by ourselves – yet still be able to have the "homey effects". You'd be able to bring my breakfast in bed to me – and when we didn't feel like "eating out" you could cook for us! What I would want most is to have everything as much like our own home as possible.

Of course, we shall have to spend a short while visiting Janesville – you can understand that! However, we must first think of ourselves; it will be our life and we want to get as much from it as we can without the influence of our families! Then too, much as our anxiety seems to mount daily, we must execute a certain amount of self-control and not count on anything 'til that day of days arrives! Goodness knows that it is a definite part of my daily routine to plan and think of OUR DAY!!

Honey, please keep submitting your little ideas. I don't know how I'd live without 'em. I love you so very much and am merely existing 'til I can be with you again!

Goodnight, Babe, David.

Friday, August 3rd

Darling:

Wow – you should have seen what the mailman brought today; two letters from you and another little V-mail from Nellie Williams! I guess I don't know how to write and express myself as clearly as I'd like; if we were together it would be very clear, rather simple, to explain how I feel and tell you then things I want so much to tell. It seems so futile to try to say how much you mean to me – and how everything is 100% brighter just to received one of those "morale building" letters!

I enjoyed reading the two items from the newspapers; especially Bob Hope's dissertation on life in the ETO. Aside from the "glorious food" that he depicted (anyone who raves about 10-in-1 rations must have rocks in his head), the columns summed up the situation quite clearly! If I were able to write like that – you might have more incentive to meet the mailman every day.

I love to spend my free time daydreaming about our future – although it is nothing to pine about! Time and time only can clarify our hopes and ambitions. Oh, we'll both be so proud – I can say "This is my wife" and let the people say how lucky I am to have such a wonderful mate. We're perfectly suited, you know!

If we should carry through our plans we could have a little party in your family's apartment. After my folks left we'd invite Edith and Edna, Jeannie and Gerry, Fenworth Paul (if he's around), Verna, Lee, and Essie, and hundreds of others. "Tuffy" is at Chanute Field, only 150 miles from St. Louis, so I don't have any doubts but what he'd be able to run down for us as best man. 'Course we'll have to find a hotel for Mother and Dad – and probably your Mom and Dad. My folks probably will leave early the next day and we'll see them a week or so later. Actually, we shall have a day to wait getting the license and other taking care of last minute details such as flowers, etc.

Oh, what a wonderful dream—the dream come true! It must be that way 'cause I love you and gosh, I miss you too.

Always, David.

Sunday, August 5th

Dearest Patricia,

Gosh, I'm getting terrible about writing; I don't feel particularly humorous and there aren't a whole lot of varied subjects to expand on so, aside from the missives to you, I am doing absolutely nothing! Before, when we were rushed and hardly finding a night's rest, I was writing to at least a dozen people – now it has narrowed down to one or two. Last night I started one to your mom and the Simpsons and after completing about three lines – I gave up. Honestly, Honey, it is hard for me to write when I'm not in the mood.

Early this morning, Roy Frantz got me up for church; the second consecutive Sunday which, I think, becomes a new all-time record for me in France. Roy played the organ and wanted some moral support and this new chaplain is about 6000% better than the one with us during the war – so I went; half by force and half by choice.

We were paid and I have another $100.00 for our account – the total now is somewhere around $700! Golly, Babe, I wish I knew what your plans and finances for school were. I don't want to dig into your personal affairs but I do think it is foolish to have all these available funds on hand when you might be able to use them nicely. There is nothing I can say or do to convince you (as you requested) how much I'd like to help, if even just a little. Oh, I realize it might be classified as "unconventional", but if it would be okay if we were married, we can say that we're engaged and have very definite plans – it's practically the same thing! In regard to the school "intentions" that you poised in a recent letter – I guess my consul would be, decidedly, to go back – this fall if possible. The instability of the present situation may have offered a reasonable excuse for delaying your decision, and I know that you are entertaining a certain agony but I think we can still say that the education you are able to get now will be advantageous to us – and our potential family. Perhaps I am inclined to place too much emphasis on education – but if my suggestion is of any importance I would say – don't let anything stand in your way; it will mean so much more than can be measured on a monetary scale!

I am not feeling too well tonight – nothing physical, probably just a mental depression. It is times like this that make me feel pathetically alone and when I have to think deeply on how Patty would console a very mixed up mind. Gosh, what I really need, probably, is a good kick in the pants to straighten me out.

To say I'm lonely and missing you would be a gross understatement – perhaps that's what is ailing me! I love you now and ever.

David.

6th August

My Darling Patty!

Received two luscious letters from you today – and I am feeling much-much better today. For some reason I was flattered and surprised to hear you say that I should write your pop again – toute suite! I do think that he approves of me but it was almost too much to hear that he "was thrilled" with the last letter I wrote; that was the one I stuck my foot in my mouth and, in general, messed up very badly. Actually, I really enjoy writing to him and I was more than pleased to have you say it.

Contrary to what you may have thought, I am not wanton for time – in fact, that is about all we have plenty of. If the urge would only come I could write a dozen letters every day.

There was a time when I suspicioned that I'd like to do professional writing someday – but I am becoming steadily convinced that my work would be too easily influenced by "moods" – that wouldn't be conducive for a regular income.

Now, in regard to "our plans" – whenever they might materialize – I have had some thoughts: Dr. Lampe could perform the ceremony with your folks & mine – and a few of our friends. I still cling to the original idea of making our vacation plans at Lake Ripley after spending a week or so in St. Louis and a few days in Janesville. There we'd be close to a place to dance or perhaps an evening of brew – and we could be by ourselves – exactly my every desire. Much as we would like to visit our parents – I want much more to visit with you! Wholly independent of ALL others.

I got the money order today and this will total $690.00 to the penny! Perhaps for a few months I won't be able to send quite so much 'cause we're not flying now and I'll miss the extra fifty percent you get when you fly. With this additional pay I draw more than a Second Lieutenant – all of which will come in extremely handy someday!

I hope that "someday" is soon because I miss you a great deal and love you with all my heart and soul. Goodnight, Darling.

David.

. . . .

August 2, 1945

David dearest,

Summer is coming to an end, and I'm preparing to head back to U of I for another semester. I was hoping that you would be home by now, and we would be fashioning our little home, maybe thinking about having a baby … but you continue to be in Germany, with an unknown date of arrival back to the States! I am so lonely, and I just don't know what to do without you. Why doesn't the army let you go, so that you could come back to be with me?

Jeannie and Charles seem to have broken up … I don't know what is going on with them. Jeannie met a man on the train—one Arnold Douglas—that she seems smitten with. He is nineteen years her senior! What is she thinking? She has always been a free spirit and a rogue … I doubt that she will ever take the path of the regular gal. Us Wise girls tend to want to spice things up a bit! We never settle for a simpleton … that is why I chose you!

Yours always, Patty.

Tuesday, 7th August 1945

My dearest Patty!

Whatta place this turned out to be: along with the clouds of dust, the wonderful library, numerous formations, we now have a new addition – an ice cream commissary (how did I manage to link up to all this?) Believe it or not, we are able to purchase it in either CHOCOLATE or VANILLA flavors AND, as if this wasn't enough, Cokes!! 'Course there is a catch – namely a line a mile (more or less) long since we have only one for the entire base. Rather nice, though, once you get to it!

Tonight we walked over to a USO camp show and, frankly, I was quite disappointed. The "Young American Lovelies" were heavily painted and obviously toughened from their appearances over here. There is only ONE American gal that I am particularly dying to see … YOU!

Now I must run ... I love you – oh, so terribly much – and I miss you, tremendously.

David

ps – Please keep writing – and praying!
David.

Thursday – 10th August 1945

My Darling Patty:

Received a letter yesterday – thank you, Babe! I was sorry to hear that Charles and Jeannie are still having their troubles – gosh, it wouldn't be very pleasant to exist under such circumstances. For myself, I don't know what sort of suitable consul could be given to the matter – but it is most definite that they should come to some sort of agreement now! It appears that they'll have to decide the matter themselves. It seems so ridiculous for people to have such apparent differences and still try to keep the thing going! Yes, I'm so very happy that we are not disputing – love is so much less painful that way!

My plans to write last night were thwarted when we took in a show by Shep Fields and his Orchestra. The performance was superb and it was my first chance to see or hear an all woodwind-reed band. Perhaps you remember the negro pianist that I have referred to several times – he, along with several other GI's, answered a plea by the orchestra leader to come up for a "jam session". When we finished about a dozen encores, Shep Fields called him before the mike and enthusiastically declared that was the best bit of piano playing he had heard in many, many years. A lad from our Squadron played the bass viola and in response to the clamor of the audience, he sang "Night and Day" with the orchestra.

In the paper that came yesterday I spotted this news item on the society page about Pres Lustig joining the marital parade. Cripes, Honey, soon we'll be the only single members of our acquaintance; the article is enclosed.

Reports of rumors are coming over the radio of an impending Japanese surrender – but we are still awaiting official notification whether or not the

"Big 4" will accept the thing! The first news came about 2:00 p.m. and general havoc was raised for a few minutes – now it has quieted to the normal conversation 'til further developments are announced.

I shall write more tomorrow, Patty – I must run over to the library with an overdue book.

All my love, David.

Saturday PM – Aug. 11th

Dearest Patty:

Holy smokes – I'm completely messed up wondering what the day or date is; after asking three different guys (and obtaining three different answers) I finally consulted a calendar and I think my bearings are straight – although I wouldn't swear by it! It is rather peculiar how you could get into such a muddle, that is until you think back and discover that one's activity will not vary one iota during a dozen days running. Our routine is so unchangeable that I have started to exist in a sub-conscious state. I know by instinct when it is time to get out of bed to eat; I have a systematic way of walking to the shower room complete with the number of steps and the necessary oblique and flanking movements (for dark nights); 'til mail call when I seem to acquire and employ all the potential energy that vests stagnant during the other twenty-three hours and forty-five minutes.

One of those "builder uppers" came in the mail today so the urge to lie in bed has suddenly left and I can write to my best gal!

The dental "processing" that you underwent is very much like my own case; about the same time I had a filling in one of my molars. Darling, I nearly screamed (GRACIOUS) when I heard that you wanted a gold filling in one of your front teeth! You have good, whole, perfectly formed bicuspids and there is no reason why you should detract from their looks by adding ornaments. If you really have a small cavity please have it filled with porcelain.

In regard to your pop – I can visualize the thoughts and feelings he has but there must be something that will arouse him from becoming too bitter and hopelessly lost. With his brilliant background and abilities, there must be a place for him! This "advice" is not my department for I'm sure he'd be quite hurt to think that I took it upon my shoulders to become involved in your personal affairs. It kinda scares me to think how such an intelligent man with a brilliant career can be stopped over such a trivial controversy. It just doesn't sound like the Harry we knew to give up even though the prospects are dim! Everything will turn out okay … I know!

After this you and I have a lot of steep thinking and working to do. Honey, we must fact the brazen reality and understand that I don't even have a prospect of a job, my education is incomplete, we want to get married. There is nothing I fear more than the fact that perhaps I won't be able to give you all the things you deserve and all the things I'd like to give you! You are going to be half of this corporation – I'd like your ideas – certainly you have thought this over. I dislike talking about it because it seems so futile to be morbid before we examine the possibilities open to us. I have confidence (if you can call it that) it's something that must be thoroughly understood.

I love you very much. Always your – David.

Book Sixteen

2016

January 3, 2016

Dear Barby,

Today I went to pick up Mom to take her to breakfast (much to my frightened state – who knows how she will act out when in public and away from her comfortable surroundings?) She had a bit of a meltdown – asking me for David (Dad), and Roy, and when she could go home back to the condo. The waitress was very kind. She acted as if we were in Elk Rapids, and we were going back to the condo after eating. It is nice to have people to "play along" as we travel this path to the unknown.

I got her back to the home, and she thought she was in Elk Rapids! We walked around outside, and it was just like being back 10 years in time. Priceless.

Love to you, Elle.

ps – she told me on my way out that she was sure that Dad was dropping by to take her out to lunch. Apparently he called her and told her he was coming. I would really like to see that jet pack that is transporting him from Heaven to Whitewater.

. . . .

March 7, 2016

Dear Barby

Mom is increasingly agitated and unable to understand her surroundings. Every day she is asking about Dad – and Roy – wondering where she is and what is what is happening. She is calling for her Mommy, and begging for a new life with them. The present is erased, she just wants to revert to the past.

Do you remember when we met those boys when we were sixteen years old – on the beach of Grand Traverse Bay? We went for a moonlight walk with them – our intention was to hold hands and flirt – their intentions were to get laid! I almost feel like we were reinventing times gone by, when our parents were courting and the girls had to set the boundaries for those fast boys who didn't really give a hoot about us. If my parents would have been paying attention to our surroundings, we would have never ended up in the situation we were. Kudos to you for giving that boy a good slap and got us on our way home. Who knows what would have happened had you not stood up for us? Me, I never learned to set my own boundaries, so fortunately, I had to rely on you - thank you for having some street smarts!

e.

May 7, 2016

Dear Barby,

I received another call from Hartstone today. Roy has died – again – Mom is the grieving widow, attending the funeral but she doesn't know anyone there at the service. David, Roy's son, is coming to get her, but he must be stuck in traffic. Mom says that someone brought her to this funeral home from her condo, and she is being driven back home later tonight. Are you coming to the service, she asks. I tell her that I am on my way.

My goal is to keep her calm and comfortable, but this doesn't seem to be working. Does it require more drugs, or do I just keep playing along and acting like life is how she perceives it? I'm always second, third, fourth guessing myself – I know I am sounding like a vinyl record with a long scratch.

Your cousin, Elle.

June 5, 2016

Elle,

Truth is going to sting a bit, but YES, you are sounding worse than a broken record. More like fingernails on chalkboard, squealing tires, and an activated smoke detector all wrapped in one. Although I love to hear from you, I think that this has become an obsession for you, and you need to work harder at letting go. That doesn't mean that you stop loving your mom – but take a break. Try to go a week without visiting – then eight days, then ten. I know you think you are helping, but really – are you helping your mom, or easing your guilt? Think about it while you are on vacation from visiting.

Harshly, but lovingly, B.

July 15, 2016

Dear Barby,

You were right – it was time for a break. I actually stayed away for almost three weeks! I am now armed with a new frame of mind and a new peace – a calm has swept over me that assures me that this is all in God's hands and I can't do anything to change it. Unfortunately, it took me almost six years to get here.

Now, Warden, it's time to break Mom out of the asylum. Armed with four mini-bottles of Sutter Home Chardonnay, we drove to a nearby park, atop the highest point in Whitewater. The world was at our fingertips. We drank, reminisced, and enjoyed a beautiful spring day, imbibing in our favorite beverage, and talking about days gone by. She seemed to enjoy the time together, and gracefully pretended that she knew me. That is all that matters. It's all about love, love, love.

Write me when you can. Thinking of you and sending love, Elle.

ps – does anyone else write old fashioned letters anymore?

September 2016

Dear Barby,

I'm taking Mom to Ken Strohbusch's funeral. She hasn't seen his wife, Mona, for almost seventy years … I thought it might be something that would spark a memory or provide her with a glimpse of days gone by.

We arrived early to meet with the family. Mom and Mona had a tear-filled reunion, and as I was walking her back to the pew, Mom said, "Are we going to see Mona?"

There was a 21-gun salute, and lots of stories about Ken's life after World War II. Mom has no filter left - she would blurt out things like "There's no way we're going to the luncheon" or "This is taking too long".

The problem is that Mom recognizes her shortcomings, and she is becoming more and more isolated. She wants to be left alone, and yet, she is lonely. What a horrible cocktail of emotions - love, hate, anger, loneliness, and confusion.

Your cousin, Elle.

October 2, 2016

Dear cousin Elle,

I do think it is too disruptive to take people with Alzheimer's out of their familiar surroundings, so I think you ought to make the decision to just keep her in the facility. What if she had some kind of meltdown, and you were unable to handle it? Go with your gut feeling and stop taking her out. I hate to say it, but she won't know the difference.

I wish I could help you more, but this is quite a helpless situation. My advice is to love her and take it easy on yourself.

Love you, Barby

Book Seventeen

1945

Wednesday PM - 15th August

My Darling Patty:

Gosh, you're probably thinking me damnable negligent in the past couple o' days; well you are half right 'cause three days have passed since I last wrote – now for the excuse: Roy Frantz and I had a seventy-two hour pass to Paris AND I couldn't find a place to write. You see, we were billeted in a series of French hotels quite far from any Red Cross and they don't have writing facilities for their guests.

Honey, it's kinda funny (to me, at least) but you remember telling me about the "bedbugs"; well, you don't stand alone now. When we arrived in town we got a recommendation for a hotel from a Red Cross lady – so we went there. The place looked reasonably clean (as French quarters go) so without question we paid for two nights!

After washing we took in a show and returned about midnight. I was dead tired so I got in bed (a double affair – Roy and I had to sleep together) and fell asleep. Poor Roy stayed awake 'til 4:30 committing murder on the vermin while my sleep went unperturbed! Finally, he became exhausted and dropped off in a sound slumber. I woke up shortly after 9:00 a.m. and found him covered with "bites" – on his face, arms, legs, etc. Man, whatta sight he was! Me? Not a single blemish.

Thirty minutes later we started in a quest for another place and found two rooms in the Hotel Louvre some seven hours later. This was much more satisfying and we got a good night's rest.

The end of the war was announced at approx. 2:00 p.m. (Paris time) and I read lengthy items concerning the gala celebrations in town. But from what I could see, life in Paris was continuing as nonchalant as ever. Roy and I bought a bottle of Bordeaux Vin Blanc and quietly toasted a scheme that would get us home and in civilian clothes in the near future.

Obviously, we don't know how we'll be affected by this turn of events but we are still hoping 'til something official is released to smash our dreams or booster our morale. The best news is: Le guerre est fini!

Coming out for Paris we got a ride with a fellow returning to Reims – driving a General's Staff Car, a 1942 Plymouth! Gosh, it was complete ecstasy after bouncing around in a Jeep in these past few months. Roy sat in the back looking like he owned the vehicle and coyly returned salutes to GI's along the way! If there is to be another war I want to be a general … whatta life they lead!

For the first time I think I can understand how difficult it is for you! Whenever we saw a show or had a drink in a sidewalk café, I'd think more than ever how much I'd like you to be there with me. I guess that when one is around excitement, lights, etc., one really can appreciate how lonely it is to be alone. Back at camp there is absolutely nothing that I'd want you to see or be associated with. I do appreciate what you are up against and can recognize how much harder it would be for you to stay home than it is for me. If it would ease your mind at all – I have done nothing that would be classed "out of line" since I last saw you – not even as much as a date. More peculiar, I haven't had the urge; you'll probably think me inhuman!

There is only one thing I want – YOU – and when I come home that will come true. Then I'll be glad that I sent most of my monthly honorarium home 'cause we can spend it for the good times we've been forced to miss during these past three years.

I love you, Babe, and miss you terribly much –

David.

Thursday – 16 August 45

Dearest Patty:

We arrived back in camp last night quite late after managing to catch a ride in a GIG semi-trailer truck from Reims; a GIG let-down from General Sander's vehicle in the a.m. As quickly as we could run down to the Red Cross, we indulged in some coffee and donuts. Gad, we were nearly famished since a Spam Sandwich and coffee doesn't seem to be enough to eat once per day.

This morning I awoke bright and early – ate breakfast, and picked up three letters from you, a newspaper from you, and a letter from my Pop. They are going on a two-week vacation at the end of this month, probably to northern Wisconsin.

Do keep looking at things you want and need. There will have to be a thousand little things that we'll need – mostly for you and us! I am pretty well fixed for clothing for a while. But dishes, silver, glassware, bedding, etc., are things we must have!

Have you thought at all about wedding invitations? Could we get them in very short notice? Then, too, should I go home first and get the car; we might need it! Also, we must think about the time (of day) element. Naturally, we'll be expected to have dinner with our families – and would we have a party for Jeannie, Gerry, Essie, Lee, Fenworth Paul, Edith and Edward, "Tuffy", etc? You know that my parents would object to the drinking angle so maybe they could go on home while we would see them in a week or so! Personally, I'd like very much to have a few "schnapps" that evening – like Ginny and Dick (gosh, we have to invite them, too). You must have a list of people you'd like to have come since most of your friends would be available.

I have a "school problem" to talk about tomorrow – it really is too much to take up in this letter. I am terrifically lonely for you and I do love your letters – keep 'em coming. I love you, Darling.

Goodnight,

David.

. . . .

Friday PM 17th August

Dearest Patty:

Before starting in the usual hum-drum of my regular missives I might explain that we're sitting on the side of a hill in front of a stage, waiting for the biggest USO show in the ETO to begin. It is 6:30, two hours before the "curtain rises" but 8000 (approx.) GI's undaunted by the wait have already gathered and are busying themselves reading, playing cards, or writing! Oh, yes, the show consists of Hal McIntyre's Orchestra with "The Rockettes" fresh from Radio City in New York. These "Rockettes" have earned quite a reputation for themselves – you have undoubtedly heard a great deal more about them than I have.

Yesterday I said that there was a little problem that has been bothering me for some time, namely, about returning to school. I don't know how much you've thought about this but it might prove to be a major part of our lives in the near future!

First of all, it would be a good scheme to determine exactly what I shall finish my course in. By that I mean whether I should be conventional and continue the history course and ultimately teach OR take a chance of taking a few writing courses and get a degree in journalism followed by a year at some place like Columbia U. to get a M.A. This is important and you must help me decide. As you know, or perhaps you didn't, I am eligible for four years under the GI Bill of Rights but, obviously, we won't want to use all of it unless I can be working and studying nights. 'Course if I was teaching I could employ my time during the summer to prepare for something with more advancement.

Then there is the little problem … WHERE? I think this has been bothering you and we haven't said much about it so I'll tell you how I feel and hope you'll be just as honest and tell me what you think. To be absolutely truthful, I'd like to get my B.A. from ole Milton C. (you did mention that you might be interested in attending there as well). There is a great deal of sentiment behind that – perhaps more sentiment than good sense. There are a lot of good contacts I could gain from the professors there. Later we could to go Chicago or New York for the post-graduate work. Now, perhaps, I have stepped way out of bounds but I'm depending on you to be just as outspoken on your suggestions!

I have had a wonderful sleep this afternoon in which I dreamed we were together again – when I awoke I found myself hopelessly disillusioned and missing you more than ever; I love you very much – Always, David.

Sunday, 19th August

Darling –

Oh, Babe, you are doing splendidly in this recent spree of writing – gosh, I'm averaging a letter per day – almost! You are well aware of the anxiety and tenseness that you are entertaining – most of us are going through the same thing and the very words of those letters you send are morale boosters to no end. Thank you, you'll never know how much they mean to me!

Today I have been assigned as Squadron CQ – which proves an old idea that a GI's capacities are limited only by the imagination of the administration! More or less my duties are comprised of chasing about the area looking for individuals for details, etc. – or driving a Jeep out to the motor pool to exchange guards. Originally, I planned to write many, many letters but here the day is practically over and my accomplishments total practically nil.

This being Sunday, naturally, I went to church and joined a communion service that was offered as thanksgiving for the ending of hostilities. Aside from this being my fourth consecutive week to attend services – I believe this was my first communion since the day that your pop officiated back in Janesville; or should I be ashamed to admit that?

The Chaplain told us that the Jap emissaries are due in Manila at noon today to sign the final documents. We've been reading the *Stars and Stripes* from cover to cover to discover anything that might tell us for sure that V-J Day is actually here!

Everything seems to add up to one thing: how quickly I can be with you again. I miss you so very much, and I love you tremendously.

Always your,

David.

Monday, August 20, 1945

My Darling, Sweet David,

I have to start this letter by saying how much I love you and miss you. A piece of my heart and a touch of my soul seems to disintegrate as another day passes with no word of your return.

With the uncertainty at hand, I am going to make some suggestions that you might not want to hear, but in the long run, might make our future plans more solid and practical.

Perhaps we should wait at least until after the semester before entering into marriage. I'm hoping by then I will be better organized in my mind for the future, and the cloud of ambiguity that surrounds our impending nuptials will be made more clear. You can come home, get settled, find a part time job, re-enroll in classes, and I will join you as soon as all of the dust settles. After discussing this at length with my parents, we feel that this might be the wisest choice.

This idea does not diminish the love that I feel for you – I am just trying to ease some of the pressure and anxiety you are experiencing as you go through this muddy puddle that is interrupting our joining together forever. Once the storms of the Occupation cease, and our paths are dry, we will be able to better define our future. But it is just a thought.

Yours forever, Patty.

Tuesday, 21st August 1945

Dearest Patty:

Effective today censorship in the ETO is *finis* – stopped – done! I guess a guy should get kinda used to it after a while but I, for some reason, could never quite stomach the idea of someone between us learning of our personal affairs. I have many complaints I could fashion on this subject but since it's over, I'll pass over them in favor of things you're probably more interested in and things I'd rather write about!

We are still in our Assembly Area awaiting movement orders in the next few weeks.

There is no positive information whether we shall be called upon to occupy Germany or if we'll continue on orders re-routed through the States. My "points" total fifty-one at present, which isn't too encouraging. On the other hand, my classification of "938" (Gunnery Instructor) isn't authorized in any Air Force unit in the 9th A. A. F.

If we can believe the papers (more often than not, an unreliable source) – men with fifty points will fall under the Discharge Point Plan in the next six months (*Stars & Stripes*). Meanwhile there is little we can do but knock our heads against the wall, hope, and pray that the time will be short.

Saying "I love you" is a matter that I could shout before the entire world but it seems so much nicer to be able to say it to you without someone reading it first! Gosh, I'm lonesome for you.

David.

. . . .

22nd Aug – Wednesday PM

My Darling Patty:

No letter from you for four days (I think it's four now) but don't be alarmed – there haven't been a half-dozen letters from the U.S. for the entire Squadron in that time! I know that you are writing as faithfully as ever – and it's a little too early to attach any definite meaning from this latest shortage of mail. Naturally, a continued absence will weigh very strongly and you will start getting those letters back with an explanation from the postal officials.

I am proud of myself – an interlude of boasting – for having written four missives yesterday: 1) Patty; 2) Mother and Dad; 3) your mother, Rae and

Bud; and 4) Mrs. Williams – the kind old lady in Miss Pickett's category who has written at least a letter a week for the past three months. Isn't that good? 'course I still have a few more before I can be totally free of "mail debt". This afternoon I could have written more except that they'd be filled with complaints and foolish issues cause by a damnable cold in my head and chest. Frank Meyers, one of the guys in the tent, has nominated himself my fairy God-pater and is planning to rub my back and chest with Vicks. I have my flannel pajamas that haven't graced my form since last winter; Frank found them in my belongings and insists that I wear them. It isn't part of my constitution to be sickly so undoubtedly by tomorrow I'll be able to resume my regular active life.

Pop sent a Gazette last week with the Dorothy Dix article enclosed. I had the strangest feeling as I read it – almost like someone had written it about us!! Oh, I know that's foolish 'cause we'll have a thousand dollars or so to back us when we embark on our marriage career! I can't understand why anyone would seek consul from such an abstract character.

Babe, my darling, we'll need lots of courage and ambition (and we do have both, I'm sure) – to get married; but two people so much in love cannot be stymied. I do love you for beyond reason – how could anyone help it? You're so wonderful!

Nite, sweet…David.

DOROTHY DIX SAYS

Money Needed for Marriage if Home Is to Be Peaceful

Dear Miss Dix: I am 19 and my boy friends is 22. He has just been discharged from the A. A. F. and has decided to return to college on the G. I. Bill of Rights plan and finish his education, as he believes that that will prepare him better to make a living for his future family.

We are very much in love, but don't know whether it would be taking too much of a chance to marry before he has a good job and has finished his education. Whether we would regret later our being married and his going to college at the same time is very hard for us to decide. What do you think?

FIANCEE

Answer: No human being is enough of a prophet to tell how any marriage will turn out. We have all seen marriages that seemed made in heaven, so auspicious were all the circumstances surrounding them, that ended in divorce and we have seen other marriages that we thought predestined for failure that were glorious successes. So there is no cut and dried follow-this-rule-and-you-cannot-fail advice that you can give any young couple who are thinking of going off the deep end.

Generally speaking, however, every marriage, like every other venture, has a better chance of being a success if it is adequately financed. That doesn't mean that boys and girls should put off marriage until they have made a fortune and can live in a swanky apartment with period furniture and ride in high-powered automobiles. But it does mean that it makes for domestic peace and happiness for the bride and bridegroom to know where their next meal is coming from and not to have their nerves torn to tatters by the bill collector hammering on the door.

Of course, lovers who marry on a shoestring delude themselves into believing that love is enough and that after marriage, they will be content to live on bread and cheese and kisses, wear shabby clothes and desire no other amusement than holding each other's hands. But they fool themselves. After marriage they are just as hungry for beefsteaks as they were before and crave amusements just as much. When they can't have them, because they married before they were ready for it, love is very apt to fly out of the window.

Many a marriage that would have been a success is wrecked by the lack of a little money. And many a man of talents and ability has his career blasted by marrying too young and being so tied down by wife and babies that he could not climb the ladder to success.

So maybe it is wise to wait for your wedding cake until you can afford it.

A few weeks after I get back to your home cooking!
Maybe I'll love you twice as much!

August – Friday

My Darling Pattykins –

Gosh, I don't know how to write these days; the mail situation hovers in the same trend – which means none! None, at least, since last Sunday and no immediate signs of receiving any more! In all outward appearances this might be very significant – on the other hand we may just be having another of these spells similar to the days following V-E Day. Our hopes are high but, don't want to start any false alarms and have you disappointed should they decide to keep us in the Occupation Army for a while.

Yesterday afternoon I received the Air Medal. I had the orders for the thing nearly three months now but they just got around to awarding the medal itself yesterday. It wasn't enough to undergo the regular ceremony – the Squadron Gunners had to make a farce of the thing by holding a "special formation" consisting of eighteen gunners, a cook, seven French KP's, an orderly room clerk, and a half-dozen or so bystanders. With all the solemnity and pomp of a Holy Rollers meeting, the presentation involved close order drill, salutes, handshakes and a long, drawn-out oration of the "Trials and Hardships of a Gunnery Instructor". Meanwhile the Squadron cook wracked his Frenchmen to a position of attention and they were quite happy to be a part of what appeared to be a (excuse the repetition) gala occasion. Those darned nuts really had a screwy citation. Now I guess I shall keep it with me in anticipation of carrying it home personally! On the next page I'll try to draw a facsimile:

My darling, I love you! Your letters were such a major part of my life that I'm twice as lonely for you. Please love me like I love you … always!

David.

Saturday PM – 25th August 1945

Dearest Patty!

You remember when Tommy and your other roommate were sick – you thought that maybe you were a bad influence. Well, it looks like I've already started to become a good prospect for the near future. I just about cleared up my cold (with Frank's help) and last night I went out and "caught" a baseball game. Somewhere about the fifth inning one of the batters foul-tipped the ball, hitting the instep of my foot. Ye Gods, I thought it had gone right through – beating my arches on the terra firma. However, the game was moving too rapidly and the pain left. After the game, the gunners had a five-gallon can of beer so we had a "sing session" 'til nearly midnight when I got in bed. I don't know whether it was the sudden relapse or I was lying in the wrong position, but the pains started returning and it throbbed so it was impossible to sleep. One of the fellows was on CQ so I got up and sat with him 'til 3:30 a.m.! Then I fell asleep and woke this morning feeling fine – not hardly a trace of the agony of the preceding night. Not very interesting, but it highlights the wholesale absence of activity … still there, Darling?

Sandwiched between horseshoe games I saw a movie, "The Great John L" with the conclusion that it stunk! Then I am reading *A Tree Grows in Brooklyn* – which isn't as bad as I anticipated.

Three or four letters trickled through today but none for me. The very thought that I might be able to see you before long (Oh, blissful dream!) is enough to stave off any disheartened attitude. Perhaps even though we know we won't be moving directly to the CBI it is still too early to say that we'll be coming to the U. S. right away. You know that's the No. 1 thought and I can't refrain from writing it in every letter. Just don't get too anxious.

I miss you, my sweet, so very much – and I love you – that you will know better when I can tell you AND show you.

Your guy, David.

Sunday nite, 26th Aug.

My darling, darling, Patty:

The V-mail letter that I mailed this afternoon will have reached you and you can attach whatever significance as you see fit. Perhaps, too, the things I have to say about in this letter will have been completely altered and the contents will be obsolete – However, I have a lot to say, some questions to ask, etc. This afternoon three letters came and I don't know how to feel, think, or react; like you say, sometimes it's so difficult to express a thought and have it understood in the same manner it's written. That is what happened to me today, so the best solution seems to be to have a discussion on the matter!

1. Your returning to school. Honey, I'm all for it ... BUT according to the way things stand now we shall be coming back to the U. S. sometime in September or October. WE mailed cards to the Postmaster of N.Y., N.Y. today to have our mail forwarded to our home addresses (!!!) and turned in the address of "the place we'd stay on a furlough"! I don't want, as I have reiterated time and time again, either of us to become overly optimistic but things appear brighter now that we have been able to surmise since the war began.

That's where the problem begins: your letters speak of waiting 'til after I finish my school term "when I'll be better organized in my mind for the future". Perhaps I should say you're right but DAMNIT – when I asked you to marry me I was so very sure that that was the way BOTH of us were thinking. Obviously, you were aware that I didn't have a job and my mind keeps thinking that this was not entirely your idea. I can't explain beyond that point 'cause I'm not sure how the situation stands now. We have been the bearers of good judgment for nearly five years and I don't think that either of us would be unaware of the "risk" in starting out on this marital career (incidentally, on bended knee I apologize for my ignorance on the previous misspelling of "marital". Thank you for correcting my atrocious mistakes). This all brings me to the Dorothy Dix article I sent a few days ago ... I am more certain that this was written about us!

I couldn't understand why, after these months and years of planning and scheming, you suggested that we undertake "the wisest step". Babe, do you mean that all these ideas and thoughts were just playthings to act as conversation or material for our letters? I must admit that I had given the matter grave consideration and I've convinced you personally had the same impression. Maybe I'm all wrong – perhaps I am being an absolute ass to think that I am capable of accepting the responsibilities of a husband, but I had every hope that we could work out our problems together; it would be much more successful, and much more FUN!

You asked me to tell you how I feel about the thing … so here goes …

I love you, my darling, more than I am able to tell you. You are the reason that makes me think there is good left in the world and offers a reasonable answer (if one can determine an answer) for fighting the "evil forces"! Myself, I haven't done anything in the ugly war, nor do I claim any rewards or think the world owes me a living – the only way I have been personally affected is by spending some three years away from you. Those have been the three longest years of my life! I thought it was one way to tell if I was worthy of you. Now the war is over – there are a few things I was able to prove: morally and spiritually I am a better man than when I first knew you. I am better equipped to accept your "wonderfulness" and to face the world with a clear conscience. What does this add up to? I asked you to marry me once before – I am asking you again! You must decide whether we shall wait or if we'll be married when I get home. You must decide whether to return to school this fall or chance that I'll get home. If you are in Iowa, our time together will be arranged accordingly since we won't "take the vows" if you are there! If your father – or anyone else – tells you how to decide I won't utter any objections but I honestly hope and pray it's what YOU really want.

Whatever happens I know you want it that way so my love will not be dimmed one iota. All these things have been playing havoc with my confused brain – I want you to know how I feel. I'm sure that your love is unaltered – more likely it is giving way to what would appear to be common sense.

If I have made a mistake or misconstrued the rightful meaning of your letters – I am sorry and you can forget that this letter was ever written.

Now since you won't be writing much longer – DO keep writing until I tell you to stop – I may not get your ideas or corrections. There may be some letters in the mail right now that will clarify everything. Do not become disheartened as nothing here is meant to be morbid. I have had "my say" – and then some. These ten pages merely signify one thing—I'll always love you – so much that maybe I'm too stupefied to be practical. I guess I'm in for a real lecture to get straightened out.

Goodnight, sweet! Always your guy,

David

Tuesday, 28 August

Dearest Patty:

I was kinda hoping that a letter would come during the last two days saying that you thought I would be coming home – and there might be some ideas or plans for US in the near future!! I can't help being sorry for the letter I wrote on Sunday – it might not have sounded as it was intended and now while I'm in a more reasonable state of mind I know it was a small depression (mentally) and I know you'll do whatever seems the best thing to do.

According to the information we received today we are on orders to go to the Pacific "indirectly" – or by way of the U.S. This being true we'll have some sort of priority for a ship and should return according to the original schedule!

I had a letter from sister Anna and Mrs. Williams today. The Webley's main concern was about the "very sweet letter" they received from my Patty thanking them for the birthday card on your birthday! They were excited 'cause you were so enthusiastic and also 'cause you "couldn't wait 'til I come home" – is that the honest truth, Darling?

Perhaps I have told you several times about the 669th Baseball team and that I have been playing a little with them. Today we played a return game with another Bomb Group; they had beaten us 4 to 1 the last time – but we won 3 to 0 this afternoon! Perhaps that is one reason I didn't mention it before – another might be 'cause their pitcher, under contract with the Cleveland Indians in pre-military days, struck me out twice and I popped out to the third baseman. Today, though, I got two hits from the same guy; maybe I am too proud over such a seemingly minor feat.

Now I've done enough boasting. My darling Patty, just think – in maybe one month or two months I may be holding you close to me! If you decide to go back to school you had better write to my folks and give them your address.

Then I can call you or write and we'll be able to make arrangements to see each other! We'll probably be sent to Fort Sheridan or Camp Grant after a day or two of processing at the port.

We'll have to crowd in so many things in a short time in case I do go to the Pacific after all. Love you very, very much – always. I'm getting myself a little more excited – for you.

David.

Wed PM 29 August 1945

Dearest Patty:

By this time you should be thoroughly fed up with my discussions of the "sudden change" in our affairs. I never meant to be insistent or to carry this to a point where you'd become disgusted so now would not be a very good place for a change of policy. If you'll permit me just this one fleeting message I promise not to repeat these words again!

This entire issue came up in answer to your letter of Aug. 20th and its abruptness caught me a little off guard. Perhaps it's because I have never wanted anything so badly in my life and I dread the thought of delaying the matter another two, three, or five years. I have wondered and worried how it would be possible for me to support a wife. The main reason seems to be a "degree" which looms up as a barrier! Tonight, after serious consideration, I have come to the conclusion that I don't give a DAMN for a degree – that is such a petty thing to ask for in a lifetime!

Perhaps I was more hurt and surprised that your mom is of the same thought. I can hear her words echoing – the statement she made just as I left to go to the station last December 31st. I suppose she knew what I wanted to hear and she said it.

I keep thinking over and over again about the confusion and disaster in your recent years and obviously my greatest wish is to steer you far away from that as I possibly can. On the other hand – a degree is absolutely no guarantee of security on a life-long basis – or is it?

That's all of it, Patty, now you are free to think of me as you wish. I'm jealous – not of losing you in a romantic sense; it's the influence of your father.

We can plan further when I get home – and talk this thing through – WITH your father and mother! Then whatever conclusion we come to will serve as a blueprint for our entire lives.

This a.m. the gunners and the only pilot left in the 669th took a trip to St. Quentin to get "flying time" for the month of August – worth some $50.00! We arrived in time to hear the Operations Officer "ground" all planes due to weather. It is a trip of approx. 140 miles so we're starting out about 0600 hours tomorrow to try again! Our equipment is being sent to the port of embarkation so we'll know in a very few days what the exact status of the squadron is.

I love you Patty – above all else remember that!

Ps – I never received an answer from the letter to your father – the last one was back in Arizona. I never said "I wouldn't marry you before I finished school" and there couldn't possibly be a discussion if I didn't get a letter.

Saturday PM 1st September, 1945

My dearest Patricia –

Missed writing yesterday because of another vain attempt to get flying time at the 397th Bomb Group. We were late in getting started in the morning so we missed the early flying period! Around noon a frontal storm moved in so we just waited around to see if the weather would clear up. It didn't and we found our weary way back near midnight. Lights were out and I was so dog tired that I didn't care to try to write a conglomeration of woes – which it would have been.

We received our month's pay for August and it seems terribly little without the flying pay that we accustomed ourselves to. If we ever get to an airfield and find clear weather we'll be able to make up the time and collect back pay. Meanwhile the monthly allotments to the First National Bank will suffer accordingly.

I was glad to hear today that I was listed as "expected". I can't tell you anymore except that in two or three weeks we'll either be permanent fixtures in the ETO or we'll be sailing for home. Should things proceed as we hope – I shall be sent to Camp McCoy (Wisconsin) for disposal: reassignment, furlough, etc. If I remember correctly, this is about 100 miles NW of Janesville and I could get Dad to come to pick me up!

There must be some form of mental telepathy existing between us. A short time ago I wrote about what schools we might consider for "the final lap". When that reaches you you'll probably be quite disappointed – but since you were frank in your discussion of deal – I shall try to do the same.

I mentioned Milton because of the "contacts" available. Should I transfer now there would no way I could gain enough sources to aid me very much. More important than a degree is the contacts one can make; in one year it would be practically impossible for anyone to make recommendations of capacity, initiative, or "likeliness" to make good.

It's difficult for me to visualize spending two to four more years in a college or university. Especially since it is quite probably that I won't re-enter 'til the fall of 1946 – at the earliest. That will make me twenty-four years old – very near twenty-five when I enter and I would like to make my debut to the working world before my beard and hair get too gray. Perhaps I'm much too pessimistic about all this but things have changed to make everything more difficult. "Where there's love there's a way" says the old adage – we'll make out okay.

Pop and Mother were on their vacation when he wrote, having a gay old time at Dodgeville with John and Minnie. They planned to move on to the lake to finish out the spree.

Miltie was in his usual good humor and has great things in store for us. I shall enclose a part of his letter in which he mentions you. Ivan Malaydik is the bass to our quartet and the boy under contract to the St. Louis Browns that I mentioned several times before. The three of us were "buddy buddy" in Arizona.

Now, my love, you have endured enough for one night – more tomorrow. Always I love you.

David.

Sunday 2nd Sept

Darling –

This happens to be the 2nd day of the month and the four year, seven month anniversary for us. Do you realize, Patty, that this makes us closer to five years than four – so we can tell people that it has been "near five years"! Foolish perhaps, but I like it!

The lights have gone out so if you can't read this thing you'll understand my plight – I'm trying to use a flashlight and it isn't panning out too well.

This morning our Chaplain informed us that he had been designated to serve in the Occupation Army. He made a lot of jokes about his assignment but when he spoke of having two children – one of which he hasn't see – I could detect a distinct "sickliness" in his voice. Since he joined this outfit a couple of months ago I have missed but one service. He's a lot like James VanderGraff and all the fellows are agreed that he's a "good egg". If you could see the turnout for Sunday services you'd be amazed. He asked us to pray for something that was dearest to our hearts – so if God heard my humble pleas you will be well-protected and guided 'til I come home to take over for Him!

(The lights are on again).

With the absence of activity, I have waged a war against something that bites me in my sleep. This morning I awoke to find my legs speckled with blotches, so I washed, aired, and sprinkled insecticide powder all over my sleeping bag. Tonight I'll learn if it was a total victory on the "rodents" or discover that it was mosquito raids.

At 0300 hours we received the news that the surrender document was signed with the Japs. Now it is beginning to dawn on us that we may soon resume our lives on a normal scale – and by normal I mean for you and me to be together again!

I do miss you terribly much and I want you to know that you're the primary object of my every dream and plan. Am enclosing a negative snapped "candidly" – to prove that with imagination and determination nothing can stop us. Sorry that I couldn't get the print but it belongs to the "victim", George Martin, one of our gunners.

My regards to your father, Jeannie, and of course, Gerry!

I love you, Doll, David.

Tuesday PM 4 Sept 45

My Darling Patty!

I can't understand why you aren't getting letters from me! It will be a shock when you are imagining that we're on our way home and letters come floating in dated Sept 4th and later. You can be sure that I shall be writing every day 'til we're forced to quit!

Last night we had a beer party for the men in the squadron and even though I drank very little I awoke with a terrific headache this a.m. Quite a few of the fellows suffered the same effects so we attributed it to the stuff being "too green".

I said earlier that I'd try to think up something "special" to tell you and it just popped into my head to mention that yesterday orders came out promoting David K. Heenan – 16056965, 669th Bomb Squadron, to a staff sergeant (ok, Heenan, you're so subtle). This will increase my monthly salary considerably:

	Sergeant:	Staff Sergeant:
Base Pay	$78.00	$96.00
Overseas Pay	15.60	19.20
Flying Pay	46.80	57.60
"Old Fogey" (3 yr in army bonus)	7.02	8.64
Total every month:	$147.72	$181.44

And furthermore, I became the first "overage" (not listed on T. O.) to make a rating since V-E Day!

Must quit, I love you very much. Goodnight, Doll.

David.

Wednesday PM, 5th September 45

My Darling Patty:

Tonight, the squadron is having a beer party as kinda a going away present for everyone. While the other fellows are over drinking I thought it would be a good idea to come over to the Orderly Room and write a letter to the girl who is always foremost in my mind. It is easier to type than to write with a pen – at least you'll be able to read it when it is finished.

Every once in a while, I am overwhelmed by a brilliant thought which originates in my own little head; today I have been thinking how you will be situated if and when I should get home. As things stand now I am awfully afraid that you will be going back to school in a couple of weeks and there will be nothing for us to do but forget about all the plans we had in the beginning. Actually, I am quite well aware that I account for very little and this must register in your mind very strongly – only my honey, I want you to consider that I haven't had a good chance to apply myself against the working world and even though I'm not worth a great deal at present, with your help I promise to be the hardest working man on the face of the earth.

Much as I dislike the idea of you not being on hand to greet me when I get home, perhaps I am all wrong in expecting you to sit around waiting for me to come breezing into St. Louis on the train like we dreamed about when there is still a possibility that we will be chosen to take an active part in the Occupation Army. All this will be decided for certain tomorrow when we will learn who is destined to stay and who will be allowed to go back home.

Obviously, you'll think that I don't have any reason to write this letter but there are things that I would like to tell you. Darling, I really don't care what they decided to do with me (as for that our marriage is being barricaded) and there are certain people that think we would be more intelligent to let this plan ride until we can maintain absolute security. I have said this to you before and I shall repeat that I am accepting you as my wife with the full understanding that for a while we'll have a few obstacles but for you I can do anything – anything that you would want me to do.

Patty, you can understand that I love you and gosh how much I miss you. It will always be that way. You may as well make up your mind that someday we'll get married and nothing will stand in our way. I am ready now – the rest is up to you. I'm lonelier (sic) for you tonight than I have been in many, many days. It seems to mount up with each succeeding day.

Oh, Patty darling, I love you!

Always your guy, David.

Friday 7th September

My own Patty:

This is one letter I didn't want to write – and without going any further you can probably guess why! That's right – the thing I had hoped and prayed wouldn't happen, DID and we're to leave here within the next two days for outfits in Germany. I don't know what happened except that we're being split up to make way for "high point men" going home. Some of the fellows are going to the 324th Fighter Group – brother Don's outfit. Others are going to Bombardment Groups, while I claim the distinction of being the only member of the 416th Bombing Group to the Ninth Air Defense Hdqrs – I don't know what my new job will be and truthfully, don't care much.

If there is one thing I'm happy about it's that you can go back to school and no problems of how we could see each other will present themselves. Actually, I am glad you'll be back studying 'cause time will pass much faster for you.

This probably will not mean that I'll be stuck here "indefinitely" – from the latest newspaper reports, no man with over forty-five points will be slated for occupational duties and it's quite likely that we'll get our chance to get home sometime this winter.

Perhaps I was most impressed by the number of high-point ground personnel who heard that the lower scores "had had it" – came around asking for my home address, etc. Roy is going to carry my Air Medal and a few other odds-and-ends to the U.S. and mail them home! You see, there has always been a resentment between flying personnel and the ground members 'cause they always felt we "had all the gravy". When you think about the Air Corps sleeping bags, extra fruit and egg rations we had during the war, extra money for flying, special passes, etc., while they were often deprived of these privileges, there may have been logical reasoning behind this. The gunners always felt they were taking plenty of chances to get killed on missions while the others never saw combat. Anyway, I decided to dedicate myself to promoting better feeling between the two and today I'm almost convinced there was partial success!

Meanwhile I'm not asking getting any mail from you. I've heard from the family but none from St. Louis for some five or six days now!

Please, please keep writing to my present address 'til I forward a new one. I promise to let you know more about this as soon as I can gain any information myself.

I'm so terribly lonesome for you and I love you with all my heart.

Always! David.

Sunday nite 9th September 1945

My dearest Patty,

Tonight, I know absolutely nothing more than I did when yesterday's letter was written – am still awaiting movement notice to join my new outfit in Munich. Instead of being wholly disgusted with everything I have decided to try to make this into a reasonably "good deal". You remember some months back when the University of Paris (Sorbonne) was my main theme in every letter. Well, if we shall be here for a period of three months or longer I intend to apply for admission when the first opportunity arises. If we are slated for relatively short period at this place before moving back to the U.S., I'd like to get a furlough to Ireland to visit Grandfather Heenan and some of Dad's other relatives. Tomorrow we are almost certain to leave here as all the "high-pointers" are scheduled to move to the port of embarkation within the next couple of days.

It has rained steadily since yesterday afternoon so we didn't get up for church this a.m., as we have the last six Sundays! Besides, our chaplain departed for Germany and I have no use whatsoever for this other bird.

All this absence of mail makes me wonder whether you are holding back because of that V-mail letter or a negative reaction to something that I wrote in an earlier missive. You know that you are perfectly justified to accept or reject any ideas that may appear in my letters written in the varying extremities of the mood I'm in. Whatever you do, don't let that hinder your writing; if you get whole-heartedly disgusted, feel free to express yourself and I'll try to understand – to the best of my ability.

Always remember that you're always No. 1 in my mind and heart. I'll always love you and think of your as we last saw each other at the station last December – gosh, it is as vivid as if it happened yesterday.

Goodnight, Doll,

David.

Tuesday, 11th September 1945

Dearest Patricia,

Darling, whatta mess we're in around here. Everything has been thrown into a massive turmoil and mental chaos. Within three or four days the ole 416th will leave for a port and proceed to the U.S. – that is, everyone holding seventy points or over. The remainder of us are entertaining a certain amount of anxiety as to when facilities will become available to transport us back to Germany. All of this is weighing pretty heavily on my letter-writing – as you can see by the more frequent "days between".

This morning I was on and off movement orders four times and finally ended up at Base Headquarters with the group of fellows scheduled to depart to learn that there were no accommodations. Some thousand fellows from every conceivable branch of service boarded trucks, leaving me stranded with all my luggage in the middle of a huge parking area when they learned I wasn't to ship.

I called the Squadron for a truck to pick up me and my belongings and came back to the guys I bade "goodbye" some hour and a half ago!

It's a funny thing but the thought had never entered my mind that I'd be sorry, emotionally so, to take leave of the old outfit; but as "Soup" Reiter, Kenny Flaig, Roy, and those crazy gunners came down to see me off, I found the Empire State Building lodged in my esophagus! Perhaps tomorrow we can go through the same act and I'll feel more stable.

I have acquired a new ailment to complain about – in yesterday's baseball game I slid into home plate and got up with a "charley horse" in my thigh. Nothing serious but an inconvenience when I try to move about too swiftly. When we get to our new "homes" I intend to hang up my spikes for something more suitable for a man who refuses to believe that he's getting old and feeble.

I must shut this off 'til tomorrow (if we're not on a train or plane by then). All my love,

David.

Sunday night – Sept 16th

My darling Patty:

At last I have reached my destination – weary but glad to be settled for a short while! Lugging four bags around for well over forty-eight hours that grossly approximate 400 lbs. proved to be anything but a convenience; however, I have a lot to tell you about and perhaps it would be best to start at the beginning so you can follow this thing through!

The letter you sent on Sept 7th arrived Friday morning – shortly before I left the 416th! After nearly two weeks of being completely wanton of mail, that little morsel did wonders making me feel better. I can easily visualize the discouragement and bitterness you are going through now that we can outline my immediate future with more certainty! I have tried to look at the whole thing as being "tough luck" but you can get that there is more behind it. Friday night the 669th left Camp Chicago for Marseilles and will be home in two to three weeks. Try to be very "objective" when you look at the thing and say, "It's one of those things that happens in the Army!" Currently my main worry is when I might get another letter from you!

To get back to the story of my trip: I departed from Camp Chicago at 10:30 Friday via truck for the train station (keep track of the changes and add 100 years to each – you'll know how many times I hauled that damnable luggage). Being the only member of the 416th coming this way I had to content myself with some pretty dull company (my own). Three hours of train riding and I hit Challous par Marne where a delay between trains left me to gnaw on a "K-ration". About 5:30 that afternoon my "express" came grinding in and I boarded the coach.

The trains in Europe obviously were constructed for people who are dead serious about traveling. The benches are wooden and have cracks to afford plenty of ventilation around the bottom half of the "fanny". After riding a few hours, one acquires a permanent wave on his hind-side! Anyway, it was on this leg of the journey that I spotted a big, husky PFC and when I learned that he was traveling clear up in Germany – we became fast friends. (He could carry his bag and two of mine with little or no effort at all) – so like I said we were destined to be "old buddies" for the duration of the trip.

The train was crowded so, being the heel that I am, every time we'd make a stop I'd feint a deep-sleep and sprawl all over the place to keep the fourth man from joining the three of us already on a two-man seat. This went on all night; between that bench and the bird across from me munching on "hard tack" I felt slightly haggard when the sun came up.

We maintained this dashing rate of speed that put us four hours behind schedule over a course of 125 miles and finally reached Frankfurt, Germany. Our trip had taken us through Strasbourg, Mannheim, Heidelberg, etc., and this was the first opportunity I have had to get a close look at the results of the bombings by the great American Air Forces. I had seen pictures of bombing results from Intelligence Section and had flown about 500 feet over some of these places but never 'til now did I realize the wholesale destruction and mass ruin. Piles of bricks and rubble are everywhere – railroad tracks are twisted and knotted – bridges are almost a thing of history as they can't very well function half down and submerged by water – shells of buildings remain in a few "less bombed areas" – rough boards cover places that <u>used to be windows</u>! Everything is gutted or completely demolished! Honey, <u>Germany was whipped – thoroughly thrashed</u>!! As I watched small groups of German men digging slowly through the huge mounds of wrecked homes and industrial areas, the thought dawned on me how futile life must seem for these people. It will take fifty years – at least – before she'll be strong enough to exhort herself as a world power. Most of the people realize the bitter cost of war and the grim reminder of American troops everywhere will not let them forget soon their bitter mistake! I really didn't mean to get into that so strenuously, so I'll continue my story.

At Frankfurt no one was too sure where I should go but I finally managed to get on a German civilian train (with a 1st Lieutenant medic) that would come within fifty miles of the IX Air Defense Command. By that time it was getting dark so I called for transportation and made the final lap in a Jeep over a pass that might have been a road at one time. We bounced along 'til my stomach rested on the seat with my fanny and near midnight finally reached our stopping point.

I am just learning about all the "good deals" there are in this Army. My quarters for the night consisted of a BEDROOM of a very modern German home. It seems that when the U.S. came in and wanted a house or number of houses – the occupants were told to leave ... and did! To make a long story shorter, I didn't sleep very well—this sudden luxury was too much after eight months in a tent. They don't have mess kits but use trays and there are German girls to serve us. Nice deal!

I heard about a truck coming to Schweinfurt (my new home) so I hauled my bags from my room to a point some half mile away (by hand) and came down here. Now they looked at my orders and no one, including the Adjutant, can figure out why a gunnery instructor was sent here. We'll know more about that tomorrow.

Meanwhile I have been assigned to a room where I shall live for my stay here. A Master Sergeant is my roommate and it seems pretty nice. This was formerly a dormitory of Hitler's SS troops – but it appears that they have no more use for it! My bed has springs so tonight I expect to do much better on the sleeping angle!

Oh, yes! While in Frankfurt I saw A. Hitler's private train (now General Eisenhower's). Wow, whatta beauty. It is a light green and about 100 PW's were climbing all over the thing simonizing it. There are about twenty cars with facilities such as double beds, business rooms, dining rooms, observation cars, etc. – I'll buy one for you like that someday!

If I can get my new address tonight I'll put it on this envelope – otherwise I'll send it tomorrow. My hand is cramped but not too much so to keep me from saying – I love you – I love you – now and always.

David

Tuesday, 18 September 45

new address: 29th Tow Target Squadron, APO NY

My Darling Patty!

When they first informed me that I was to be moved out of the IX Air Defense Command, the thought never confronted me that possibly I might be tossed into some administrative job – much less completely away from flying. When I got to Bad Neustadt (headquarters) one of the fellows "wised me up" and I took it on my own shoulders to get out of the place and proceeded here to Schweinfurt, the only air base under the IX ADC. As you heard in my last letter, no one knew exactly why a gunnery instructor was sent here and for three days the 1st Sergeant has been attempting to gain some information or orders to keep me at this place – and I think he is getting some good results. But there is one conflict – since they have absolutely no use for a gunnery instructor, they traced through my records and found I was a graduate of radio school!

The trouble started when I was assigned to the Communications section this a.m.. They took me over and introduced me to the Commanding Officer who immediately described his anxiety to get a Radio Operator/Mechanic since they seem to be pathetically on the short end of men to repair radio sets in the B-26's and C-47's. Trying not to shock the poor fellow too much out of this beautiful dream I reminded him that it was two years since I had last cast my glimmers on one of these things; I couldn't bring myself to tell him that even though we had never done more than change a tube! "Oh," he says, "It'll all come back to you in a couple of days." So, like it or not, I am destined to become a radioman once again.

Three days have passed and I am fast coming to the conclusion that these guys are the hardest fellows to become acquainted with of any I have run across in the Army. They're so much different from the Air Corps men in that they all act as individuals – rather than teammates. Up 'til now I have used that "jolly-good fellow" approach – but it isn't working worth a damn – so that will have to give way to something else. My Master Sergeant roommate, who affectionately refers to me as "you", or sometimes, "Hey, you", has lead quite an interesting background in the Army. He worked as a crew chief on a B-17 IN RUSSIA when we were running shuttle runs from England and landing there. He also served in Egypt, Iran, England, Italy, North Africa, France, and Germany in the same capacity – quite an interesting chap!

You will find my new address on the envelope – gosh, I'm already starving for a letter from you.

I love you very, very much – David.

Friday PM 7 Dec 45

My dearest Patty:

Yipe, yesterday we took "influenza shots" and boy, I've been feeling like crawling on all fours to propel myself from one place to another. Actually, it affected me like a slight case of the flu – and I can sympathize with your recent more severe attack. Unlike Mrs. Howell, the 1st Sergeant doesn't seem to give a damn if I go to bed or work my fingers to the bone. This means I have to use a little good judgment by myself; last night I crawled in bed at 1930 trying to get rid of this weak-helpless feeling.

The "replacements" that we've read about in the papers have begun to show their first signs of existence. Today we welcomed six young boys into the section with point scores ranging from 9 to 21! It's almost sad to tell these guys that you're happy to have them with you – especially when you can see how unhappy they seem to have been selected for occupation duty. The recruiting officer told me that most of these kids will have at least one year of overseas service before they can hope for a return to the U.S.

We have a big party in the bar tomorrow night to help the 55-59 pointers bade farewell to the outfit. I could be very happy about the lowering of the point score except for the fact of conflicting rumors that rage unchecked. Some of the fellows cling to any bit of encouraging news but I keep hearing the Colonel's saying: "You'll be here quite a long time yet." This sort of squelches any enthusiasm that might arise from one of these malicious stories that circulate.

My legs still ache and I feel chilled all the time so I think I'd better make this a short letter.

Patty darling – you're very wonderful and I need you so much! You're sweeter than a ton of dextrose – and I love you so very much.

Goodnight, David.

December 8, 1945

Dear David,

I just received your note dated 12/2. I think it is adorable that you count the months that we have been together! What will our real anniversary be … our first date, or the date we marry?

Thank you for the money … it is desperately needed! With that in hand, I'll be able to pick up a few trinkets for Christmas. I know your instructions were that I get something for myself, but I want to be able to put something under the tree for everyone. My treat this Christmas (what I have written to Santa Claus about) is that I will find YOU with a bow on your head, waiting for me!

Sending love, and wishing you were here, Patty.

Saturday PM, 8 Dec 45

My darling,

Things look so much brighter tonight … the chills, leg ache, and fever have almost completely subsided and I find life might be worth living after all! I asked myself how Patty would prescribe treatment if she were here and came to a conclusion of heated fruit juice and early bed call. It worked, Honey … that's what you would have done, *n'est ce pas?*

Saturdays, as you know, we are only supposed to work a half day … this is swell when there isn't any work to do. We still are in the final stages of clearing up inventory, requisitioning parts, and in the "morning distribution", we fell heir to twenty "radio facility and navigation charts", each of which have a dozen or more corrections! Naturally, I got back to the barracks around 1800 and we're near not finished.

I have accumulated a lot of candy and gum which I made in a package to be sent to some English children for Christmas. When we were over there I woke up one morning hearing a couple of "biddies" discussing the black market. Apparently, she was trying to buy some chocolate for her kids and when the merchant or vendor quoted "two and six" (approximately fifty cents) for one bar, she said, "I told 'im to stick it up 'is bloody aws!" (excuse me, Honey, I'm merely quoting the gal and clarifying my point). This conversation stirred up something in my innards and then and there, I decided to forego what pleasure that candy brings for some Limey kid. This package is complete with twenty-four bars and I gave it to the mailman tonight.

Tonight they have a big brawl in order in the bar upstairs to help the 55-59 pointers celebrate their departure for God's country! In my present state of mind, I think the occasion calls for one or two snifters.

Saturday p.m. is the loneliest night of the week ... oh, what wonderful Saturday nights we have to look forward to! Patty, I love you, darling.

Goodnight, David.

Monday, December 10, 1945

My dear David,

It was a difficult day to digest on December 7th this year. Flags were flown at half-staff, and all of us remembered what a tragic day that was just four years ago. Now here you are, paying the price of victory ... but foregoing your college education! It is a sad situation. I hope that all of our efforts pay off!

I just received your note dated Dec 2, I'm sure that God understands your lack of motivation to attend services. I am trying the best I can to write faithfully, but sometimes the words just don't come. Please don't berate me for my ineptitude at writing. As I have said many times before, writing is not a strong point of mine.

The newspaper is reporting that General Patton was involved in a serious car accident in Germany a couple of days ago. We here in the States are praying for a speedy recovery.

The new song by Bing Crosby is all over the radio … it's called "It's Been a Long, Long Time" … have you heard it? Every time it plays, I think of you!

I have three big tests in the next week … pray for me! I'm wading in a sea of books and notes right now. It's hard to focus when I know that, after this is all over, I'll be back home with my family. My heart aches from missing all of you!

Kisses … LOTS of kisses to my love! Patty.

ps – My literature professor – Dr. Schwartz – thinks that I really have something going!

Tuesday PM 11 Dec 45

My darling, darling Patty:

Oh, you're so wonderful and I have a few nice things to tell you; partly to let you know how much I miss you and partly to explain myself for not writing over Sunday and Monday! Three superb missives arrived – so much like I always want to think of you. Chronologically, the explanations come first and the best part at the end.

Saturday, as I told you, we had a party to help the 55-59 pointers bade farewell to the 28-29th Tow Target Squadron. In the first ten or fifteen minutes the boys had consumed a dozen shots of REAL scotch, so I just took leave of the celebration for a more sociable evening. You see, it has been quite a number of months since I could do things like this without fear of dastardly consequences. About ten minutes later my CO who has become quite an old buddy dropped in with a quart of cognac – complaining that he needed some assistance!

Well, we drank and talked, and the longer we talked, the drunker we got. He told me all about his wife who he married two weeks before he left the U. S., and I told him how we planned to get married last Christmas.

When this bottle was gone, he was still thirsty so we went up to the bar to join the party. Mind you – I am still not in condition for such excess indulgence.

Shortly, Hoagy, Lt. Carmichael, decided to make a speech on the subject of "VD". So up on a table he hops and delivers his address. Once or twice he wavered pretty close to the edge of his podium and nearly fell on his ear. Most of the guys were pretty gleeful and decided that we weren't drunk enough; you can see that I wasn't so bad 'cause I remember most of the details. We did exactly that and somewhere around 12:30 a.m. I, with Lt. Butler and Corporal Fischer, started dragging him back to his sack. This action went over with Hoagy like bowel gas in a church service.

Finally, we reached his room and the fun began. Butler started slapping him to sober him enough to get in bed – Carmichael swung at Butler catching ME square on the beak. All of this being a mistake – I was tempted but didn't cold-cock the guy – and now I am sporting a <u>cracked </u>nose with two scabs. At least it doesn't stick out quite so far. I reported on sick call yesterday a.m. and the flight surgeon said it would heal straight providing I didn't get "bumped" again or I don't sleep on the thing! Enough of that – now for last night when the letters came!

I had to go into town to get things underway for your Christmas present. This was my first nocturnal jaunt into the city … and the LAST! To mention any more would give away "the secret"; anyway, I walked back to camp (some four or five miles) and it was too late to write all the things there were to say!

I wrote and told you all about our Thanksgiving Day – and yours was hardly more home-like. Gosh, it's too bad that you couldn't get together with your family over the holiday and I could see that the original "big time" that was planned didn't work out too well. Honey, I'm so sorry it turned out that way but you can rest assured that next year we'll have a real thanksgiving in our OWN home!

Incidentally, some of the fellows here are getting letters saying that their families are receiving mail that was sent back! This probably accounts for the six weeks that so little mail came from you. Then three letters were post-marked the 3rd and 5th, which is seven to ten days en route.

I generally don't mention anything about my coming home – mainly, of course, 'cause of the results of the last time I told you that we were coming back. Perhaps this is wrong – but it would be worse to build up false hopes. Accordingly – there is little information except unfounded rumors. By cold calculation I figure that it will be between March and June but the current grapevine would have us believe that I'm an extreme pessimist

I'm so glad that you like your perfume – it isn't exactly the thing I was looking for and there is still a ray of hope that the "right" scent will be available before we're out of the ETO.

Honey, I still have a couple of things to talk over but there are four "drunks" in my room and it's terrifically hard to concentrate. Tomorrow will bring another longer epistle.

I love you so much … oh, so much.

David.

Wed. PM, 12 Dec 45

My dearest Patricia,

Last night when I came in from choir rehearsal I had planned to finish the letter that was started early in the evening. My roommate had acquired a bottle of cognac and was proceeding to get himself and three other guys inebriated to the eyebrows. The place was rowdy and there was little hope of getting a reasonable missive written – so I cut it short to complete today.

Your last letter was primarily concerned with this business of going to school at Columbia. At the time we were in New York I took a trip down to Greenwich Village with Max; I guess I never expressed myself on my sentiments of that place. We wouldn't want an apartment in that district – it has a notorious reputation and besides there are many nicer sections that are much more conveniently located. You are apparently learning a lot about the "other half" … not all people in Brooklyn have the renowned "accent". The fellow that I room with now lives in that section of the city and speaks as flawlessly as anyone I have ever known. After spending three years in this Army I wonder if I'll be able to qualify in any entrance examination that they offer. Perhaps when I finish my B. A. things will be slightly more accessible in my mind and it won't be too difficult.

The flattened nose that I explained in such length is beginning to assume its normal shape but is getting a sickly green-yellow in color. Every morning when I get up I race into the latrine and look in the mirror to see if perchance I slept on the wrong side. The hair on my head is turning gray while I worry whether or not it's healing straight

Things down here in the Communications Department are looking much brighter in the last couple of days but it is too good to last. The new fellows are getting the drift of their work and exactly what we will expect of them. They seemed to have a little trouble acclimating themselves to the way things are done over here but some meetings and "guiding instruction" (a big, long whip) they appear to straighten out more each day. Our work is reaching a new low as there are very few planes flying now. At the first of the year we can expect to either move to southern France or send a couple of flights of airplanes to Tow Targets in that area. The weather is so bad that nothing is getting off the ground.

Darling – the thought just struck me that you'll probably be in St. Louis over the Christmas recess and the little part of a Christmas gift that I plan to send you tomorrow will not reach you in time. This part is cash to supplement a few dollars I asked the folks to send. You'll be able to use it when you get back. The third part will be mailed in a week or so … it's the REAL present that I thought of all by myself. Perhaps you are being built up for a huge let down- honey, it isn't much, more a sentimental gift than anything else.

Patty, I do hope you'll have a Merry Christmas! I shall dream of our next Christmas when we're together – I love you with all my heart.

I love you,

David

ps – the sore throat is a thing of the past! Je vous aime beaucoup, toute l'annee.

17 December 1945

My dearest Patty…

VERY MERRY CHRISTMAS!

Gosh, it will be much nicer next year. I love you, Patty!

David.

Dec 18, 1945

Dear David,

I laughed out loud when I read your rendition of Lt. Carmichael and his antics. What a night! I'll bet that you had a headache the next day … but I'll also put money on the fact that Lieutenant didn't even get out of bed!

Oh, I'm so sorry about your "accident" involving a fist and your nose! I would describe your previous schnoz as having "character" … I don't want to see a "flattened" version of a good thing! I hope it bounces back to normal.

I am back home in St. Louis. Daddy ended up coming yesterday to pick me up. We had a nice drive home, catching up on family news and other minutiae. He still feels quite strongly (and he mentioned a number of times) that we get our schooling out of the way before getting married. He understands (as do I) the importance of an education in these troubling times—he wants me to have a "Plan B" so that, God forbid, I am ever in the position of having to take care of myself. I know in my head that he is right, but my heart seems to be wanting to take a different direction. Can't we do both? From your last letter, you don't seem to be too keen on heading to Columbia U. Where could we go together?

You keep mentioning this special Christmas gift you are getting for me … can't you give me a hint? What could possibly cause you so much trouble, having to go into town numerous times? I'm not worth all this effort!

I'm afraid that I won't be sending a package to you this Christmas. I hope it suffices to send a HUGE hug and an infinite number of kisses your way! Next year, we will have our own tree, in our own house—we'll be in school together, and we'll have each other! Won't it be grand?

Sending love your way … always! Patty.

Wednesday 19 Dec 1945

My Darling Patty,

I have just learned why all this trouble came up over this mail situation. One of the fellows told me that he and his wife have a system in their letter writing and he received letters numbered one, three, and eighteen … which might give you some idea of the way we are getting mail. Now I am sorry that this business came up where we had a misunderstanding. You probably find it difficult to understand how one could get so worked up over such a matter, but that's the way I feel about the thing. I think that now it would be safe to tell you that since Nov. 3rd there have been exactly twelve letters that have reached here. That is an average of two per week and I know that you MUST be doing much better than that, so honey, please forgive that outburst of two or three weeks ago. I'll try to see that nothing like that ever happens again.

This afternoon, I was talking to one of the "old married men" that is in my squadron about a number of different matters and he gave me some pretty good advice that I was needing. He said that he and his wife were "blissfully ignorant" and everything that they know came from experience. I have thought that perhaps we should discuss our problems with some authority but he seems to think that we would be just as wise to follow nature's course and only seek advice if something is wrong and beyond the depths of our power to solve the question. We have let this matter of talking about getting married slide, pending the plans of Uncle Sam, but I think that the time is ripe for a little more consideration on the subject. Personally, I think that we can do some serious planning for a big marriage celebration sometime in March or maybe even before. You said that perhaps we should wait until the end of the school term before we do any anticipating of such a step … that was quite a while ago and I hope that you have become as enthusiastic about the thing as I have. Of course, there is the matter of you finishing your current semester but you may as well know that I shall have a whale of a time trying to restrain my impulses for three or four months.

Tomorrow the 55 to 59 pointers are leaving the outfit for a fighter group going to the U.S. This means that I am among the ranks of the "high pointers" and according to all the stories circulating around camp, we'll be next in line for a transfer back to the "zone of the interior". I talked to the commanding officer of the 28th Tow Target squadron and recommended that I forget about my ambitions to go down to southern France since (by his own words) the 50 to 54 point men will be the next on the list for departure from the ETO and it should occur sometime in January. Take this for what it's worth but don't make any extensive plans from it. You know there is nothing I want more that to be with you.

The more I talk with people about you, the more I wonder if I'm worthy of such a wonderful gal. Darling, you can't possibly imagine exactly how much you mean to me. It gets more painful each day when you know that your turn is about to come up next and realizing that you must wait until the army makes up its mind what to do … I have so many things to say on this matter but after the last time that I built up your hopes and let them down so miserably, perhaps it would be better to wait until there is more definitive news.

Things are going quite according to schedule. They have sent my boy "Hoagy" to school which has interrupted our normal routine but I expect to have him back in a couple of days. We have planned a big blow-out on Christmas Day and I have acquired a quart of scotch for the occasion. He has a couple of bottles in store, so everything should work out okay. I told you before I left I would hold my drinking to a minimum … well, sweet, I shall start controlling myself a little better when I am home with you.

Goodnight, Patty … I love you. David.

Friday PM, 21 Dec 1945

Dearest Patty,

Tonight another letter came … dated Dec 10th which is a big improvement in the situation. I especially noted that you graciously opened the salutation "My dear" and ended with "my love"; whoa, Honey, could you spare all that affection? Slowly and thus can understand how you might have felt when the letter was written. It came at the most inopportune time though; right when a gob of sympathy or "mush" should have been in order. This morning I woke up with the beginnings of another ear ache and I feel plenty rough tonight.

Why in Hell am I so susceptible to this monotonous plague? It's disgusting and I feel ashamed to admit that the thing reoccurs at periodic intervals that are getting more frequent in ratio with my years.

Tomorrow I shall have to report to the flight surgeon for treatment and probably the hospital for the Christmas seasons. There is so much work to be done and playing guardian to these rookies doesn't make my departure any more pleasant for the other boys.

Your latest "romance" with the literature professor forces me to let you know that there are persons pursuing MY hand … I hadn't intended to even mention it, but perhaps you can get a good laugh from it! In the past week, I have been the recipient of three letters from a little Limey gal who has taken a terrific stand "to get to the United States no matter what the cost." One night my crew chief and I happened into the Red Cross lounge – while sitting at a table eating doughnuts and drinking coffee, a couple of girls came over and started to talk. Realizing that they were hostesses we magnanimously joined into the conversation to keep them earning their pay. At 10 o'clock we walked a block down the street to put them on their subway. This one gal asked if she could write to me and I condescended to give her my address – that was all of it – I didn't see or hear from her the rest of the time.

Then one day the first letter came in … and the second … and the third, keeping in line with my usual policy of negligence, the first remains unanswered. She accelerates her zest and "mush" with each succeeding missive until she speaks more familiarly than you and I do after going together for five years! I don't think it would be violating any rules of correct conduct if I sent you a piece of her correspondence – in fact, you should be acquainted with people that try to steal me from you! Then, too, perhaps you should know that she's hoping for her seventeenth birthday to roll around!

Before you receive this epistle, I shall have written and tell her that I already have a fiancée who would disapprove of these antics!

Patty, honey, I'm not feeling so well and I think that the best way to get rid of this ear ache would be to climb in the sack and dream that you're here, putting compresses on it.

I love you very dearly and am getting more and more anxious for that big "5th anniversary" to come … there is a slight possibility if we both pray hard enough … gosh, you're wonderful!

David.

ps- Perhaps I should let "Lillian" continue to write it might give me some novel ways to tell you that I love you … are you getting tired of my old style?

Dearest David,

I haven't written to you for almost a week, so I thought I'd better set to and write now. There has been so much to do cleaning the past week that I feel almost worn out now it's over. The wedding was lovely yesterday, I do wish you could have been there. We had some photographs taken, so as soon as I get them I will send one to you. The weather was absolutely freezing cold, and I'm sure I've caught another cold, but I guess I'll survive!

I'm having to work all day today, but it's the last Sunday I'll have to work as I'm leaving here next Saturday, and I'm going to find myself another job. I like the work, quite well, but it's the hours that get me down. Anyway, Dave, I thought if you were to come over on leave, I just don't want to have to work during the evenings, like I did last time you were here.

I think I shall go back to an office again … don't you think that will be the best plan, Dave? At least then I shall be sure of having all my evenings and weekends free, just in case you happen to come to London.

I'm just wondering if you will be able to get any leave, and when it will be. I'd love you to be here for Christmas, Dave. We're not having many people at home this year, there will be just the family and about four other friends of ours, so I'd be ever so happy if you could be here, too.

I think you would like my family, Dave, they're quite an ordinary bunch of people but I know they would like you, and make you feel very welcome.

Well, my dear, what have you been doing during the past week? And what's the weather like over there, Dave?

I haven't been out at all, except to go to work for the past week. We've all been so busy at home, making preparations for the wedding, but now the wedding's over, I guess we can relax again.

I seem to have come to the end of the news I have to tell you, for today, honey, so I suppose I must just finish off this letter for another day. I'm hoping I'll soon get a letter from you, but of course, much rather you were here.

There's so much, really, I'd like to say, but it sounds so terribly sentimental, Dave, so I'll just say goodnight, and God bless you,

All my love dearest, Lilian. xxxxxxxx
Via telegram

24 DEC 1945

MERRY CHRISTMAS, SOLDIER! SOON WE WILL BE CELEBRATING EVERY DAY TOGETHER ... I CAN'T WAIT! YOUR PATTY.

26 Dec 1945

Dear Pat,

Not long ago, you started a system of numbering your letters – and, apparently, at the same time, began a different approach in your style of writing. You will be interested in knowing that Nos. one, three, and six have arrived- figure out what has happened to make you persist in being so formal in these letters. There are two things that you acquainted with that "get under my skin": smoking and drinking. It wasn't too steep for my stalemated grey matter to realize the bit of applied psychology of the cigarette burn through one of the letters- and the subtle reference to drinking beer on Friday afternoons.

I don't mind being a subject for these stimuli but I draw the line when your letters accelerate in their "coolness". It still bothers me to think that perhaps you went on your Xmas vacation receiving the series of "mistakes" that I sent. The reason this seems to bother me must be that I have never seen you so wholly indifferent – more like you were receiving coaching from some source on "how to make your letter sting." I have undoubtedly been guilty of this offense many, many times and am not too narrow-minded as to see just a single viewpoint. If at any time I have ever seemed to slight you in my affections – or seemed "tired of everything" – I should hope that you would kick my fanny via air mail. Perhaps you are submitting a means to culminate this whole affair; then I should suggest a straight punch; that is all I have to say on that matter. I hope that it was merely the result of having received those foolish letters a month or so ago.

I wrote to the family requesting that they start getting my clothes cleaned and pressed pending my return to the States. With these in stock for immediate usage, I shall be able to hold off from an entire new wardrobe until things start to get stabilized. Naturally, there will be certain things that I'll have to get right away, like shirts, ties, socks, etc., but I have sufficient trousers, coats, sweaters, and that stuff to hold out for a couple of months.

The mail clerk told me today that I would be much wiser to mail the blouses in an envelope – a brown heavy paper affair – so I have started a quest for one or two this evening. They will be in the mail within a day or two.

I think I told you about the three boys that were killed in the airplane wreck on Xmas eve – anyway, there is going to be a memorial service for them tomorrow afternoon and the chaplain called this afternoon asking if I would sing a couple of numbers with the quartet. After Christmas services, I swore that I would never become obligated like that again, but here we go. You can bet your bottom dollar that this is the last time. The only reason I said I would help to relieve the chaplain a big job for hunting up someone else on such short notice. Naturally, this will necessitate another rehearsal, which they are holding tonight at the Red Cross.

"Hoagy" and I went to the dispensary this a.m. – he to get a physical checkup, and me to get a decision on my ear status. They're not going to wait until January 18th and tell me that it will take an examination in the hospital before I can go home – not if I can help it. The doc did quite a bit of digging and truthfully it didn't bother me at all until I left the place. He forgot his own strength and dug out a piece of the ear drum, causing it to bleed making more of the mess than the original discharge created.

Things are okay in the Communications section since they told me that we would leave soon. Now everything would be perfect if only a letter would come saying that all is forgiven and we can resume our normal living. Gosh, it isn't all pleasant to continue this way. Certainly, it doesn't make either one of us very happy to carry on this way.

My sweet Patty – let us forget the whole mess and believe it never happened. I love you very much and I miss you tremendously.

Always your guy,

David.

---

30 Dec 1945

My dearest Patricia,

Since the surge of letters arrived in which you were pretty disgusted with everyone and everything … I haven't done so well in receiving mail so tonight I don't know if you are happy again or still on the war path. The *Stars and Stripes* carried an article last night that 62,000 pounds of mail was lost in the big storm in the Atlantic. This probably means that some of the letters you wrote will never find this place. Gosh, Darling, although there isn't anything special in these scripts I hope that you aren't undergoing the same misery of missing the daily info sheet as I am.

This morning I got Hoagy out to church … the first time he has been in to a service in quite a few months. The shock was apparently too much even for the good Lord. Right after church let out, the sun came out and shone brightly for the first appearance in the last couple of months. He is searching for an answer to a lot of things connected to religion so I told him the best way to solve his problems would be to go to the chapel on Sundays. He thought that was a pregnant suggestion and plans to be an ardent "attender" from now on. While sitting there half-heartedly listening to the sermon and sorta day-dreaming, I thought back on the times that we used to go to church together and the way it will be when we go again. All of a sudden, I began feeling tremendously lonesome, almost like I was sitting there with a bunch of total strangers. I thought how foolish it is to try to make yourself believe that you can have a good time over here. There is always something missing, just like an arm or a leg. Boy, we have lost a lot of time in a year, and we have so many things to do to make up for this past period.

All day today my mind has been reaching back for all the events of a year ago this day … how could one forget those precious moments that marked the beginning of a long separation. You were making last minute preparations for going to school … we ate our last meal together in that little restaurant on Delmar. We went out to "Art Hill" and smooched, gosh, do you remember how cold it was that night? Then the next morning I said "goodbye" to our mom and the house and your father and I drove down to pick you up … I told you that you shouldn't go down to the station with me and, by coincidence, you were dressed when we stopped at 0800 hours. Then we met with Gerry who had saved me a spot on the train and you came out to see me again after we had said goodbye once. Gosh, Babe, it's so vivid but it must have been a thousand years ago.

In case you're still wondering, I'm very much in love with you, and very lonesome, waiting to be with you again!

Goodnight, darling … David.

December 31, 1945

Dear David,

It is the end of a long year that we have been apart. Sometimes I am so unhappy that we are not able to be together, and yet sometimes I think that it is the best for our relationship!

I'm going out tonight with Jeannie, her and her new beau, Arnold. We're going to paint the town, in celebration of the end of 1945! Let's hope that 1946 brings more peace and happiness to us all!

Your Patty.

Book Seventeen
2017

January 12, 2017

Dear Cousin of mine –

I have told you this before, but I will repeat – there is nothing you can do to change the lot in your mom's life. You need to figure out a way to understand that there is no turning back. We are prisoners of Mr. Alzheimer's, and we have to make the best of it! Love your life, embrace the days you have with your mom, don't beat yourself up over the woulda, coulda, shoulda. She is in a safe place, and you have to be happy with that. It is in God's hands now. I love you dearly, B.

January 28, 2017

Dear Barby,

I just finished getting Mom out of cataract surgery. As expected, she had no idea of what was going on, but I felt that saving her vision was well worth the risk of just letting her travel down the path of blindness.

"Pat? Are you awake?" The nurse gently cajoled Mom into consciousness as she came out of her anesthesia from surgery. "Can you see me?"

"I think I'm alive," she responded, groggy, but fuzzy from the procedure. "It was a great success!" the nurse announced. "I'll bet you can see 100 times better than before!"

"I couldn't see? I didn't know that," was her response.

Elle.

February 17, 2017

Dear Barby,

Today Mom asked me when Dad was going to arrive – she thinks they are going to the movies, and maybe smooch a bit! Too much information for me! I have decided to follow the path of "just go along" – so I laughed and talked about what she was going to wear, whether or not she was wearing lipstick, etc. We giggled like teenagers, but it made her happy, if only for a moment. At this point in time, that is my only goal – to bring her a smile, the thought of a kiss, the love that she has treasured throughout the years.

Tell me if you think I am traversing down an evil path that fills Mom with false hopes. It's all I can muster at this point in time.

Love, Elle.

June 15, 2017

Dear Elle,

I read your last letter with a heavy heart. It is a tough road when you are no longer recognized – and there is no easy answer to how to handle the questions and confusion. I would say that it will bring your mom the greatest amount of peace for you to agree with all of her requests, i.e., "Sure, we can go to Elk Rapids! Let's look at a calendar and figure out what days work best!" or "Dad just went out for some milk, he'll be back soon. Would you like to look at these photo albums?"

One piece of advice that our cousin, Paul, gave me that I have always cherished is that once they have departed this world, your mind slowly erases these last few difficult years, and in its place are memories of when she was Mom. He was right. Now when I think of my mom, I remember her funny stories, the delicious smells from the kitchen, her pretending not to notice when I would sneak out at night to cruise on Main Street. You will get to that point, too. Patience plus love plus understanding – that is the equation that will help you to survive these tumultuous moods and unpredictable behaviors. I hope this helps.

Love you, B.

September 7, 2017

Dear Barby,

I arrived at Mom's, and she is in a catatonic state—rocking back and forth, reciting over and over: "Where is my dress? Need my dress!" Then she thought I was her nanny – she asked me to find her blue Chiffon so she could get ready for David to return from active duty! I should be thankful for the rare times that she speaks any more, and I am pleased that her memories float in happy places.

Ellen.

December 4, 2017

Dear Barby,

Mom continues to have more apparitions and hallucinations as she nears the end of her life. Hospice has been called in to help. She has reverted back to her childhood years in her mind, reliving times of old and fearing the inevitable. She no longer recognizes me, but she still knows the dog! When we come for a visit, she welcomes his sloppy licks to her face – she pets him and asks, "Do I have the good end or the bad end?" Although she is still eating, she no longer gets out of bed, and staff informs me that she sleeps 23 hours a day. At least she doesn't appear to be in pain.

I have resigned myself to be thankful that I have a clearer understanding of her life, her ambitions, her relationship with Dad, and the curious way that they chose to demonstrate their love.

When I was a teenager, I would occasionally go out on the bay with our little Sunfish sailboat with Dad. When it was time to turn around and head back to shore, he would yell, "Ready come about?" to which I was taught to answer, "Come about!"

I think I have had my "come about" moment.

I tell myself that she had a wonderful life – full of adventure, drama, and fun. What more could a person ask for? She loved her two husbands, she traveled the world, she loved, lived, and soaked up every experience with joy and verve, even to this day!

At this point, she is a shell – living, yet absent. Tough coated, but vulnerable inside. I hope and pray every day that she leaves the life of the living to join her family members on the other side. It is what she has been asking for during the last few years, and I hope that her wish to God is granted.

Elle.

Book Eighteen
1946

New Year's Day...1 Jan 1946

My darling,

In contrast with last week's holiday we spent a very sober and quiet evening yesterday. For some time we had planned to have a bridge game in my room to avoid the only other alternative for entertainment – soaking up brew at the bar. Originally it was Hoagy's idea, but he took off on leave for Switzerland at noon and we were short a man; while debating whether to play three-handed or chase down one of the soberer (sic) individuals, our C. O. dropped in and solved the problem. He came well-equipped with a quart of scotch which we split between the four of us – no one got drunk, and we had a wonderful time.

Just 365 days ago, I started a new venture—something that I had never tried before— keeping a diary. Since this marks the first anniversary of the record I decided to re-read the thing and see what was going on a year ago, and throughout the time up 'til now. Most of the stuff seems so childish and ridiculous when I note the reactions to new experiences; then too, there were some bits of "sentimentalism" that cropped out so very frequently when I'd get lonesome and homesick to be with you. In our old age, we can take the thing out and laugh as we reminisce what seems to be a monstrous catastrophe now.

Jan 1st: arrived in Greensboro at 1830 – just under the wire. Am lonesome already for Patty ... how will I be able to stand being overseas and away from Patty for two or three years?

Feb 2nd: our fourth anniversary – four wonderful years! Confined to camp or I'd call Patty. She's wonderful to have stood me so long.

Feb 7th: Sailed at 1345 on U. S. S. Mt. Vernon. Bade *adieu* to the "old lady in the harbor" who was almost hidden by fog. At last we're on our way after waiting three months.

Feb 8th: Out at sea this morning and practically nine out of ten guys are seasick ... thank goodness it hasn't hit me yet! I was assigned to guard 100 prisoners brought on ship from some guardhouse in New York at the point of a gun ... nice guys! Yipe!

Feb 14th: This is Valentine's Day – I hope that Patty received the card I sent from Ft. Hamilton. Diana and Harrison have been sick since we left port.

Feb 16th: Happy Birthday – cripes! At least we're on land again – that's consolation after all that water. Docked at Glasgow Docks in Liverpool approx. 1600 hrs. English band out to meet us.

Mar 2nd: 49th anniversary – left stone for France today in C-47's. Saw the "White Cliffs of Dover" ... English Channel. Landed at the famous field Le Bourget where Charles Lindbergh landed in 1927. Noticed the immense bomb craters all around the area. Warned to watch for mines and demolition charges still remaining in camp.

Mar 4th: This is really roughing it. The mess hall stinks like a hog pen and the food is like swill. Still not sorry – this is better than Yuma.

Mar 20th: Left Reims at 1400 for the 416th Bomb Group – rode with paratroopers! Tex and I slept in a transient tent at 668th Bomb Squadron ... cold as HELL.

Mar 23rd: This morning we got a first-hand view of the airborne Rhine crossing. The whole sky was black with C-47's, C-46's, gliders, and we made three missions in direct support of the crossing. Those guys are really catching hell tonight.

Apr 8th: First flew two missions – hit oil tanks at Plauen this morning and gave direct troop support at Shoensha this p.m. Flak reported but I didn't see any. Lt. Harper, pilot this a.m., Capt. Shepard this p.m.

Apr 9th: No. 3: Marshalling yards at Paluen – flew as gunner in Major Roney's ship. Saw bombs land and there will be no more activity at that yard in this war.

Apr 15th: No. 4: Marshalling yard about eighteen miles from Switzerland at Ulm. Was four miles from the border at one time. Got three hrs, thirty-five minutes combat time. Heavy flak but they say it was inaccurate – Good God, it was as close as I ever hope to see that crap.

Lt. Dubose was my pilot – the best pilot I have ridden with so far. West and Hodgson left for the 397th B. G. today.

Apr 16th: No. 5: Flew gunner with Capt. Wheeler in camera ship – no flak! Target: Supply depot and Kraut garrison excellent hits, except for our flight – smoke at 2000 feet. Haven't heard anything from Patty for five days – would give anything for a bit of news.

Apr 21st: Original target was Hitler's summer home at Berchegarten, but later briefing was called and target changed to a marshaling yard at Salzburg. Seventy-five miles from the Russian lines. 20 and 40 mm flak concentrated at us over German airfield. Mission diverted because of bad weather at A-69 so we landed at A-53. Longest mission in history of Bomb Group: five hrs, forty-five minutes.

May 4th: This evening, Chet, Roy, and I went up to the Red Cross and when we returned, flares, rockets, and tracers were illuminating the air. Official notice came over the loudspeaker that the war is kaput. We broke into a couple of hoarded bottles and had a big session in the officers' tents.

May 11th: Talked to Lt. Whitten about going to University of Paris and it looks like things are pretty well set.

May 24th: Packed up our belongings and flew down to new airfield – A-59 near Pontoise, about twenty-five miles from Paris.

May 28th: Willie and I came down to Arbonne – the bombing range for seven days detached service. Met a little character named Alexander Kalina who seems like a nice little guy. Have made friends with the bartender in town who earned the distinction of being the first man in France to set up a drink for me.

June 15th: Worked to get clothes marked for inspection. Lost 500 francs in a poker game – too lucky in love, I guess.

June 17th: Reported to sick call with an otitis media – pulled guard duty tonight but this damned thing is going to toss me back in the hospital again, I fear.

July 21st: Today is Patty's birthday! Gosh, I hope she got at least one of the bottles of perfume that I sent in time for the occasion.

July 27th: Up at 0500 for movement, reached Camp Chicago at about 1100 hrs. Place is dusty but tent and mess set up is better than in Pontoise.

Aug 2nd: Our four and one-half year anniversary. Oh, that I could tell Patty today how much I miss her and how much I love her!

Aug 22nd: Have incurred a terrible chest cold. Brought out my flannel pajamas and had Kenny rub my back and chest with Vick's. Cut six heads of hair today … God, how I hate that job.

Sept 3rd: A ball game with the 670th Bomb Squadron, which we won easily 2-0. A big beer party for the squadron "going away celebration" ensued. Sang with Captain Stewart, Lt. Meall, and Ransom for the boys. Orders came out promoting me to Staff Sergeant.

Sept 14th: At last, I got on my way as a handcuffed volunteer to go to Germany. Departed Leon at 1128 hrs leaving Clem, Rondeau, and Klingman at the station. Riding on one of the famous "40 & 8's" that were built for anything but comfort.

Sept 17th: Spent the day running from the room to the orderly room trying to find out what they intend to do with me. Expect to work in Communications Section as a Radio Operator – whatta joke. Like my room but roommate seems slightly elusive.

Sept 25th: Checked "869" and dressed for a trip to the U. K. Trip was three hours and forty minutes. My first trip to London – stayed at the Red Cross Club "Portman Square". Rode underground and walked out to Piccadilly Circus, Regent Square, Trafalgar Square, and Charring Cross. Saw a V-2 bomb set up for exhibition. Walked in Hyde Park and heard famous "Soap Box Orators".

Oct 18th: Received a nice long letter from Patty with an explanation of our August row. Everything is okay but she is hesitant to believe that I understand her viewpoint – it was all a big mistake for which I assume most of the responsibility.

Oct 29th: Received a letter from the family who know about my plans to get a leave to Ireland. I have never seen Dad get so excited over anything.

Nov 6th: 60 -69 pointers left today – the time may not be as long as I had anticipated.

Nov 26th: Flew to England with Gen. Richardson.

Dec 18th: 55 pointers left for the U. S.

Dec 21st – Dec 31st: The 50 pointers will be eligible for discharge.

Dec 25th: Christmas in Schweinfurt – next year I will be in our home … with Patty.

That's all I've got for now … I'm sure this is all old news to you, but it helps me to remember where I came from, what I have accomplished, and what is in store for DKH Jr!

Happy 1946, Darling … it won't be long until we are together FOREVER.

David.

January 1st, 1946:

My darling Patty,

There could be no better way to start the New Year than to profess the loneliness I'm going through without you. We can be assured that this year will see us accomplishing the many things that we've hoped and prayed for during the past five years. My New Year's resolution is going to be pretty rough … if possible, I want to be able to love you 1,000,000 times more than in 1945. You are so much a part of my life that I want nothing to stand in our way of being the happiest people on the face of the earth! Any little differences that have developed in these past five years must and WILL be completely wiped out.

My darling ---I love you so very much!

Always your guy, David.

2 January 1946

My darling Patty:

What is this army coming to now? You are probably reading accounts, though not quite so "colored" as the stories in the *Stars and Stripes* of an open rebellion of the troops in defiance to the recent War Department notice that redeployment had to be slowed down. These protests, nothing short of mutiny, are about to test the powers of the authorities who have been able to speak with a thunderous voice during wartime while their subordinates quake in their boots lest the wrath that they had heard about in thousands of lectures fallen on them. I have tried to be philosophical about the matter and found it's disastrous … I don't know how interested you are in hearing my viewpoint on the subject but if you'll bear with me I shall attempt to summarize it in a few short paragraphs.

The best place to start is to consider the bad aspect:

The entire future of the Army rests with the way they handle the outcome. They can't give in without being very subtle since their power-to-be can easily be determined. Ultimately this can lead to "strikes" and completely ruin the United States' chances to maintain the honor of having the finest and best disciplined army in the world.

The occupation armies in Germany and Japan are making the whole United States look silly. Those people aren't used to seeing an army that can stage mob demonstrations and mass meetings completely out of control of their commanding officers.

It defies all principles and laws set down by the "Articles of War" which, in turn, shows the weakness of the government.

Naturally, though, these things come secondary to a guy that feels that he has done his part in winning the war and now the task of maintaining the peace should fall on someone else. A lot of the boys think that they are being victimized by Pentagon commandos who are quite comfortable and can't visualize that the plight is half as bad as the GI's try to suggest. They are damned sick and tired of reading in the papers that the "loyal home frontiers" quibbling over the difference between $1.50 per hour and $1.75 while they sweat out an indefinite period of service overseas for $50.00 per month. Many of the guys are wondering just what their occupation policy is; as far as they can ascertain they are merely serving over here to relieve a shortage of employment in the U.S.

Our Tow Target Squadron is a perfect example of a farce. In the four months that I have been a part of this outfit, they have toted targets exactly two weeks. This hardly is congruent to a feeling that you are really accomplishing something worthwhile.

I am sorry to portray such a dismal story … the only thing I have that I can hold on to for hope and a positive future is…YOU! I love you, my darling Patty!

David.

January 1, 1946

Dear David,

I am back at the U of I, and just opened your letter dated 12/26 … let's call the whole thing off! I just can't seem to do enough to please you! You'll be better off not having a gal that you have to answer to when you finally get back to the States. I can't imagine what my life will be like, not having you a part of it, but obviously I cause you so much heartache that it is better off that we are apart. Not only do I not correspond enough, but now you send me love letters that you are receiving from another girl? I just can't do anything right.

Pat.

3 Jan 1946

My darling Patty,

In my enthusiasm of making a resume of 1945's activities I forgot to mention how we spent New Year's Day. Other than being a holiday, it was not much different than a Sunday or a day of rest. Getting a good start, I broke the first New Year's resolution by singing in the quartet after a staunch vow that I had finished with them. The Chaplain is looking for some way to fill up his morning services so he calls on us to take up some time in the service … you are probably tired of hearing the same old menu that I rewrite after each holiday. It was the same yesterday except that we paid for our greediness last night. Apparently, something was spoiled or dirty, and today about ninety percent of us are feeling the effects of dysentery.

My case was quite light, only requiring two nocturnal missions. Some of the fellows really are going through agony. They lined all of us up this morning and gave us a paper cup filled with some medicine to counteract the trouble. The flight surgeon says it was the result of the turkey dressing staying in a soiled container overnight. Whatever it was, a lot of boys paid rough dividends and are quite willing to settle for stew if that must be the price for eating turkey.

Honey, I was thinking that perhaps we could get an apartment somewhere in Janesville right after we get married. Whenever the local paper arrives, I have been searching through the classified ad section for ideas of rent and location in and around the town. I plan to get a part time job to help defray any incidental expenses since it would be next to impossible to try to maintain decent living conditions on ninety dollars per month. Little as I know about the cost of food and other living expenses, I feel that it is much better to try to get along on normal standard of living than having to budget on every turn. I want you to have things that you want and small luxuries for myself without worrying about the money angle. Supposing I could find work that would bring in an additional forty or fifty dollars per month, that would supplement the sum that Uncle Sam provides give us some $130 or $140 samolians to work on. On the basis of that our expenses would be:

rent …. $35.00
Food … $50.00
Cigarettes, permanents, etc. … $15.00
Clothes, medical care, etc. …. $30.00
Total: $130.00

Considering all these things we would still have a thousand dollars (or thereabouts) to have in reserve for cases of emergency. Cost of living in a town like Janesville is much lower than in a bigger place like St. Louis. My father raised an entire family on slightly more than $200.00 per month and I can't remember the day when we stood short on anything that we wanted. During the summer months, I could probably find a job that would pay enough to see us through the cold winter ... it's hard to figure on the basis of my personal expenses while going to school because I ate all of my meals "out" and the room was quite inexpensive.

Every day I haunt the authorities for some ray of hope to pass on to you about this redeployment business. So far, there is nothing more than the material that I have already forwarded ... one thing that we can be pretty sure of is that nothing can possibly go wrong this time ... God, I've prayed too hard for anything like that to happen.

I talked with the C. O. this morning and managed to get two of my boys promoted. One of them ... my roommate. This was a moral victory since he denied an earlier request Hoagy put in for the same two boys.

Darling, darling Patricia ... I'm about ready to burst with enthusiasm at the prospect of seeing you soon. I love you too much 'cause I think I'm getting an enlarged heart to hold the enormous affection for you. Am still hoping to reach the U.S. by our fifth anniversary although it appears dubious right now.

Goodnight, Babe, David.

Sat P.M. 5 Jan '46

My darling Patty:

The night before last, ol' DKH was the recipient of several letters – among which were nos. 2 and 5 dated Dec. 10 and 14th. From this you might get a small idea of the way the mail comes in. These two came exactly ten days after 1, 3, and 6 with a blank in between. Gosh, it seems like you would have received one of the "apologetic documents" that were mailed to let you know that it was all a mistake. Naturally, everything should be straightened around long before this gets to Iowa City, so the sooner it's forgotten the better for all concerned. From the reports that some of the boys are getting, the same conditions exist in the mail going from here to the States. Gad, whatta mess

Uncle Sam is developing 'twixt the member of the armed forces and their loved ones.

For some unknown reason, I was selected to represent the Tow Target Squadrons at the base "Enlisted Men's Council Meeting". Since the end of hostilities, a new form of army government has been put into effect whereby (at least on paper) the base policy is determined in part from the ideas submitted by enlisted representatives of each outfit. Flanked by the base C. O., the catholic and protestant chaplains, and two or three other bald-headed "advisors" … it was a little bit of a problem to figure out the purpose of such a gathering when after two and a half hours, we were still discussing the potentialities of such an organization and the influence it could swing when it started functioning. I thought there was legitimate business that the "council" could start … namely, an effective system for supplying hot water for showers. For something constructive like that, you are laughed at and they point you out as a classic example of dementia which, for all I know, may be a form of hardening of the arteries. Therefore, I made my report of the proceedings to our first sergeant with a request for them to find another delegate that has more time and patience for such crap.

When I reached my room, I learned that a trip was scheduled for Berlin the following morning. Since I had never been there and since it would be an opportunity to get away from it all for a day or two, I raced down to the Operations Office and asked to be put on the orders to make the trip.

The departure and flight were uneventful save the impression one gets from seeing the effects of the terrific bombardment the place suffered from the AAF. Berlin would compare in size with Chicago and probably was as densely populated at one time. You can look at square miles of territory that are absolutely destroyed – in most cases, completely leveled to the ground. We landed at the Templehof Airdrome which is, without a question, the biggest airport that I have even seen. Before the allied bombings the entire perimeter of the field was outlined with hangars, administrative buildings, assembly plants for aircraft, etc. Naturally, about one half of the original building remain though they are burnt and scarred.

Yours always, David

January 5, 1946

My darling Patty…

We were assigned to billets in the one "whole" building within ten square miles of the Airdrome. My first ambition was to get out to see some of the places of interest including the Berlin Stadium where the 1936 Olympics were held; the place that Lou Zamperini tore down the swastika, where Hitler decorated Jesse Owens, etc. Truthfully, I was more impressed when I first saw Madison Square Garden in New York City. It gets dark in Berlin quite early and we were warned not to roam about too far without some form of "equality" (a gun) – so we paraded back to our room.

As soon as the last rays of sun streaked across the sky, we learned that the main past time is "black marketing". Darling, one carton of cigarettes sells for a price ranging from 1000 to 1500 marks; translated into English, this means that they pay from $100 to $150. I have never sold a thing on the black market since I've been in the ETO but if we had brought any cigarettes I would have set a precedent last night … one of the guys stationed here told me that some soldiers have sent thousands of dollars home. They're amateur gangsters and try to impress the fact by talking out of the sides of their mouths and bragging about the "haul" they made in a single night. I thought that I had seen enough of that stuff to get hardened but even Al Capone would sit up and take notice of novices "legally" collecting three or four thousand bucks in a night. That's one of the main reasons that currency control books had to be inaugurated limiting the amount they can send home with their monthly pay. At least we can spend our savings with a clear conscience that it is "clean money"!

Patty, I don't think that we'll be so seriously affected by the alleged housing shortage, but that's one of the first things we'll check on when I get back. Oh, blessed thought … I love you so much.

David.

6 Jan 1946

Dearest Patty,

What a lazy day this has been; for the first time in many moons I slept through breakfast and nearly through dinner. Now at 4 o'clock, I have accomplished practically nothing ... last night after writing your letter I finally got around to sending a message to Paul Thompson and Kenny Strohbusch sending them our congratulations. Kenny and Mona were married last August and Paul was married in the latter part of September.

We had a little poker game last night and today I am the possessor of a $50.00 check that I mailed to Dad to put in the bank. The "victim" was Hoagy's roommate, Lt. Butler. German money isn't much good now so that will probably buy a set of dishes or something when we go shopping to set up our own household. Incidentally, I still have my entire pay left from the valiant service performed in the month of December and I want to send a small amount to cover expenses for a trip at the first possible moment when you are free after I get home. Please do not object to these small bits – I have wanted to send something right along and perhaps I can fulfill this ambition in part by remitting it now. You mentioned in one of your lesser moments that you wished to send the money back to my folks, boy that would be No. 1 on the list if you were seeking a means to make me miserable. Someday, we'll probably wish that we were able to dispose of our money so lightly!

I don't think that I told you about the big talk I had with the C. O. who said that it will probably be late in the month before we take leave of the Tow Target squadrons. This will mean a much later date than I originally anticipated. You can completely discount any idea that I'll be home in time for our fifth anniversary. This put a crimp in the plans I had for making second semester of school and I shall probably find work to occupy the time until fall term arrives. I don't know what your plans will be and it's hard for you, I know, to make any decisions until the army divulges theirs. The papers are filled with news that the brides of GI's in this theater will start moving home at the beginning of the month which will hamper our transportation to some degree. Some of the fellows in England have started a campaign by sending cables to the War Department, their Congressmen, and well-known columnists such as Winchell and Drew Pearson to see that the soldiers are given No. 1 priority for a ship going home. You have probably heard a lot more about this than we have but it is bound to carry some effect.

Sometime this week, we are sending eight men down to Istres, France, to start their duties towing targets for Ack-ack battalions and fighter planes. At least it will offer a respite from having so many men under our feet all of the time. They had planned to send me down with them but since we were declared eligible for release, they decided against it. The main consolation I have is that soon I can toss the responsibility on someone else's graying locks.

Gosh, Babe, you're wonderful and the reason that this subject is so prevalent is because I can hardly wait to be with you again. I guess I have to admit that I have a serious case of homesickness, and you know why! I love you more than any other material thing in the world.

Goodnight, Patty. David.

January 7, 1946

Dearest David,

I'm sorry about the last note I sent you suggesting that our relationship be terminated. I'm just so frustrated, and so lonely! I talk nonsense sometimes!

I'm glad that you got Hoagy back to church and that it gave him some much-needed hope that he is obviously not finding in a bottle of scotch. Will he and I ever meet? I feel like I know so much about him that he will be an immediate friend.

I received your letter dated 12/30. I'm not sure how it is okay for you and your buddies to go out drinking, yet I make one reference of a night on the town and you are all upset about it? I guess I won't tell you anymore about the very few times that I go out with friends and try to forget about this horrible situation we are in. Forgive me for trying to have a normal life!

And by the way, you reference my "coolness" … how about your preface to your letter, where you start "Dear Pat" … are you playing the same games? I will not stand for your demands for me to be cooing to you when you are treating me as a mere acquaintance.

Which, by the way, reminds me about the letter you sent from your girlfriend, Lilian. I wish you both the best if that is what you want.

I am going to believe that you were just playing a trick on me, and I too often reminisce about those last hours together prior to your departure. I wonder, should we have gone ahead and gotten married? I know my parents were disapproving but having you as my husband would have made me incredibly proud and maybe it would make this separation a bit easier!

Does the *Stars and Stripes* carry the column written by former first lady Eleanor Roosevelt? She is now serving as our representative to the United Nations, and she writes a column that appears in the local newspaper called "My Day". I find her to be fascinating and courageous! I'm enclosing a portion of her address to the country that appeared a couple of days ago:

The little people are the ones who fight the wars, they are the ones who work their hearts out in production, they are the ones who suffer most during the wars and afterward. They are the ones to whom a little more hope for a better life now and in the future will mean a little more joy and a little more ease in an existence which in the past has never been without anxiety. They are the ones who will be willing to adventure in new ways because they have less to lose, and yet they are the ones who create stability for those who have had much in the past and hope for more in the future.

Doesn't she write beautifully? How I wish I had her gift. I feel like she is talking to me.

I have new classes this semester, namely, Sociology, Economics, Math, and Home Economics. So far, they seem to be pretty interesting … but as always, it is a bit difficult to concentrate when my mind drifts off to your return home. It can't possibly be much longer!

Have I told you recently how much I appreciate your letters? If you didn't write as often as you do, I think we would have a hard time getting back together. I feel like I understand what you are going through. Some of the other gals in the house have guys overseas, and they don't hear much about what is going on. Sometimes, I share your words with the other roomies in the house—they feel like they already know you! How lucky am I to have a fella that loves me, writes letters, and is cute to boot!

I am going to forget about that letter you sent from Lilian (unless she is your choice for a spouse … then I'll forget the whole thing completely) and hope that you only sent that letter out of spite and frustration. I really don't want to call the whole thing off.

Sending love, Patty.

Monday night 7 Jan 1946

My Darling Patty:

Good news! Another letter came tonight! Written from St. Louis, it was postmarked December 27 which is a big improvement in service over previous mail. In a way it brought very sad news because now I know that you spent Christmas holidays feeling much the same way as I did, which wasn't good. Honey, you don't know how sorry I am to know that I contributed to making your vacation less enjoyable and now that you're back at school you might realize from the letters that accumulated how things stood. I was surprised, but happy, to hear that the family enjoyed the makeshift card that was sent. I had planned to cartoon several for my friends but they seem so childish and "uncomical" that I was almost ashamed the next morning after the message was on its way. The main reason that I stopped sending those drawings in letters was because I thought you looked upon them as silly; I can see they aren't very clever. At any rate, if you were being nice or if they did appreciate it, it does my heart a lot of good to hear you say it. Now I shall probably subject you to more frequent pictures ... don't say you didn't ask for it!

You read the newspapers and there is little use in trying to add anything to the War Department announcement that came out after I had mailed yesterday's letter to you. I might say that I took the order standing up since there isn't much one can do to fight such a decree except in your own mind. Reading a part of the text of General Collins who stated that there are "very few" men left overseas now, I smiled ... there are so many things that he isn't acquainted with. My bomb group received SIX battle stars which put most of the fellows over the hump. Everyone from the latrine orderly to the Commanding Officer were awarded stars just for being in the outfit while the pilots, navigators, and gunners were flying combat missions to make these battle stars possible. I saw so little combat that it hardly warrants mentioning – but in a single mission I saw more than any of those jokers saw in eighteen months overseas.

Also, according to the *Stars & Stripes*, General Marshall had previously announced that all servicemen with two years of service would be sent back to home ground by 30 March. Now the powers that be seem to be backtracking on that pledge, and it is causing all kinds of havoc! Apparently, there are demonstrations going on at every base in the world!

Last night's letter told you to discount any plans that I would be back in time to celebrate our fifth anniversary. Tonight it is quite safe to say that you may revert back to the original date I am set to be home in March or April at the earliest. But you don't want to listen to a dozen pages of sob stories, so I shall try to refrain from talking about it too often in the future. It is for things like this that I asked you to continue writing until I told you otherwise.

The money order that I spoke about earlier has been applied for and I want to make a request. When it arrives, please use it to buy a dress, suit, or whatever you wish and there will be plenty of time to send a little more money to make the trip that we talked about. The reason I repeat myself so often is to make sure that you get rid of any silly ideas about disposing of it in other ways. I beg you to do this for me.

And that about sums up everything for tonight except to tell you that since the "announcement" that 50 pointers will have a delay in their return, I have become homesick twenty-fold. Oh, darling, I miss you so very much and I love you with all my heart.

Your guy, David.

January 9, 1946

Dearest Patricia,

Each month that I spend here means that much more accumulated cash and today another money order went in the mail for our account. Perhaps you might have wondered why I never mention the sum that has mounted ... well, originally, I planned to save it as a big surprise and now I don't know the total close enough to estimate within $200.00 ... so I guess it will be a surprise to us both. And along with that money sent home there was plenty left over to send a small check to you. Any little thing that I am able to send makes me so happy 'cause that way you can make use of it rather than letting it grow moldy in some bank. In this way I can show you in a small way that I appreciate the many things that you have done for me. Please do not think that I am trying to cheapen this thankfulness by remitting cash … I have a vague idea of how unpleasant it is to be without funds for incidental expenses and it's the only available means I have here at hand to help.

We have just finished taking an inventory of all our communications property with the astounding results that we are only short on a couple of non-expendable items. The way things are handled down there I marvel that we have enough stock to warrant counting. This makes about three day's work before we can say that the job is complete. Much of the stuff we possess has been scrounged from Normandy to the Elbe and there is a lot of radio equipment that has no papers to show its origin. Last week we turned in approximately $50,000 worth of radar supplies that weren't charged to anyone as far as we know. Records now show that they are trying to track down some of the material that just disappeared. Someone is going to find himself owing the U.S. government a pretty big sum of money … or else the government is just trying to "make" work, much like they did during the Depression. You see, the commanding officers of each outfit are personally responsible for every "issue" item in their particular unit. Thank God I don't have to worry about that … though I hate to see some of these boys take the rap for another guy's negligence. Poor Hoagy is up to his neck in trouble until we straighten out this latest deficit.

My darling, darling Patty … certainly you are back in school and have been able to get our differences aligned to make thing run along the old groove. There should have been at least a letter a day when you arrived for all the time you were in St. Louie, plus some that were in the postal system and were slow in getting there. There weren't many days that I missed writing at least a few lines … unlike you!

Gosh, I miss you … I love you so much.

Goodnight, Babe, David.

Thursday, 10 January 1946

My sweet baby daughter Patricia,

How kind of you to forward your letter from David dated January 2nd ... partly knowing that I am quite lonely here, but it is also quite reassuring that you rely on your dear old pop for some paternal advice every now and then. I will tell you that it is a life lesson to release your young ones into the wild vestiges, much like an untamed animal that instinctively turns its back when a cub reaches a certain age. You have to have faith that they will know how to fight and survive in this gone-crazy world.

My major concern as I read through David's suggestions for you to relocate to Janesville is ... what about YOU? Not once in his diatribe does he mention your departure from college or what you will do while he is pursuing his dreams. Does this not bother you at all?

Another thing that furrows my brow is his constant pestering of you never providing enough mail. Methinks that you could write twice a day and it wouldn't be satisfactory. I understand his isolation and loneliness ... I've felt something similar (yet not so drastic) in the past few months. But I would never berate your mother, or make her feel guilty, for skipping a few days of correspondence. Good Lord, if she wrote on a daily basis, I may have wanted to tear out the little bit of hair I have left on my head out of sheer boredom. I love the gal, but there is only so much of meaning that can be said.

David speaks of "discussing plans" but I fear that, in his mind, the discussion has already occurred. He has your future mapped out without any input from you.

Believe me, I am not opposed to your future nuptials with David ... I think that Mother and I have proved that we are ready to make him part of our family. My only lingering concern is your well-being ... becoming an educated, self-sufficient person in this ever-changing society. As the map of my career has illustrated, nothing is certain, and one must always prepare for the least expected turn in the road.

Your devoted father.

Thursday, January 10, 1946

Dear David,

Well, your "order" to stop writing hasn't arrived yet, so I will continue on my mission to keep you apprised of goings on here at home. I hope I don't sound brash, but really, the browbeating that I have taken for my failure to produce enough mail has been quite hurtful. I'll continue to do my best.

One of the biggest stories circulating in the news is that there have been numerous demonstrations on the part of the soldiers as a result of the announcement that demobilization is being slowed down. The military is trying to suggest that there are insufficient numbers of boats available to ship our boys home ... but some evidence points to the contrary! Some reports say that there are up to twenty transport ships that are sitting idle on the west coast, just waiting for orders to deploy. The other part of the story is that President Truman is backpedaling on his previous promise to get all troops on their way back home by March 20 ... now the papers are "Saying it isn't so!" Who are we to believe anymore? These demonstrations seem to be getting more violent and vociferous ... I hope they get the attention of our elected officials.

Your Patty.

Sunday night, 13 January 1946

My dearest Patty:

Tonight I find myself planted here in "CQ" – much in the same predicament that you "enjoy" each week. There is never a dull moment around here though. Fifteen minutes after I reported for duty a guy came in yelling for someone to call the "MP's" ... it seems that one of the fellows got a little drunk and decided to show his boss that he was tired of taking orders. To prove his point he went into his section chief's room with a gun and in his drunken stupor, was ready to make sure that he never took another order from the guy. It all ended up that there wasn't any ammunition in the carbine but the department head, Bausch, wanted to make sure that this would never happen again and was insistent on calling the Military Police to have the inebriated boy put in the guardhouse. It all came to focus when I promised to put the guy in bed and Bausch went to Schweinfurt on a pass. Yipe, perhaps I should be thankful that "CQ" only comes around once in three months.

Keeping tabs on all reports coming in from higher headquarters on the re-deployment situation, we listened to the commanding officer give a talk last night on the Washington reaction to the demonstrations staged by the "GI's" over here. It seems that now, rather than drop the release of servicemen by points, they plan to make smaller units and make sure that the highest point men get first priority. I am leery of all reports referring to these re-deployment statements by authorities seeking to pacify the soldiers – and I hope you can weigh any information that I pass on with the same degree of trust. Anything can happen, and probably will.

This morning, I was supposed to join the quartet in singing the morning service … naturally, I missed the thing by sleeping overtime … making a big hit with the Chaplain and the other three fellows that were lucky enough to wake up in time. I told them that they shouldn't depend on me anymore since I hate to be obligated. They don't seem to understand that time means anything to anyone but themselves and were quite put out.

My roommate, "Billy" Mitchell, received two more battle stars this afternoon from his old outfit giving him a grand total of 60 points … making him eligible for an immediate release and probable shipment to port before the end of the week. He gets a big thrill out of being among the select few having enough points to get out right away and has, for the past twelve hours, reminded everyone within hearing distance that he has joined the "high score" category. I am very happy for the guy, since he has been over here for over twenty months … it's about time they gave the lad a break. Quite a number of the men are getting extra "battle stars" when they learned that the requirements were changed to make more eligible for honors and points. Gosh, I wish there were some way that I might qualify for one more star – it wouldn't take long to get us out then!

Honey, I have been thinking that perhaps we might get married between terms of your school year … this spring, if possible! We can set up housekeeping after a good long vacation for both of us and make plans to go back to school in the fall of this year. There are so many things that I have dreamed about that we could do together – things that we have talked about before when I thought that I'd be in the U.S. last September. Dad says that he is saving out a good golf set to serve as recreation in the spring and summer. Naturally, this will only be a small part of my plans since there are many things for us to do that both of us enjoy. We can get a cottage for two – and after we get a rest we'll proceed to tear up the civilization that we couldn't enjoy before. We'll make up for everything in a few short months and then try to keep ahead of the rest of the world in showing other people how to live … The very thought of it starts my blood boiling and I forget all my troubles and can only think of you. 'Course I am depending on you to keep scheming for things that you have wanted to do and it'll be really complete.

Even though I'm on "CQ" Sunday nights, I feel closer to you than any other day of the week … I guess it's the soft music and familiar programs that we associated with Sunday that we used to listen to together. You probably think I have grown into a silly old sentimentalist by constantly referring to the "old times", and even more in the future … if these things start to bother you please understand that it's only because you are the closest thing to my heart and mind … I can't help thinking of the good things we have to look forward to!

My sweet … I miss you so much and I'm terribly much in love with you!

Always your guy, David.

- -

Tuesday, Jan 15, 1946

My dearest Patty:

Finally, the long-awaited message arrived – in two letters dated Dec 29th and 1st Jan – between the two, I felt relieved, happy, perplexed, doubtful, and a dozen or more associated emotions. Naturally, any mail from you is anxiously awaited and always greatly appreciated. There is no need to go into the difficulty so best we keep all comments strictly up to the moment; so with that in mind you can settle back while I unload whatever there is left to be said …

All of a sudden, I find that perhaps we don't know each other as well as I thought. It wasn't hard to see in those letters that both of us wrote that we were a little bit doubtful whether it would be wise to continue making plans for getting married. You once told me that if there was ever a question in your mind you wouldn't hesitate in putting a stop to our relationship. Now I'm not too sure that you weren't on the verge of doing just that. Acknowledging the fact that the blame rests primarily at this end, it was probably easier for me to think that it was just an undesirable interlude in our lives, and not anything quite so drastic as it hit you. Although I had not anticipated any lengthy misunderstanding, the thing that bothered me most was that you spent the holidays under the misapprehension that things were still not improved. As I told you, there was nothing over here that even suggested that the day was Christmas, other than we all got polluted and had a day off. You should have been in a position to be very merry and obviously I was the cause of a poorly spent vacation.

About that time you suggested the perhaps we call the whole matter off – and I must admit that I was nearly ready to make the same suggestion to you about that time. My diary of last year dated Jan 2nd said: "this year will be the real test of whether our love will hold" … and it came very close to doing just that. It seems almost foolhardy to destroy the thing that we have fought for five years just when we are so close to being together "permanently". At least without a chance to prove to ourselves that is what we want. You have changed immensely in the past twelve months and I feel sure that I can equal, if not surpass, your "changing"; now is the time for us to get accustomed to the idea that we have a lot to face … I think that we're both intelligent enough to accept this and will have no difficulty in maneuvering a reasonable understanding. That's what I want – so badly! That's the way it will work out, I'm sure!

Last night we were the guests of one of the more prominent families in Schweinfurt – I became acquainted with Mr. Boguschewski through my old friend, Dave Henninger. He is an official at the famous Schweinfurt ball bearing factory that was completely demolished by Eighth Air Force bombs. He and his wife live quite comfortably (in comparison) in a small apartment in the outskirts of town. We sat around about three hours talking and drinking their very scarce supply of wine. Both of them are studying English with the hope of reaching America someday … like all Germans, they disclaim any part of the Nazi following and are quick to accept any pity that is offered them. They are convinced that Germany will never rise as a world power again (that's what they said!) They took us through the different rooms of their abode making certain that we could appraise the damage suffered from the bombs. He is making a frame for a colored picture for me "to remember my stay in this area." We came back to camp in a big snowstorm less our cigarettes and candy that we took to show our appreciation for the invitation.

And this, my dear one, is the ending of another letter. Am awaiting further developments in my next letter from Iowa City. Goodnight.

My love, David.

- -

Wed nite 16 January 1946

My dearest Patricia,

Things have taken a decided turn for the worse since yesterday – but I shall not delve into the matter further than just to mention the catastrophe – Carmichael and I turned in recommendations for several promotions and had a lengthy and heated argument with the authorities to get them okayed. Today the ratings were posted – without the names that we suggested. This probably seems quite unimportant but it serves to show us precisely how much their appreciation for the work we've done actually registers. Effective today, I have done my last bit of work for the Tow Target Squadron. There is no extra charge for this little addition to the letter I had planned to write – I just thought you'd be interested in knowing that we're mighty unhappy around this quarter tonight. Some of the fellows have really warranted an increase in pay.

I heard from a guy, whose cousin is a janitor in the Commanding Officer's quarter, that a date has been selected for the departure of 53-54 point enlisted men. Considering the source of information, one could hardly make a mistake in passing on the news – it must be authentic! Anyway, it is fun to listen to things that would tend to rush our ETD (estimated time of departure). Next Tuesday, January 22nd. This, I might add, should be taken with a grain (or dose) of salt. We have a fellow in the orderly room who is among the high point veterans and keeps us well informed of the latest developments. He has started to turn in all his excess equipment and has our morale from tumbling completely into the depths of doubt.

Mitchell, my roommate, has had his "battle star" okayed by the "wheels" and will be going home on Friday. He will probably be in the United States by the time that this letter reaches you, judging by the speed which mail has been traveling of late. Naturally, he is walking on air and is anticipating big things from the civilian world. It makes the room several shades lighter (atmosphere) just to hear him explain why it's necessary to rush the old vets home … when all the trouble originated about the delay of returning men to the U.S., several of the fellows used this as an excuse to stage a personal protest and proceeded to adorn their faces with weird types of beards and moustaches. Being quite willing to join in any kind of a rebellion, I, too, had a monstrosity creeping out of my chin and upper lip. This demonstration lasted about five days, when it was a matter of shaving or going crazy with "the itch". This put me in a category of "chicken" (which you may or may not have heard about) but at least I feel slightly less raunchy and self-satisfied to be "one of the boys" again. Some of the guys still sport their appendages and are looking more like a Smith Bros. advertisement every day.

It is getting late and I have a heavy day of lounging ahead … so I must bring this conglomeration of assorted topics to some kind of conclusion. Goodnight and

All my love, David

January 17, 1946

Dear David,

Did I ever tell you my new address? I'm no longer at East Lawn Dormitory … Mrs. Howell's home is at 325 N Clinton, still in Iowa City. I'm not much farther from campus, but it is a bit more private than in the dorms. I remember your stories about how rambunctious the dorm residents were at Milton … it isn't much different here! Mrs. Howell runs a tight ship and doesn't stand for any shenanigans. I kind of like it that way … it's a bit more like home.

There is a group of people who have formed a club called the "Bring 'Em Home Movement" – they are putting pressure on Congress and President Truman to speed up the return of troops from Europe and the South Pacific. If there is a local branch, I'm going to join!

School is going well. I'm particularly enjoying my class in Home Economics. Do you know how much is involved in running a household? You have to budget for groceries and other essentials, plus keep up with the laundry, dishes, dusting, mending, and (if God allows) children! I don't know if I am up to the task.

Must run ... there is a study group meeting for our upcoming Sociology exam! Sending lots of love your way, Patty.

Friday, January 18, 1946

My dear Patty:

Holy Joe, I'm having a big dispute in my mind over the course to follow tonight! There are a few things that I want to tell you in this letter so it should be written and mailed. On the other hand, the effects of getting out of bed at 0530 this morning to see Mitch on his way has rendered a stupefying and musty feeling on my brain ... meaning that it would probably be a better idea for me to hit the sack. If you find several places in this missive that don't seem to make sense, you'll understand why!

A couple hours after I got the boy safely on his journey, another guy moved in to fill his bunk. We had promised two of the new fellows our room as soon as we left – when he departed they flipped a coin to see who would move in first, and I was the loser either way. The boy, named Kosinski, now shares these humble quarters and is he a character! His very presence would stunt a conversation between Socrates and Aristotle, and his appearance reminds me of an actor out of a Frankenstein horror picture. Within twelve hours after he came in, he had pilfered three rosy apples I had nursed from a big meal we had a couple of days ago. He raises hell when I dial the radio for music in place of a Russian newscast that neither of us can understand. In general, he is making my life quite miserable. We are on the precipice of coming to an understanding ... do not get the idea that this is being "catty" – he just needs to be straightened out like all the newcomers from the routine they had in tech schools back home.

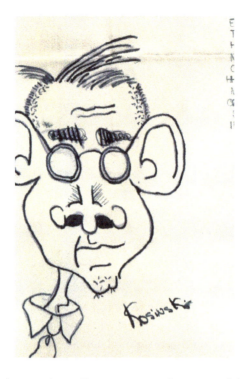

Today I bought an eight-millimeter camera from one of the boys in the 29th Tow Target Squadron … perhaps you remember the camera I had some years ago. Or the pictures that are brought out for guests in place of the usual family album. There are some shots of Harriette that are really terrific and never fail to bring a near riot and a strain on the family ties. Actually, I think they're very funny and will make excellent entertainment in years to come. That's the main reason I wanted another movie camera … this model is a German number made by a company fairly well known in the U.S. – an AFGA – some of the more ardent followers of photography say that I got a good buy – I'm not in a very good position to judge one way or another because of very limited knowledge of such things.

An officer from 11th TAC, our immediate headquarters, paid an unannounced visit to the different departments this afternoon. Fortunately, we had just completed our inventory a few days back and things were reasonably accessible … he nearly hit the roof when he got a look at the way some of the sections kept books. Overall results were not satisfactory which means that we can expect an inspection from one of the big wheels of the command. Should a close investigation come, they would find plenty of discrepancies; some in communications 'cause I don't know the procedure in making the books balance. There are absolutely no records of the source of much of our equipment before Oct 31st of this year and about a half million dollars' worth of unaccountable material. No one seems particularly concerned – Carmichael and the commanding officer have to foot the expense of any equipment that shows up missing and neither of them seem bothered in the least. With this in mind I have ceased to worry, too.

There is no change in the re-deployment information that you don't already know about. The scheduled date of January 22nd still remains at the head of the rumors that circulate with increasing crescendo. When anything certain is distributed, I shall forewarn you on the outside of the envelope. But if we do get to come home … beware! I'll be on the first train to Iowa City to claim my girl!

That is the end of the news at this end of the line. Except that I miss you very much and I love you, darling …

David.

19 January 1946

My darling Patricia:

This is it!! After months of planning, praying, hoping and speculating, I can give you the first reasonable answer to the question we have wondered about … when will it be that I shall depart from here to be on my way to home and to you? Yesterday morning a "TWX" came in with the information that all enlisted men having 53 or 54 points would be made available for immediate release from their work and would report to the 36th fighter group at Kassel, Germany, not later than January 23rd, to be processed in preparation for their return to the United States of America.

This short notice means that there will be a lot of things to do before we climb into the truck that will portage us on the first leg of our journey.

Tomorrow morning I shall turn in all the flying equipment that I have had to carry from one end of the "ETO" to the other ... I'll be darned if I'll haul that crap back to the States. Then there is the matter of straightening out the clothing issue from quartermaster supply; when my friend, Henninger, was Supply Sergeant, I found that a lot of extra clothing got into my locker. They check quite closely on these things so there isn't any sense in trying to carry a bunch of stuff up there that they'll take away sooner or later. My radio, iron, and this typewriter I am willing to leave to some of the boys that will be around here for a while, these things would bring unbelievable sums if one decided to sell them but, it is easier to dispose of them as a present and not bother about bickering over a few dollars ... they need the stuff ... I don't.

Perhaps the thing that will sound sweetest to your ears is that we can dispense with this mail difficulty for this letter is also the notice for you to stop writing to this address. Among other things, I filled out special forms yesterday that will be sent to the central postal directory to send any mail that arrives here to 1027 Ruger Ave (my parent's address). That will be a stable point for any mail that arrives regardless of where I might be. I shall continue to write, every day, if possible, to keep you informed of the things that we're doing and the progress we're making ... The C. O. is very optimistic about the early sailing date that is scheduled for us but I plan on being over here for another month before we board ship. Feb. 20th and March 5th ... this, I realize, is not very definite but neither is my faith in the things that the army tells us.

This is the first letter I have written about this matter – naturally, I wanted you to know first. I didn't write last night for two reasons:

1) There still might be a mistake and I thought that it would be wiser to wait another day awaiting further news ...

2) Carmichael and his roommate, Lt. Butler, "forced me" to go over to their room for a couple of "quickies" ... It wasn't very late when I got back, so that really didn't account much for the failure to write.

Honey, I do hope that you are as anxious as I ... the uncertainty implied in our most recent letters will be just as strong a certainty in the next few weeks. I can say now that my love for you was never dimmed a single candle-power, and I'm looking forward so much to reaching an understanding that will be perfect harmony for both of us.

I love you! xxxxxxxxxxx

David Jr.

- -

20 January 1946

JUST RECEIVED ORDERS THAT I AM TO DEPLOY FOR ANTWERP AT 0900 HRS TOMORROW … DON'T WRITE ANY MORE LETTERS AS I DON'T KNOW WHERE I WILL BE. THIS MUST MEAN THAT I AM HEADING HOME. WILL LET YOU KNOW IF I HEAR ANYTHING FURTHER.

DAVID.

- -

22nd January '46

My darling Patty,

We're in Kassel, Germany! Shortly after I had finished my letter to you Sunday afternoon, the first sergeant broke into the room with the news that the orders for leaving had been changed from Tuesday to Monday. This meant a complete change in plans that I had made for packing, turning in equipment, etc.

Feverishly we sorted excess clothing from the absolute bare requirements and by 0130 hours things were reasonably well organized. At times like this, one forgets about being tired, hungry, and only constant visitors keep your palate from becoming parched! With January liquor rations still undistributed, I thought the entire squadron would be "on the wagon" … but no, I never saw so many and assorted types of alcohol in one place … and this continued unchecked 'til they got too tired to too drunk to stay!

At 1100 hours our bags and baggage were outside waiting for the trucks that were to carry us on the 150-mile jaunt. From then until 12 o'clock we stood around shaking hands and listening to half-hearted jokes from those who were staying behind about the miseries we'd encounter in civilian life and how we'd be begging Uncle Sam to let us back in the Army within sixty days.

About noon, our transportation came and we left on the first part of a long trip. Eleven men and two officers shared the truck I was in with luggage and five quarts of scotch and cognac. We kept warm except for our feet – mine haven't thawed out yet! The trip was uneventful as we raced sixty mph in a two-and-a-half-ton truck over mountainous roads covered with snow and ice – five hours of riding interrupted by "rest periods" and one stop at a Red Cross.

It was dark (approx. 1830 hrs) when we arrived in the gates of the 36th fighter group. We ate and were assigned to rooms built to accommodate four men; we numbered seventeen when a final tally was taken.

Honey, they have HOT WATER here … twenty-four hours per day! This is a big treat for men from the Tow Target Squadrons who thrived on a shower every other day … and had to shave with ice water! The building is modern (by this I mean an inside toilet) so our stay shouldn't be too miserable.

But, I've been evading the most important thing … rumors! Boy, they fly thick and fast, even more than back in Schweinfurt. The former CO of the 28th Tow Target is our most reliable source and he swears that we'll leave here (all 500 of us) for Antwerp Friday morning, Jan. 25th … where we are scheduled to arrive on the 26th! Our stay in port is uncertain but shouldn't be over a week. This will mean (if this proceeds as per schedule) – a much earlier date than my wildest dreams could visualize. I'd be a "civvy" by Feb. 15th!

I shall continue to write and let you know just how things stand.

Incidentally, this is being scribed on a blanket as I sit on my cot. If it's illegible – please forgive! My sweet, I love you very much.

Always, David.

Here I am in Kassel and Schweinfurt … you can see I've put on a few pounds.

29th Jan '46 Tuesday pm

My dearest one:

So far, so good! We're proceeding per schedule; we left Kassel, Germany at 0600 Saturday, reaching Antwerp last night at 10 o'clock. We traveled in box cars, spending sixty-four hours taking the recoil of every bounce on the road! This mode of transportation has a priority following prisoners of war, freight, salvage, deployed persons, etc., so about half of the time we were side-tracked. For some reason I couldn't find a comfortable position to sleep; so many guys are crowded into one car that any self-respecting sardine would complain. For health's sake we arranged our blankets on the floor so you had feet, rather than "head to head", in your face. Our food for nine meals was "c-rations" and the stew they served us last night was kinda refreshing.

Now we're at Camp Top Hat, awaiting some news of Packet No. 5144-32 – shipping!! This place is very much like Camp Chicago where I was with the 416th Bomb Group. Shows, beer halls, ice cream counters, etc. dot the area for recreation during "off hours" (any time other than time allotted for sleeping and eating).

We have been "charmed" but this is apparently the spot we'll get stuck past the scheduled departure. A list is posted each day of available shipping and expected ships. Personally, I think it will be around Feb 5th when we get our call.

There is nothing we can do now but wait and hope! Every night I dream I'm already a civilian and the picture of us together is perfectly clear. When we reach Ft. Sheridan, I shall try to call and we can make arrangements to get together from there. I should like to meet you in Chicago but if this isn't okay with you, I shall go to Iowa City as soon after as possible. There are a couple of things one has to do immediately after becoming a civilian, like reporting to the Draft Board, etc. Then I shall climb into civilian duds!

Must quit, am loving you very much…David.

30 Jan 1946

Darling!!

Finally they have crammed the last bit of processing that we could possibly be subjected to and we're free to come and go as we like.

Today we had part of our currency changed into Belgian francs – enough to guarantee cigarette and coke allowances. Our next money will be U.S. queenbacks, which will be doled out on board ship.

An infantry colonel is the commanding officer of this place, so when they make announcements such as "prescribe your own uniform" or "you are our guests and can expect and demand treatment accordingly" ... it makes one raise an eyebrow and wonder what in Hell cooks. Laundry, shoe shining, clothes pressing, etc., are among the conveniences afforded the transients stopping here on their way home; all these menial tasks are ably performed by Kraut "POW's" who wander around camp unmolested by guards. None of them even want to escape – they're getting three meals per day, a bed, and clothing appropriate to the weather. This is MUCH better than they'd do back in Germany!

My only regret is that we don't have more things to keep us busy. There is so much time to think and dream that the hours and days pass slowly. In all probability there will be another week of this before boarding the homebound vessel. In that period I shall continue to make plans of things we can do in a very short while. Oh, how I wish we could spend the next three or four months together ... married! It will be bad just to know that you're in Iowa City and I'm not with you. If only we could have made some plans for this – and you could have taken a recess from school for the remainder of the year. That's what I'd like – but I guess it's foolish to suggest it.

Patty, I'm counting the days – minutes – seconds ... I miss you and love you,

David.

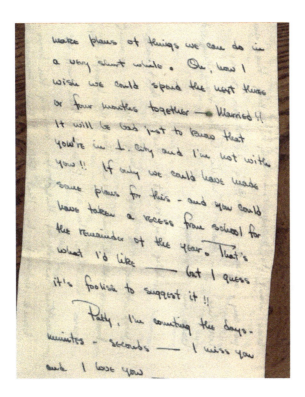

5 February 1946

My Darling Patty:

After a long train ride, then a bus ride, then hitchhiking a bit, I am finally in Brighton, awaiting another ride to Antwerp, for my deployment. There is no sense in you writing, as I may be here for a day, or I may be here for a month.

Regardless, when I get stateside, I'm heading to Iowa City, where I will make you my bride!

David.
via telegram –

15 FEBRUARY 1946

LEAVING TODAY. MILTON COLLEGE HAS ALLOWED ME TO RE-ENROLL AND KEEP MY PREVIOUS STATUS IF I REPORT IMMEDIATELY. DAD IS PICKING ME UP IN CHICAGO ON 25 FEBRUARY, ANTICIPATING A TEN DAY SHIPPING. IT IS HALF WAY THROUGH THE SEMESTER BUT I THINK I CAN CATCH UP.

PACK YOUR BAGS AND WE'LL HEAD TO ST. LOUIS. BE READY TO MAKE PLANS TO MARRY SOON THEREAFTER. I CAN'T WAIT!

DKH

Friday, February 25, 1946

Darling Patty,

It has been a hectic, exhausting week – but I'm enjoying every minute stateside! From the first glimpse of the beautiful Lady in Green, welcoming us to Ellis Island ... through the seemingly endless train ride to Fort Sheridan ... all thoughts were on you and our upcoming *rendezvous* (I'm practicing for my return to Milton ... and French class!)

Dad is allowing me to borrow the car on Friday, March 8th. I hope that gives you enough time to pack and be ready to return to St. Louis. I thought it would be best if you had some time with your parents before I whisk you away to our new life ... TOGETHER! in Wisconsin.

You'll be busy for the next few weeks making preparations for the wedding, honey, anything you want is fine with me! The best date for me would be April 13th because I have exams during the last week of March and into the 1st week of April.

Now we can splurge and communicate via telephone to solidify all the details! I'll call before Friday to let you know my arrival time so that we can leave for St. Louis immediately.

All my love, David.

26th February 1946

Dear Mom and Pop Wise:

For a long time I have waited for the day that I could write the joyous message that the U.S. Army and yours truly had come to the parting of the ways. At exactly 1900 Saturday, 23 February 1946 we left the ceremony in a most undignified manner waving our discharge papers and proceeded toward home. This culminated three years of service to the day and there is little to say pro or con about that period, primarily I'm only interested in the future which shall monopolize most of this text.

At you probably already know, I called Patty from New York and again from Camp McKoy making arrangements to see her as soon as possible. She got here early Sunday morning and our meeting hardly met the expectation of many months of dreaming – IT WAS A THOUSAND TIMES BETTER THAN MY HIGHEST HOPES! We had been writing each other trying to describe how we might have changed but it was all in vain. Pat is just as wonderful as ever; I can't see where she has changed an iota! Apparently, she finds that I am still tolerable and we had a marvelous reunion!

Today she had to go back to school SOOOOO we have made plans to come down to St. Louis this weekend to see you. I am wiring ahead for reservations and we'll call you sometime Friday evening. Pat told me about the new position with Washington University and it sounds like a wonderful deal. You have a lot of things to tell me about the happenings of the past year plus and I am very anxious to see you.

The transition from government issue to civilian togs wasn't nearly as exciting as I had anticipated.

Your future son-in-law, David.

15 March 1946

David,

Patty has arrived home (thanks to your decision to remove her from school and to bring her back home) after completing one half of a semester at Iowa City—do you really think this is a wise course of action? There are "male" plans that are made, but are you really looking out for your bride? I question your motives, although I understand your feeling that you want to establish a home, and I know that in the future, you will support her.

Please let me know what you have envisioned for the next few years. My support of your "plan" depends on it.

Harry.

Monday, 8 April 1946

My darling Patty:

Just wanted to dash off a line to tell you how much I miss you and that I love you very much … Saturday night, I attended to the proposed little job of taking care of nephews Ricky and Greg, which reached its climax when I fell asleep and couldn't have heard them if they were crying and swimming in their respective beds. Sunday sat around talking about all the things that passed in the past four years. Last night I rapped off the book report plus about six pages of French.

I have been angling for another apartment; this one over Olson's Drug Store and it looks like a wonderful place. All that is standing in our way is a little matter of waiting for the plumber to come in and finish the bathroom which will probably require two or three weeks.

Tomorrow will be a busy day with French, a debate in Speech, picking up my suit, rings and your hose if it's available, two Glee Club rehearsals, and the concert at night. We had another practice tonight and it still sounds like all terror.

Paul and Mary are still uncertain as to what their plans will be, but we can count on Paul being there at least long enough for the wedding. Tentatively my plans will be to leave Milton with Paul about 11a.m. Friday and arriving in St. Louis Friday afternoon. The car deal fell through so I guess we'll be depending on rail transportation as a means of getting back.

The test that I studied for and took didn't turn out as well as I had anticipated. It seems that I confused a poem by Keats and included it as a part of Shelley's works. I wasn't too disappointed to receive a "C" – it was more than I deserved for the amount of time that I spent in preparation.

The boys have taken up the cry of reminding me that only five days remain before "the day". I try to live up to their expectations of looking nervous, but actually it's more anxiety than nervousness. This is short but perhaps tomorrow will bring more news and more time to write. It is 1 a.m. and I'm ready for bed.

I love you, David.

ps – please give my love to Mom and Pop Wise.

PPS – The sore throat is a thing of the past – thanks to faithful gargling and taking care of myself.

Je vous aime beaucoup, toute l'annee!

Wed night, 10 April 1946

My darling Patty:

This, I think, will be the last letter that I ever write to Patricia Wise. According to my calculations there are two days and twenty-two hours before you're my WIFE … more about that later! There are a few things that I must get off my chest and then we'll talk about the more pleasant aspects.

1) The apartment: I did a bit of shopping around and really fell into a good deal. The apartment above Olson's Drug Store is one block from the college, and she is holding it for us and we can occupy the place as soon as the plumber gets in the toilet and shower facilities. I talked with Mr. McVicar, the plumber, and he figures about ten days before he can get over there. The place will require some painting and cleaning but we have all kinds of pledged workers to finish the heavy work. There are three rooms and a bath (which unfortunately, is in the basement) - in the meantime I thought of getting a double room in Milton where we can stay until the place is habitable. This is apparently a sure deal and the best that we have struck so far.

Mary is going to make the trip and we plan to leave here Friday after Paul's Econ class. We should be in St. Louis late in the afternoon or early evening. I shall call Essie's as soon as we hit the town. I imagine that Paul and Mary will want to go directly to the Hotel Jefferson and I'll probably call from there.

The Glee Club concert went off last night a lot better than any of us had anticipated – Kenny's part in particular was superb.

Now it's time to focus on the fact that, in less than three days, the two of us shall become one. Darling Patty, you have made my life complete … and I am SO looking forward to starting this brand new, exciting adventure with you at my side. We'll be making all kinds of wonderful discoveries together (by the way, do you snore? If you believe what Kenny has to say, I may be guilty on occasion). I'm the luckiest guy in the world!

See you tomorrow, Mrs. David K. Heenan!
Your guy forever,

David

Prologue

David and Patty married on April 13, 1946. Patty left the University of Iowa before completing her sophomore year to join David at Milton, Wisconsin, so he could finish his bachelor's degree. They lived in a small apartment over Olson's Drugstore, where they had three meager rooms and had to go to the bathroom down in the basement.

Back with the boys at Alpha Kappa Phi – 1947.

After David finished his work at Milton, he applied for a Master's program at Washington University in St. Louis, Missouri. He completed his studies in a year (most students took two years) and returned to Madison to complete his PhD in European History.

David, Junior, was born on August 20, 1949.

Here is a picture of David after his return to Milton (top row, 1st on left):

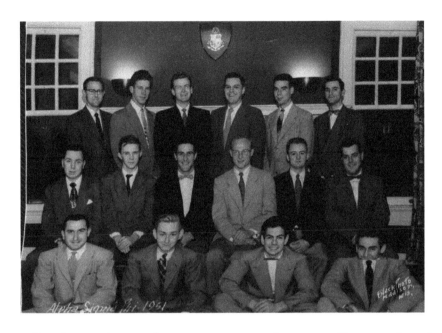

David spent the next few years serving as substitute staff at a number of UW campuses. In 1955, David was offered an Associate Professorship at Michigan State University. He accepted—with a salary of $5500 per year. David and Patty purchased their first home at 935 Forest Street in East Lansing, Michigan, for $16,000. They later relocated to 500 Butterfield Drive in East Lansing and stayed there until retirement. Every summer they spent on Grand Traverse Bay, enjoying the sun and fun in northern Michigan.

Patty returned to college in 1968 and earned her degree in Human Ecology in 1972. She accepted a job as a Foreign Student Advisor at Michigan State and retired in 1981.

David loved his life at Michigan State University until his retirement in 1981.

David died on October 22, 1988. Patty remarried in 1992 to Roy, and they enjoyed eighteen years together before Roy died due to complications from Parkinson's disease.

Patty died on June 28, 2018, just shy of her 94th birthday. She celebrated the last years of her life amongst "her angels" at a memory care facility in Whitewater, Wisconsin. God bless all of those angels that took care of her during the last years of her life.

CPSIA information can be obtained
at www.ICGtesting.com
Printed in the USA
BVHW061105170419
545792BV00019B/88/P